D1131670

COUNTY

OF

TRIGG,

KENTUCKY.

HISTORICAL AND BIOGRAPHICAL.

EDITED BY WILLIAM HENRY PERRIN.

ILLUSTRATED.

F. A. BATTEY PUBLISHING CO.,
CHICAGO AND LOUISVILLE.
1884.

This Volume Was Reproduced
From An Original Edition
In The
Library Of
The Filson Club
Louisville, Kentucky

New Material COPYRIGHT 1979
        By: The Rev. Silas Emmett Lucas, Jr.

                SOUTHERN HISTORICAL PRESS
        % The Rev. S. Emmett Lucas, Jr.
                P. O. Box 738
        Easley, South Carolina   29640

ISBN-0-89308-164-7

Library of Congress Card Catalog No.:79-66904

PREFACE.

THIS volume goes forth to our patrons the result of months of arduous, unremitting and conscientious labor. None so well know as those who have been associated with us the almost insurmountable difficulties to be met with in the preparation of a work of this character. Since the inauguration of the enterprise a large force has been employed in gathering material. During this time most of the citizens of each county have been called upon to contribute from their recollections, carefully preserved letters, scraps of manuscript, printed fragments, memoranda, etc. Public records and semi-official documents have been searched, the newspaper files of both counties have been overhauled, and former citizens, now living out of the counties, have been corresponded with, for the verification of the information by a conference with many. In gathering from these numerous sources, both for the historical and biographical departments, the conflicting statements, the discrepancies and the fallible and incomplete nature of public documents were almost appalling to our historians and biographers, who were expected to weave therefrom with some degree of accuracy, in panoramic review, a record of events. Members of the same families disagree as to the spelling of the family name, contradict each other's statements as to the dates of birth, of settlement in the counties, nativity, and other matters of fact. In this entangled condition, we have given preference to the preponderance of authority, and while we acknowledge the existence of errors and our inability to furnish a *perfect* history, we claim to have come up to the standard of our promises, and given as accurate a work as the nature of the surroundings would permit. The facts incorporated in the biographical sketches have in most cases been secured from the persons whom they represent, hence the publishers disclaim any responsibility as to their general tenor. Whatever may be the verdict of those who do not and *will* not comprehend the difficulties to be met with, we feel assured that all just and thoughtful people will appreciate our efforts, and recognize the importance of the undertaking and the great public benefit that has been accomplished in preserving the valuable historical matters of the counties, and biographies of many of the citizens, that perhaps would otherwise have passed into oblivion. To those who have given us their support and encouragement we acknowledge our gratitude, and can assure them that as years go by the book will grow in value as a repository not only of pleasing reading matter, but of treasured information of the past that will become an enduring monument.

OCTOBER, 1884.

THE PUBLISHERS.

HISTORY OF TRIGG COUNTY.

CONTENTS.

HISTORY OF TRIGG COUNTY.

CHAPTER I.

A FEW decades ago and this country was the home of the red man and his kindred, these great forests his hunting-grounds where he chased the buffalo and deer. From a wilderness infested with savages and wild beasts the country has been reclaimed and transformed into unsurpassed loveliness. The history which attaches to every section of it increases in yearly interest, and must continue to do so with the passing years. Every county has its traditions and memories; every spot, how-ever small, is more or less historical. Trigg County, to which these chap-ters are devoted, bears no mean part in the history or the importance of the State, as she bears no inconsiderable part in the history of our com-mon country.

Topography.—Trigg County lies on the Tennessee line in the south-western part of the State, and is bounded on the north by Lyon and Cald-well Counties; on the east by Christian County; on the south by the State of Tennessee; and on the west by Calloway and Marshall Counties, from which it is separated by the Tennessee River, the dividing line between "Jackson's Purchase" and the older settled portion of Kentucky. It is drained and watered by the Tennessee and Cumberland Rivers, the latter of which flows north almost through the center of the county, and the tributaries of these streams. The surface is diversified between rough and broken hills and beautiful and undulating valleys of productive lands.

The original timber was several kinds of oak, hickory, walnut, maple, ash, elm, sycamore, poplar, etc., and hazel, willow, cedar and other shrubs. Quite a portion of the county was what was called "barrens."

The geological structure of Trigg County is so similar to that of Christian County that it is needless to go into a detailed description of it, as it is fully described in the first part of this volume. A few words upon the subject in this chapter will suffice. The eastern part of the county averages from level to rolling or undulating, while that portion lying between the Tennessee and Cumberland Rivers is broken and hilly, and abounds in lime and conglomerate sandstone, the latter predominating. High, steep banks border the Tennessee River, with ledges of rocks in great plenty. The finest of limestone may be found in almost all parts of the county, but most prominent outcrops are in Wallonia and Cerulean Springs Precincts. The blue limestone makes a fine building stone, and is much used as such. There is also a very good sandstone in the neighborhood of Cerulean Springs which is utilized for foundations and for chimneys, also for grindstones. Between the rivers (the Tennesse and Cumberland) a fine quality of iron ore is found.

Iron Ore.—As early as 1841 iron ore was the source of an important industry, and several large iron furnaces were put in operation. In the year above mentioned T. T. Watson of Tennessee purchased a large tract of land in what is now Ferguson Springs Precinct, and erected the Empire Furnace. He operated it very successfully for about a year, when Daniel Hillman, also of Tennessee, bought a half interest in the business, and immediately the firm erected the Fulton Furnace just over the line in Lyon County. At Watson's death, which occurred some two years later, Hillman became sole owner. He soon after built the Center Furnace three miles west of the Cumberland River, which he operated on a more extensive scale than the others. This enterprise represented a capital of several thousand dollars, and gave employment to about one hundred men. The Empire Furnace was of a limited capacity, and was abandoned in 1861–62, and its business transferred to the Center, which is still in operation.

In the year 1845 Messrs. Stacker & Ewing of Tennessee built the Stacker Furnace on the east bank of the Cumberland River, where the village of Linton now stands. This proved a very successful venture, and a handsome fortune to the proprietors was the result. Thinking to further increase their business they sold the furnace in a few years, and commenced the erection of a very large one in Tennessee, but before its completion they became financially embarrassed and were compelled to give up the project. Stacker Furnace was operated by different parties until 1856, when it was abandoned, owing to the ore in its vicinity becoming exhausted. The last proprietors were Lewis Erum & Co., who abandoned it as above.

Laura Furnace was built in 1855 some two miles west of Cumberland River by Gentry, Gunn & Co., of Tennessee, who invested in it a capital of about $40,000. They gave employment to 120 or 130 men, and carried on a very successful business for three years. The furnace was then purchased by George P. Wilcox, who operated it until 1860–61. The civil war seriously interfered with the iron interests of this region, and for several years Laura Furnace remained idle, to the great loss of the proprietors, who were thus financially ruined. It has been operated only at intervals since 1865. Pringle & Co., of Pittsburgh, had charge of it in 1871, and Whitlock, McNichols & Co. leased it for a short time a year or two later, but did not make the business lucrative. The property is now owned by C. Beninger, of Pittsburgh, but is not in operation.

Trigg Furnace was erected by Daniel Hillman in 1871, and stands east of the Cumberland River in the Rock Castle District. This is the largest furnace ever built in the county, and at the time of its completion represented a capital of $60,000. It was constructed upon an improved plan, employed the hot blast, and required the labor of about 150 men to operate it properly. It produced a superior quality of iron, and was in operation about seven years. At the end of that time it was discontinued on account of the enormous expense required to operate it and the scarcity of ore on the proprietor's lands.

The mineral deposits, principally iron ore with limited deposits of lead, are very rich in the county, and only require plenty of capital to properly develop them. Railroads are much needed in order to develop the country and render its hidden treasures more valuable. With plenty of railroad facilities, and competition in the transportation of fuel to the works and the products of the works to market, this would soon become the richest portion of Trigg County. The day is not far distant when these rich deposits will be brought to light.

Streams.—The most important stream aside from the Tennessee River, which forms the western boundary of the county, is the Cumberland River. It is a fine stream, and as an avenue of transportation and travel is of the greatest benefit to the country. In the early period of the country's history it was the sole mode of transportation almost for the early settlers, as there were no roads but trails through the forests and barrens. Boating was carried on extensively until the era of railroads rendered water transportation too slow a method. Those who have only known the country under the railroad systems can form but little idea of the river business of early times. Flat-boats and even steamboats were loaded with the produce of the country, and passed out into the Ohio River, thence into the Mississippi, and down to New Orleans—then the great market of the country. In this respect the Cumberland River was far more important to Trigg County than the Tennessee, in that it flowed almost through the center of the county.

Little River is the most important tributary of the Cumberland in this section. It flows in a general northwesterly direction, and empties into the Cumberland near Canton. It is the crookedest stream perhaps in the world, and flows to every point of the compass sometimes within the distance of a mile. At one time it was considered a navigable stream, and small boats came up as far as Cadiz. Efforts have been made to obtain an appropriation from the National Government for its improvement, but the fact of its location south of Mason and Dixon's line has so far defeated the laudable undertaking. Its principal tributaries are Muddy Fork, Casey's Creek, Dyer's Creek and Sinking Fork. The latter receives its name from the fact that it sinks into the earth at a certain point, reappearing a mile or two distant. Along these streams as everywhere in the cavernous limestone region are numberless caves, some of which have been explored to a considerable distance. They are more fully described, however, in the precinct histories.

Soils and Productions.—Adjacent to the streams the soil is alluvium of great depth and fertility. On the higher lands is a clay soil, in the limestone region a red clay, which is very productive. The higher ridge land rests on a light clay, and is much less productive than the red clay. Wheat and corn are grown extensively, and are well adapted to the soils of the county. Tobacco however is the principal crop, and has been produced to an extent to injure and wear out the lands prematurely. It will be a bright period in the history of the county when the farmers cease raising so much tobacco and give their time and attention to stock-raising and the production of grain. The latter industries are already beginning to receive more attention each year, which is to the prosperity of the county. But there is room for still greater change and improvement.

Tobacco is considered by many one of the most valuable crops produced in the United States, but in its cultivation comes the real "drudgery" of farm life. It is never off the farmer's hands, for before he can get his crop into market he is preparing for another crop, and thus it goes on from year to year. A great need of the times is to make rural life so attractive and at the same time to make pecuniary profit in it so possible as to hold the boys and young men on the farm. This can hardly be done by the universal growing of tobacco. It is a very mistaken idea of gentility, of ease of life, of opportunities for culture or for winning fame, which draws a large percentage of the brightest boys into the so-called learned professions, or into trade. With proper surroundings of the home, with a proper education at school, with a proper administration of the economies of the farm, with a sufficient understanding of the opportunities for a high order of intellectual and social accomplishment in the rural life of this country, this need not and would not be so. This is not intended as a wholesale condemnation of the growing of tobacco, which it is to be confessed is a necessary evil; but it is merely to show the advisability of more equally dividing the crops cultivated. Grow less tobacco, and more corn, wheat, clover and grass, and raise more stock. A few years will disclose the value of the change in more ways than one.

Mounds.—That a strange and semi-civilized people resided throughout all the country in times which antedate the Indians' occupancy of the soil is established by conclusive evidence, aside from the most universal denial of the savage tribes of their having had any participation in the erection of the vast number of earthworks scattered throughout the continent. All that is known of this mysterious people has been discovered from the decaying remnants of their works; but their origin and final fate are enshrouded in hopeless obscurity. Although the pre-historic remains of Trigg County are few in number and comparatively uninteresting in detail, yet a few words here may not be out of place, descriptive of some of the more prominent ones.

The largest mound in the county perhaps is the one near Canton. It covers about one-eighth of an acre of ground, and when first known to white people was of considerable height. On opening this mound a number of axes (stone), pipes, and other relics of the Mound-Builder were found in profusion. An image was also found, which from its appearance might be a statue of the "lost link" between man and the "Darwinian theory." On the Grace farm, in Cadiz Precinct, is another large mound. This mound has likewise been opened, and in it were found a large number of relics. Smaller mounds than the two above described are found in other parts of the county, principally in the neighborhoods of Cerulean Springs, Roaring Springs, etc., etc. They are noticed further in the chapters devoted to those particular sections, and further mention here is superfluous.

Settlement by White People.—It is difficult at this remote period to fix upon the exact year in which white men first came into what now constitutes Trigg County. But from the most authentic of the scant sources of information it appears to have been as early as 1778. "The first of these were hardy adventurers from the Carolinas, who floated down the Cumberland and Tennessee Rivers on flat-boats, and after erecting a few temporary huts contiguous to the banks of the streams, remained but a few years and then suddenly disappeared, leaving no traces behind them except the rude habitations that could not be dignified with the appellation of cabins. What their object was speculation can hardly furnish a conjecture. There are no evidences of their having been hunters or trappers, and the fact of their showing no disposition to plant even so much as a patch of corn, was a conclusive proof that if they had a motive at all, it was not an agricultural one." The next comers, according to Collins, were Dr. Thomas Walker and Daniel Smith, the Virginia Commissioners appointed to establish the boundary line between the western portions of Virginia and North Carolina (now Kentucky and Tennessee), and their surveying party. "On the 23d of March, 1780, having run the line entirely across the county westward, and across Tennessee River, they closed their survey according to directions from Richmond. They made a tolerably good map of Cumberland River, the first that was ever made. One of them went down the river with the baggage while the other proceeded through the woods with the survey. Their report speaks of the Cumberland as a 'fine stream, navigable at least 700 miles above its mouth.'"

Following close after these came several families of permanent settlers, but few of whom have left any traces behind them. The site of one of the first oldest settlements in the county is in the neighborhood of Cerulean Springs, but the names of the majority of the first-comers have long since faded from the memory of the oldest inhabitants. As early as 1782 or 1783, Robert Goodwin, of North Carolina, and his sons Samuel and Jesse, were living near where Robert Goodwin, Jr., now resides, a short distance from the village of Cerulean Springs. They were, like the majority of the early pioneers, fond of their gun, and were good hunters, but when the season was over for the pursuit of game, they displayed a laudable ambition for some more permanent industrial business enterprise. They cleared up fields, planted and cultivated them, and aside from looking after their farming interests, paid considerable attention to the raising of domestic animals. They had considerable herds of cattle in a very early day, and seemed much more fortunate with them in the neighborhood of the springs than in any other localities. After the Goodwins came the Spencers, James Daniel and sons Elijah and George, John Blakely, William Johnson, Joel Thompson, John Goode, Eli Hasber, Jacob Stinebaugh, John Guthrie, David Haggerd, Samuel Campbell, Wiley Wilson, Seth Pool, Joel Wilson, William Wilson and Adam Thompson, all of whom became citizens, and had homes in the northern part of the county as early as 1800.

Between the Rivers.—About the same time of the second influx of permanent residents, quite a settlement had sprung up between the rivers.

" Allan Grace, the grandfather of W. D. Grace, lived in a block-house near the present location of Redd's tanyard as early as 1793, and there were older settlers than he." Moses McWaters and his sons John, Levi and Davis, Robert Forgeson, Abraham Lash, Robert Ferguson, James Benham and Eli Kilgore were all living between the rivers shortly after the beginning of the present century.

" The settlements on Dyer's Creek, Donaldson's, Casey's Creek and Sinking Fork were all made about the year 1798. It is possible, however, that the settlement on Dyer's Creek was made one or two years in advance of the rest. John Mayberry was living one-fourth of a mile from the mouth of the creek, and having a small field opened, the indications are that he had been there a year or so previous to that time." Near the head of the creek lived a man by name of Thedford, who built a rudely constructed horse-mill near the site of Trigg Furnace as early as 1798. His brother, James Thedford, "squatted" in the same locality, and opposite the old Empire Iron Works an old man by name of Gillahan had a cabin about the same time. A man by name of Curtis was one of the earliest pioneers of the county and made his first improvements on what is known as the Dyer farm. John Grasty came from South Carolina, and settled not far from Trigg Furnace, near which place he taught the first school in Trigg County. The Standrods came to the county as early as 1807, and settled on the road between Princeton and Rock Castle. Other early settlers located in the same neighborhood, of whom a more extended notice will be given in the precinct history.

The Dry Creek settlement dates from about the year 1798, at which time a large family of the Westers came from North Carolina, and located homes at various places along the stream. " They were a hardy, impulsive, energetic, upright family of people ; loved the adventurous spirit that characterized the inhabitants of a new country, and as soon as the settlement on Dry Creek began to crowd them, they pulled up stakes and crossed the Cumberland and Tennessee Rivers into Jackson's Purchase, where they said they wanted a wider range and more elbow room." Samuel Skinner and his brothers William, Joseph, Theophilus and Wiley, came from North Carolina, and settled not far from the village of Linton as early as 1802–03. Richard Ricks, Jesse Cox (a Baptist Preacher), William Scott, John Tinsley, William and Henry Bibb, David Rogers and Abel Olive all settled in what is now Canton Precinct at or near the date mentioned above.

Other Settlements.—As early as the year 1800 the most populous and thrifty settlements in the county were on Donaldson Creek. The most prominent families who resided there at that time were those of John Futrell, Shadrach Futrell, Drury Bridges, Josiah Outland, Enos Outland,

Joel Cohoon, James Lawrence, Basil Holland, Nathan Futrell, James Dixon, Hiram Dixon, John Wilson, Sr., John Wilson, Jr., Ben Wilson, James Wilson, John Craig, James, Joshua, Caleb and Carlton Lindsay, " Larry " Killabrew, the majority of whom came from North Carolina. James Thomas came in the summer of 1806, and settled in the same neighborhood. A further notice of this prominent family will be found in the history of Canton Precinct.

Another old settled portion of the county is in the neighborhood of Roaring Springs, and the most prominent families living there prior to 1820 were those of Elijah Burbridge, James Daniel, John Ford, Cornelius Burnett, the father of Dr. Isaac Burnett, John Greenwade, Elder McCullom, William Cook, the Northingtons, Lindsays, Dawsons, Blantons, Ledfords, Millers, Torians, Colemans, Crenshaws, etc.

The settlement at Boyd's Landing, or Canton, as it is now known, was made about the year 1799, by Abraham Boyd, the most noted and prominent of all the early settlers of Trigg County. A more elaborate account of this distinguished family will be found elsewhere in this volume. Other early families that should be mentioned in this chapter are the Wadlingtons, Cunninghams, Osbornes, Carrs, Sheltons, Norvells, Mathises, Dawsons, Sumners, Campbells, Binghams, Bakers, McCulloms, McCullochs and Thompsons. The foregoing list comprises only a portion of the pioneers deserving mention, and in the history of the various precincts will be found additional names and facts concerning the early settlements.

Pioneer Hardships.—The first thing for the family to do was to erect the little log-cabin, and while this was being done by the men, assisted by the neighbors who came for the purpose four or five miles, the families were obliged to live in the carts or in a tent of boughs, bark and blankets, or in the cabin of some neighbor. The cabin, such as it was, often without floor or permanent roof, and destitute of door or window, was very often ready for occupancy at night of the day it was begun. Blankets served for doors, greased paper for windows, while the floor was perhaps the bare earth. The furniture was such as the settler could manufacture with an ax and auger. Hand tools when possessed were always a part of the load, and nothing was more advantageous to the pioneer in setting up housekeeping in a new country. Bedsteads were often made by boring a hole in the wall, in which rested one end of a pole, the other end of which was supported by a forked stick in the ground. Upon this were placed impromptu seats, supported by one side of the cabin and the foot rail, and upon this structure hay, dry leaves and skins were placed. Chairs were mere blocks of wood with holes bored in them, in which legs were put; and tables were a packing box fortunately brought with the family, or were constructed of puncheons split from the tree, provided with legs as were the chairs.

These characteristics were true in only the earliest habitations, and were seldom all combined in any one. A few nails and some glass and hardware were occasionally brought in by some rather well-to-do emigrant or thoughtful pioneer, but the other picture had its counterpart in every settlement in the county. But with such inconveniences the people, many of whom had known something of refinement in older communities, had no time for repining or melancholy. People were more sociable then, and all were neighbors for miles around. Although the pioneer possessed some characteristics repellent to refined ideas and modern culture, yet in their social intercourse with each other they displayed those exemplary traits of character which might well be esteemed a bright legacy to a more advanced age. If they deviated from the strict rules of morality and indulged themselves in habits and excesses which have been discarded by progressive civilization, they still retained those estimable virtues which are the tokens of a generous and sympathetic people. Unpretentious and unostentatious, they tendered whatever of hospitality their humble homes afforded, and were assiduous in their efforts' to provide for those whom chance brought within the circle of their charities. Affectation had no place in the cordial entertainment tendered visitor or stranger, and self-seeking was never the incentive which prompted their open doors and hospitality. It is worthy of remark that society had not yet matured enough at that time to produce the "tramp," and the foot-sore traveler was likely to be a worthy recipient of their kindness.

The pioneers brought but a meager outfit of this world's goods, but strong in faith and hope expected to increase their worldly store and provide a home in old age. Some came in frontier wagons drawn by horses and oxen, and some used the more primitive pack-horse as a means of migration. Some came in one-horse carts, while others came on flat-boats down the river, and were many days and weeks in reaching their destination. While on their journey their encampment for the night was made wherever night overtook them. A fire was built by the wayside, over which an iron kettle was suspended, in which the frugal evening meal was cooked. The father's gun through the day provided abundance of fresh meat, for game was plenty and the deer could be had for the shooting.

Yet let the advantages of the journey be the best, it was one of toil and privation. There were no bridges over the streams, and each immigrant followed the general trail, but sought a new track for his own team. If the season was one of much rain, the ground they were compelled to pass over would be almost impassable, and the roads heavy. If dry the roads were rough, so that at its best the journey could not be said to be pleasant. Under such circumstances nothing but the necessities, and those in small bulk, could be brought hither.

It is difficult at this day to imagine a state of society where even the commonest means of social progress must be invented and set in motion, but the pioneer found this fact a very prominent and practical one in his early experience. The supplies brought into the country by the immigrants were occasionally by the closest economy made to last until the growing crop or garden could supply the necessities of the family. For years the people were thrown entirely upon their own resources. The nearest point where meal could be obtained was at Nashville and other points equally as far distant. A temporary supply of corn was occasionally secured from some older settler who had harvested a crop which sufficed until the growing corn became of sufficient size to eat. When the kernel was sufficiently firm the grater was brought into requisition and a sort of bread or porridge was made. This old grater was an eyesore to most of the children, as it occupied the greater portion of their time during certain seasons of the year. When the grain became hard and the grater no longer effective, recourse was had to the mortar and pestle. This consisted of a block or stump in which a kettle-shaped excavation was made by burning and scraping. A pestle was made of a heavy pole to the end of which a block of iron was fixed. Almost every cabin had its " hominy block," and among the earlier sounds about the house was the monotonous pounding of the frontier mill. This machine furnished several grades of meal, from fairly fine to simply cracked grains, and this was separated by sieves constructed of deer-skin tightly stretched over a frame and punctured with small sized holes. The finer part was transformed into the dodger, which was baked upon the hearth, while the coarser product was served up as hominy. Some of the better provided settlers possessed hand-mills, which were made of nigger-head buhrs. In the upper stone was made an eye and a handle inserted; the boys would grind hour after hour at this slow method. Although the streams afforded good sites for the construction of water-mills, the necessary machinery and the mechanical skill were for a long time wanting. Horse-mills came in to supply this need, and while they were called corn-crackers, did much more effective service than the name would imply. These consisted of a small set of nigger-head buhrs, propelled by a large cog wheel set upon a perpendicular axis. In the lower part of this axis horizontal levers were attached so that two teams might be attached to give the machinery motion. Such mills were constructed in various parts of the country at different dates and greatly relieved the farmers in the task of making meal. They ground very slowly, and the patron was obliged not only to furnish his own motive power, but was often obliged to wait several days for an opportunity to use it.

Mills.—Several water-mills were attempted in a very early day, but the character of the streams made the experiments rather unsatisfactory. During the greater part of the year the mill could not run for lack of water, and at other times the sudden risings of the water would wash out the rudely constructed dams. Wild meat for many years furnished the pioneer farmer his chief means of subsistence, game of all kinds being plentiful and easily procured. Deer were found in great abundance, and the earliest settler found no difficulty even if not an adept in the use of the rifle to kill all he needed without leaving the precincts of his cabin. Large droves of these animals were seen in the woods, and the pioneer, who was in the habit of carrying his gun wherever he went, need not spend much time in the special duty of providing meat for his family. Buffaloes were killed by the first settlers in the neighborhood of Cerulean Springs, and bears were numerous for many years in the woods skirting the various water courses. Mr. Goodwin states that his father killed fifty bears during one season. Grouse were found in unlimited numbers, as were also wild turkeys, and no cabin was deprived of their delicacy. Wild hogs served also to vary the frontier fare. These were animals that had escaped from the older settlements, and subsisting upon the nuts and roots of the woodland had gone wild in the course of nature. They were of a long-legged, gaunt species and kept the timber pretty closely. They were no particular damage or annoyance to the settlers, but furnished capital hunting sport and gave a relief to the monotonous recurrence of venison upon the table of the settler. Wolves were of more annoyance to the settlements, attacking sheep, pigs, cattle, and when rendered desperate by hunger, even man himself.

The streams of the county have always sustained the reputation of being the best stocked rivers with fish in the State, from the earliest knowledge of the whites to the present time. Before any settlements were made, rumors of the profusion of fine fish came to the frontiers through the Indians, to whom this was a favorite place of resort each fall and spring. Here bass, mullet, salmon, suckers, and other varieties having been found weighing several pounds. With this abundance of what are now considered luxuries, it would seem at a casual glance that the pioneer's life was one of ease rather than of hardship, but when it is considered that these were the sum total of their early luxuries, and what we deem the common necessities and find so cheap as to pass almost unnoticed in our estimate of family supplies and expenses, were to early settlers almost inaccessible and the most expensive, a great change is wrought in our estimate.

Salt was more expensive than sugar, and even the variety of game provided soon failed to answer the purpose of beef and pork. The system was exposed to the ravages of disease, and, subject to the trying experiences

CHAPTER II.

ORGANIZATION OF THE COUNTY—ACT OF THE LEGISLATURE FOR ITS FORMA-
TION—JUSTICES OF THE PEACE FOR THE NEW COUNTY—THE FIRST OFFI-
CERS—NAME OF THE COUNTY—COL. STEPHEN TRIGG—LOCATION OF THE
SEAT OF JUSTICE—REPORT OF THE COMMISSIONERS—CADIZ—COUNTY
COURT—THE FIRST CIVIL DIVISIONS—TAVERN RATES—ORDERS FOR
MILLS AND ROADS—THE FIRST CIRCUIT COURT—EARLY JUDICIARY AND
BAR—THE GRAND JURY—EXTRACTS FROM THE QUAINT OLD RECORDS—
LAYING OUT THE COUNTY SEAT—FIRST TRUSTEES—COURT PROCEED-
INGS—HON. LINN BOYD—VOTE ON RE-LOCATION OF COUNTY SEAT—
CHANGES OF BOUNDARY—MARRIAGE LICENSE—THE CENSUS—STATIS-
TICS—COUNTY OFFICERS, ETC., ETC.

WHEN the first permanent settlements were made in the present
County of Trigg, it formed a part of Christian County, and was
under the jurisdiction of that county for a number of years and in fact
until it became quite thickly settled. Christian County was originally a
large district of country extending north to the Ohio River and west of
the Mississippi. As it settled up new counties were formed and its
territory lessened by frequent drafts until the close of the year 1819,
when efforts began to be made for the formation of Trigg County.

The legislative act under which the county was created is entitled " An
Act for the formation of the county of Trigg out of the counties of
Christian and Caldwell," and was passed by the Kentucky Legislature at
the regular winter session of 1819–20. It was approved by the acting
Governor, Gabriel Slaughter, on the 27th of January, 1820. The ma-
terial part of the act reads as follows :

" Be it enacted by the General Assembly, that from and after the 1st
day of April next, all that part of said counties of Christian and Caldwell
contained in the following boundaries, to wit :

" Beginning at a point ten miles due west from the northwestwardly
limits of the town of Hopkinsville ; thence southwardly to Lindsay's
Mill on Little River ; thence due south to the Tennessee State line ;
thence west with said line to the Tennessee River ; thence down the
same to the mouth of a creek on which Levi Davis now lives ; thence up
said creek, leaving Davis in Caldwell County ; thence to the mouth of
Crooked Creek, so as to leave the inhabitants on said creek in the proposed county, except Daniel Osborne Esq. ; thence toward Simon Sher-
ford's horse-mill to the Christian County line, so as to leave the inhab-

B2

itants of Hurricane Creek in Caldwell County ; thence with the present
Caldwell line and Christian line to a point on said line within two miles
of Calley's horse-mill; thence from said two-mile point southeast to intersect a line running from the ten-mile point; thence south to the beginning, shall be one distinct county, called and known by the name of
Trigg," etc.

The remaining sections of the act, which is rather a long one, are
omitted. These, when divested of the said whereases with which they
are encumbered, stipulate among other things, that a copy of the proceedings be furnished Abraham Boyd, Ferdinand Wadlington, John Goode,
Samuel Orr, William Scott, Presley Slaughter, James Daniel, Beman
Fowler and Richard Dawson, who are named in the act as Justices of the
Peace for the said county. These Justices were required to meet at the
house of Samuel Orr in the village of Warrington on the 15th day of
May, 1820, for the purpose of effecting the permanent organization of the
county ; and their proceedings on that occasion are described on the old
records, as follows :

"In pursuance of an act of Assembly of the Commonwealth, entitled
an act, etc., etc., approved January 27, 1820, Abraham Boyd (then follow names of others), met at the dwelling-house of Samuel Orr in said
county of Trigg, on Monday, the 15th day of May, 1820, and produced
a commission from his Excellency, Gabriel Slaughter, Lieutenant-Governor, acting Governor of this Commonwealth, appointing them Justices
of the Peace for the county aforesaid—whereupon the said Abraham
Boyd, being eldest in commission, administered to the said (here names)
the oath of fidelity to the United States, the oath to support the Constitution of this Commonwealth, the oath of office and the oath required
by an act of the Assembly to suppress the practice of dueling, and thereupon the said Presley Slaughter administered to the said Abraham Boyd
the said several oaths." Thomas Raleigh produced a commission, signed
by the Governor, appointing him, said Raleigh, Sheriff of said County of
Trigg, whereupon he took the said several oaths, and together with
Charles —— , George Loftus, William Armstrong and George Daniel,
his securities, entered into and acknowledged bond in the penalty of
$3,000, conditioned for the faithful discharge of his general duties, and
thereupon a County Court was begun and held for the County of Trigg
aforesaid at the dwelling-house of said Samuel Orr, in said town of
Warrington, on Monday, May 15, 1820."

At that court William Cannon, Jr., produced a certificate of the
Judges of the Court of Appeals, to the effect that he had been examined
by the Clerk in their presence and under their direction, and that they
udged him well " qualified to perform the duties of Clerk of any County

Circuit Court or courts of equal dignity within the Commonwealth." He was accordingly appointed to the position, and entered into and acknowledged bond in the sum of $10,000 for the faithful discharge of the several duties of his office, giving as his securities John G. Reynolds, James Bradley and Thomas Asbury. The ability with which Mr. Cannon discharged the duties of his office is attested by all who transacted business with him during his administration, and his early records are among the most legible and systematic to be found in the State.

The other officers appointed at the first sitting of the court were : Fielding Harrison, Coroner, with Allen Grace, Ephraim Harsberger and Charles Linn, securities ; John Willingham, Surveyor ; and George Daniel, Deputy Sheriff.

Name of County.—The county was named in honor of Col. Stephen Trigg, of Virginia, a man of great ability and soldier of renown. The only account of this distinguished character accessible is the following from Collins' History of Kentucky: " He [Col. Trigg] first came to the district of Kentucky in the fall of 1779, as a member of the Court of Land Commissioners, and after that body had concluded its labors in the spring of 1780, determined to make the new country his permanent home. In that year he settled a station called Trigg Station or Viney Grove (sometimes called Haggin's Station after Trigg's death, because John Haggin lived there), four miles northeast of Harrodsburg on Cane Run, four miles from its mouth at Dick's River. He soon became noted for his activity against the Indians, and fell August 19, 1782, in the fatal battle of the Blue Licks while bravely leading his men to the charge. He was greatly beloved and very popular, and if he had lived would have taken rank among the most distinguished men of his time." Additional to the above brief sketch we learn that he assisted in the organization of the first court ever held in Kentucky and that he was proprietor of the original survey of 200 acres of land on the present site of Covington.

Locating the Seat of Justice.—The Commissioners appointed by law to locate permanently the seat of justice were Dickson Givens, William Thomson, Lander J. Sharp and Benjamin Vance. In accordance with the provisions of the enactment forming the county, the above-named gentlemen, after viewing the various eligible sites and taking into consideration the donations of land, money, services, etc., submitted the following report :

Having, in pursuance of the aforesaid act, met on the 15th day of May, 1820, it being the third Monday in the said month, at the town of Warrington, and at the house formerly occupied by Samuel Orr, and proceeded to discharge the duties assigned us. After a mature and deliberate examination of the many different places proposed as sites for the administration of justice at and near the center of said county, we are of opinion that the seat of justice be fixed on the lands of Robert Baker where he now lives on Main Little River on the top of the eminence above the spring, at or to include the lot wherein his stable now stands, it being the most central, convenient and eligible site for the purpose. Whereupon the said Robert Baker has this day obligated himself to convey to said County Court of Trigg, for the use of the county, together with fifty acres more to be laid off in right angles from the squares of said public square, which bond we here submit as part of the report, likewise several promissory notes given as donations.

Given under our hands and seals this 15th day of May, 1820.

DICKSON GIVENS,
WILLIAM THOMSON,
LANDER J. SHARP,
BENJAMIN VANCE.

Report approved May 16, 1820.

In the October term following the county seat was laid off on the land above designated, and was named Cadiz. The details will be found elsewhere in this volume. The promissory notes referred to were given by Presley Slaughter, Sevier Tadlock and Moses M. Waters and called for $100 each.

The better to dispense the ends of justice, the county was at this time laid off into civil or constabulary districts. Samuel Fowler was appointed Constable for all the territory west of the Cumberland River; Richard Ricks for that south of Donaldson Creek to Ogle's Mill and the Christian County line; Charles Linn for the territory from Donaldson's Creek north to Ogle's Mill and down Little River to the mouth of Muddy Fork and the Christian County line; Robert Hawkins for all that part of the county lying between the road leading from Hopkinsville to Eddyville, now Wallonia, and Samuel Campbell for all the territory north of said road on Muddy Fork. The court divided the county into two precincts for the purpose of appointing Commissioners of the Tax therein for the year 1820. It was ordered that the road leading from Hopkinsville by Shipps & Boyd's landing (now Canton) and from said landing up Cumberland River to the Tennessee State line, should be the division line between the northern and southern precincts. Thomas McFarlan was appointed Tax Commissioner for the northern district and John I. Porter for the southern.

The court continuing the next day, Benjamin Jones was released from paying poll tax; John Goode granted a license to solemnize the rites of matrimony; and Robert Baker having presented satisfactory evidence of good moral character, and being provided with such accommodations as the law required, was granted a license to keep a tavern at his house on Little River for one year, giving as securities William Murray and William Waters. The following tavern rates were fixed, to wit:

For French or Cognac brandy.....................$37\frac{1}{2}$ cents per half pint
For rum or domestic gin.................................25 cents per half pint
For Holland gin...$37\frac{1}{2}$ cents per half pint
For Madeira wine...50 cents per half pint
For port, sherry or other wines.......................$37\frac{1}{2}$ cents per half pint
For peach and apple brandy...........................$18\frac{3}{4}$ cents per half pint
For whisky..$12\frac{1}{2}$ cents per half pint

For porter per quart or bottle........ ....25 cents

For cider per quart...12½ cents

Lodging per night...12½ cents

For breakfast, dinner and supper..................................25 cents each

For horse for stallage and feeding, corn and oats, and hay or fodder for
    each 24 hours...50 cents

Horse to pasture for each 12 hours...................................37½ cents

Oats and corn per gallon..12½ cents

Ordered that the tavern-keepers of the county charge and receive according to the above rates and no more.

Remarkably cheap times those, but bless the simple lives of the honest forefathers, they knew nothing about " black strap," " rot gut," " tangle leg " and the thousand-and-one fancy drinks with which the guests of our modern hotels and " sample rooms " regale themselves.

The first order for erecting a mill was made on motion of George Loftus, and the Sheriff was commanded to summon twelve good and lawful free holders of the county to meet upon the premises the first Saturday in June, to consider the same and report thereof according to law to the next term of the court. This mill was erected on Sinking Fork of Little River.

The first public road that was asked to be established in the county was one from Cadiz to intersect the road from Dover to the old Brannon place. David Cooper, Charles Linn, Hiram Whitney and Baxter Alexander were appointed at the same time to view a road from Baker's to the Cumberland River. Another road was asked for from the seat of justice to Princeton and the county line, and Absalom Leavills, Moses McWaters, William Husk and Presley Slaughter were appointed viewers thereof. A road was also asked for leading from the county seat toward Hopkinsville, to intersect a road from Hopkinsville to Boyd's Landing. Rowland Hill said that all roads and by-paths of England lead toward London, and with the same propriety we can say that all the early highways of Trigg County led to Cadiz.

After dispensing with all other county business, on the 16th day of May, 1820, and before adjournment, we find the following general order: " The Commissioners appointed by law to fix upon a place for the permanent seat of justice for Trigg County, having done so, fix the same on the land of Robert Baker where he now lives on Main Little River, etc. It is ordered that the books, papers, etc., of this county be moved to the dwelling of the said Robert Baker, and that this court be adjourned until court in course and then be held at the dwelling house of said Robert Baker as aforesaid."

First Circuit Court.—The Hon. Benjamin Shackelford, Judge of the Seventh Judicial District, on the 15th day of May, at the town of Warrington, held the first Circuit Court in Trigg County. William Cannon was appointed Clerk, thereupon completing the county organization. No grand jury was impaneled at this court, no other business transacted and no other order made except one permitting Fidelio Sharp, Benjamin W. Patton, Daniel S. Mays, James Breathitt and William McDowell, to be admitted to practice law.

The early judiciary of Kentucky was marked as furnishing a higher order of talent—larger-minded men—than are to be found in the early political history of the State. Many of these early jurists will take their proper place in history as among the country's best men. They mingled with the rude people, assisting, advising and counseling them for their own good and benefit. They forecast and laid well the superstructure of the civil polity of the State, and in looking into the imperfect records of their lives that are now attainable, the student of history is impressed with the fact that here indeed was Kentucky most favored and fortunate. Of the above-named lawyers Maj. McKinney in his sketches of the county says: " Ben Patton was a very eminent lawyer, but has left no traces except the frequent appearance of his name upon the docket, and position that tradition assigns him of possessing splendid abilities as an orator and advocate in the courts. Daniel S. Mays has left to posterity a record in books. He removed from this end of the State to Frankfort in an early day, and was the cotemporary and rival of Mr. Crittenden in oratory, and afterward changed his residence again to the State of Mississippi; was placed upon the Supreme Bench of that State. His decisions have been ever since, and to this day are, quoted as specimens of legal ethics containing some of the most astute principles of international and constitutional law. Mr. James Breathitt, father of John W. Breathitt of Hopkinsville, was then the Commonwealth's Attorney and a very able one he was. The name of the only remaining one of the attorneys qualified at the court is here lost sight of, and to us at least the twilight of obscurity settled over his memory forever."

Second Term of the Circuit Court.—The next term of the Circuit Court was held at the residence of Robert Baker on the 23d day of August, 1820. A grand jury of inquest was impaneled and sworn, consisting of the following persons, to wit: Williams Armstrong, Sr., foreman; Whitmill Holland, John Williams, Abraham McCullom, Joel Wilson, Ashford D. Gore, James Wallace, William Redd, Richard Davenport, John Wharton, James Jones, John Hanberry, William McWaters, Thomas Woosley, Benjamin Wallace and Eleazer Gore. There were but two indictments found at this court, one against Andrew Carter for pettit larceny, and the other against Isaac McCullom for failing to keep a road in order. The latter was dismissed at the next court, and the former continued with an *alias* process.

Rezin Davidge and Matthew Mays, Esqs., produced certificates of their being qualified to practice law, and having taken the prescribed oath were regularly admitted to the bar.

The first suit filed was a case of debt of Jeremiah and Moses Brown, assignees of Sherwood Atkinson plaintiffs, against John G. Reynolds defendant. A demurrer was filed by defendant's attorney and the case thrown out of court.

The next case on docket was a suit for debt, Nathan Conduit against John Patts. In this case the defendant did not come off so well. In that day a man was liable to imprisonment for debt, and the law seems to have been enforced, as the following order in his suit will show ; " William B. Bond, special bail for the defendant John Patts in this cause, this day surrendered the body of said Patts into court and the said bond from his undertaking herein is discharged, and on motion of the plaintiff by his attorney it is ordered that the defendant Patts be delivered into the custody of the jailor, and that further proceedings in this cause be stayed and continued until the next term of this court." How long John remained in limbo does not appear, but the indications are that it had a tendency to make him keep clear of the court house, for at the November term the cause was again called up, and proceedings continuing, to wit : " This day came the plaintiff by his attorney, but the defendant although solemnly called came not " etc. This is the last that was ever heard of John Patts.

The third case at this term was for a similar cause as the ones mentioned. Ezekiel Thomas against John Hambury and James Wimberly. Court found for plaintiff with interest at the rate of 6 per centum, from the 20th day of March, 1820, until paid, also the costs.

The first trial by jury was a cause in covenant, the parties to the suit being Daniel Mays, plaintiff, and Hugh A. Reynolds, defendant. The following jurymen served upon that occasion : John McWaters, George Buckner, William Husk, Thomas McFarland, Alexander Wilson, Drew Holland, Thomas Doler, Thomas Young, John Young, William Young, John Patrick and Ambrose Mills. The jury returned a verdict in favor of the defendant, fining the plaintiff $100 and costs.

The second petit jury was composed of the following gentlemen, to wit : William Young, Randolph Guinn, Willis Minton, Hampton Wade, Henry McCombe, Thomas Armstrong, Smith Martin, David Mitchell, Abraham Cowley, Baxter Alexander, Richard Jones and John Young.

Subsequent Session of the Circuit Court.—The third term of the Circuit Court was held in the month of November, 1820, his Honor, Judge Shackelford, presiding. The following grand jurors were impaneled and duly sworn, viz.: George Street, foreman ; Jacob Torian, William Cunningham, Lipscomb Norvell, Ashford D. Gore, Archer Boyd, Luke Thomas, Whitmill Holland, Baxter Alexander, Zenas Alexander, James Sevills, Zadeck Thomas, Stephen Peall, Daniel L. Futrell, Jaconias P. Pool, Timothy Jones, William McWaters and Edmund Wells. Indictments were returned against Ebenezer Boyd for assault and battery, a true bill ; Andrew Carter, for petit larceny; a presentment against Rezin Davidge for profane cursing, a true bill ; indictment against James Jones, for assault and battery ; presentment against William Adams for profane swearing, and an indictment against Asher C. Davis for assault and battery.   Other bills were found against Elijah Ladd for arson ; Ebenezer Boyd, trespass, assault and battery; Robert M. Coleman, George Thrifk, William J. Worthington and Randolph Walker, assault and battery ; William Murray for swearing; David Mitchell and Jesse Wormack, for profanity.

Our forefathers in those primitive times seem to have had a profound regard for morality and good order.   In searching among the musty records in the clerk's office, the historian's fingers came in contact with a package of old indictments, time-stained and bearing the dates of 1820 and 1821.   A few specimens of these quaint and curiously worded documents are given, to show how the minions of the law dealt with offenders sixty-five years ago.

One John Wooldridge, in an altercation with a neighbor on the Sabbath day and yielding to the impulse of a warm temper, violated one of the commandments by assaulting said neighbor, and was held to answer to the following indictment:

" COMMONWEALTH OF KENTUCKY, ⎫ SCT.
          " TRIGG CIRCUIT, ⎰

" The Grand Jurors for the Commonwealth aforesaid, impanelled and sworn for the circuit aforesaid, at the November term of the circuit, for said circuit, in the year one thousand eight hundred and twenty-one, in the name and by the authority of the Commonwealth of Kentucky, upon their oaths, represent that John Wooldridge, late of the Circuit aforesaid, yeoman, on the fifteenth day of July, in the year one thousand eight hundred and twenty-one, to wit, on the Sabbath day in the Circuit aforesaid did assault and beat one James Gillum, which said business of assaulting and beating the said James Gillum by the said John Wooldridge, on the Sabbath day aforesaid, was not an ordinary household office of daily necessity, or work of necessity or charity, contrary to the form and statute in that case made and provided, and against the peace and dignity of the Commonwealth of Kentucky.

"Information given by James Gillum, living in Trigg County, by profession a laborer, and Samuel Moore, living in Trigg County, and by profession a farmer, both not of the grand jury."

For the above trifling and uncharitable offense, the pugilistic Wooldridge was fined the sum of "five shillings, which sum was duly paid and turned over to the proper fund."

The next indictment was for profane "cursing," and reads as follows: "Trigg Circuit Court. The grand jurors for the Commonwealth, &c., &c., at the May term of the Circuit Court for said Circuit, in the year 1822, in the name and by the authority of the Commonwealth of Kentucky upon their oaths represent that Miles Creekmer, late of the Circuit aforesaid, yeoman, on the 21st day of May, in the year 1822, did profanely curse by then and there profanely uttering and speaking the profane words following, to wit: 'Oh, God damn the fine' contrary to the form of the statute in that case made and provided. and against the peace and dignity of the Commonwealth of Kentucky. Information given by John A. Caudle, Mel Olive and John Craig, all of the grand jury." What was done with the blasphemous wretch is not known, though it is presumed that he met with a summary punishment, as the courts in those days were chary in dealing out mercy to offenders. We cannot forbear giving the substance of another indictment returned against Uncle Gabriel Davy, who offended the dignity of the law by profanity also. It charges that he did "on the 20th day of May, 1822, in the Circuit aforesaid, twice profanely curse by then and there twice profanely uttering and speaking the profane words following, to wit: 'You are a God damned liar,' contrary to the form of the statute, against the peace and dignity of the Commonwealth. Information given by George Grace and John Caldwell." He was tried and fined 10 shillings and costs, which seemed to have a salutary influence upon the old gentleman's morals, and as far as the books show it was his last violation of the decalogue.

The third grand jury was composed of the following citizens: Thomas Raleigh, Samuel Orr, Luke Thomas, William F. Dew, Elijah Whitney, Robert Anston, James Puckett, John Patterson, John Breeding, James A. Lindsay, John W. Lindsay, Henry Jones, Baxter Alexander, John Humphries, John Mills, Armstrong Noel, Benjamin Faulkner, Samuel Scott and William McWaters. About the usual number of indictments were returned, the majority of which were for drunkenness, Sabbath breaking and profane swearing. In May, 1822, the following grand jury was impaneled and sworn: Thomas Raleigh, John A. Caudle, Joel Wilson, John Craig, William Lawrence, Isaac Gray, David Cooper, George Grace, William Young, John Prescott, Henry James, Smith Martin, John Caldwell and M. Oliver.

Harmon Alsbury was admitted to the bar in 1823; James I. Dozier, 1824; James Cartwright, John W. S. Moore and Thomas A. Duncan, in 1821; Matthew D. Patton and Robert A. Patterson, in 1825; Josiah C.

Smith, Garrard Pitts, James W. Calloway and Thomas Hammond, in 1824; Richard L. Mays, Thomas Haynes and Gustabus A. Henry, in 1827; Philemon C. Frayeer and Irwin Hallowell, in 1828.

The first deed ever admitted to record in this county was from Ezra Cox and Polly, his wife, to Jonathan Ricks for 150 acres of land on the waters of Dry Creek, for which he paid them $1,000. The second deed was recorded May 30, 1820, and was from Thomas O. Bryant and Anna, his wife, conveying to Philip Ford, James J. Morrison and John G. Reynolds a certain tract of land lying on Main Little River, being a part of a 200-acre tract originally granted to George Wilson by the Court of Commissioners in 1798. A third indenture made on the 14th day of June, in the year 1820, between Edwin Noel, of the County of Trigg, and Delila Noel, Frances G. Noel, Emily Noel, Edwin Noel, Caleb Noel and Washington Noel donates, gives and grants to his six children the following property, to wit: One negro man, Will by name, a blacksmith, with his tools; Phyllis, his wife; also Levering and Jack, children of the said Will and Phyllis; and James, another blacksmith; and McKinsey, a yellow boy; also a negro girl by name of Nancy; together with the interest in his mother's estate and a tract of 600 acres of land on Cumberland River, all of which property to be divided among the children in such a way and manner as to them seems best.

Second County Court. — In June, 1820, John McCaughn was appointed Surveyor of Trigg County. At the same term George Daniel was appointed Sheriff to fill the vacancy occasioned by the resignation of Thomas Raleigh. Thomas McLean produced to the court his credentials of ordination as a Minister of the Gospel, and was granted a testimonial in due form of his being legally authorized to solemnize the rites of matrimony. Whereupon he took the oath required by law, and together with James Thomas and Drury Bridges, securities, gave the accustomed bond of £500.

At the August term, 1820, James Thompson was appointed jailor. Samuel Orr, Presley Slaughter and James Daniel were appointed Commissioners to lay off the public square in Cadiz. The order alluded to reads as follows: "It is ordered that the said fifty-two acres of land shall compose and constitute a town, and the same is hereby established as such, to be known and called by the name of Cadiz, which shall be contained within the following metes and bounds." Here follows the boundary. "The whole of said town of Cadiz containing, according to the foregoing metes and bounds, the quantity of fifty-two acres, and the part besides the public square that has by former order of this court been laid off, is directed to be laid off into lots of one-fourth of an acre square, being four in a block, and the main and cross streets of the width of sixty feet each, crossing each other at right angles; and it is further ordered that Sevier Tadlock, William Redd, Charles Jones, Absalom Leavills, David Cooper, Levi Harlan and James Harlan are hereby appointed Trustees of said town." From this date the history of Cadiz proper begins.

The county levy at this term was fixed at 75 cents, and the following allowances for the year entered upon record:

To the Clerk of the Court for ex-officio services rendered by him within the last six months..	$ 20 00
To the Commonwealth's Attorney for same time.....................	16 00
To the Sheriff for same time..	17 00
To Abraham Sevills for a Clerk's table................................	8 00
To Elizabeth Bell for keeping John White, an infant..............	5 00
To same for keeping, clothing an orphan one year from this date.	60 00
To James Thompson, Jailor, for attending court six days.........	6 00
To Francis Summers, a Deputy Surveyor, for running this county's lines as per act. filed...	46 50
To Abraham Humphries, Jr., for carrying chain 14 days.........	14 00
To William Watts for 13 days rendering same service..............	13 00
To John McCaughn for 10 days making survey......................	10 00
To Robert Baker for cash paid by him to Commissioners in fixing the seat of justice...	102 00
To John McCaughn, Surveyor of the county, for laying off the town of Cadiz and other services rendered as per acts filed.......	27 50
To Abraham Boyd, Esq., for attending as Judge of the last election 3 days..	3 00
To James Daniel for same service.....................................	3 00
To James Coleman for same service...................................	3 00
To Commissioners for contracting and superintending the building of the jail of this county...	200 00
A deposition of..	76 00
Amount to be collected................................... ....$	630 00

Say 840 tithables in this county for the present year, on which a levy of 75 cents is and shall be laid, making $630. No further business of importance was transacted at this term.

The following year, 1821, the levy was fixed at $43\frac{3}{4}$ cents, and the number of tithables was 940. The allowances at the October term of 1821 aggregated $411.25. For 1822 the levy was fixed at $43\frac{3}{4}$ cents per tithable, and 444.05\frac{3}{4}$ were collected, making the number of tithes that year 1,015. The allowances at the October term amounted to 506.45\frac{3}{4}$. At the April term, 1821, the county was laid off into four precincts for the purpose of appointing Commissioners of the Tax therein. Abraham Boyd was appointed Sheriff in 1822, with Charles Linn, George H. Gordon and John Boyd, securities.

The following incident is related by Mr. McKinney: "The 16th day of October, 1820, being the regular day in course, court was begun and held at the seat of justice; present, Abraham Boyd, presiding Justice, with

his usual attendants.   After some minor orders had been made and whilst
Matthew Mays, a young man then County Attorney, was making an examination of the conveyances from Robert Baker to the county, the Clerk
William Cannon was busily engaged in drawing up the order giving the
present boundaries of the town of Cadiz, the proceedings were suddenly interrupted by a loud yell and the discharge of a rifle in the bottom just
back of the present residence of Ed Summers.   The bottom at that time
was covered with a heavy growth of beech and cane.   For a time little
attention was paid to it.   By-and-by, however, the cry of *"bear, bear"* was
heard.   This caused a universal commotion in the court room, all hands
rushing to the door, upsetting chairs, stools, tables and inkstands as they
went out.   Maj. Mays in laughing over it used to say that everybody
was excited to death about the animal except the Clerk, who quietly went
to. work righting up his table and books and cursing the d—n heathens
for upsetting the ink on his papers.   There had a very large crowd gathered
that day, and on reaching the door a large black bear, badly wounded,
suddenly emerging from the thicket came rushing through the crowd,
scattering men and horses in promiscuous confusion as he went.   He came
within thirty yards of the little log room in which they had assembled to
hold the court, and passing over the hill he hauled up at the head of the
big spring.   Here Tommy Wadlington, with a rifle he had caught up from
Baker's store, got in another shot.   Finding matters still growing warmer,
bruin skipped from there, and crossing the river just below Lindsay's old
fishing place, was dispatched by an old hunter on the opposite bank."

At the September term of 1820, John Mayberry was recommended to
the Judges of the Court of Appeals and the Circuit Court of the Commonwealth as "a gentleman who intended to apply for a license to practice law, and is a gentleman of property and honest demeanor." Silas
Alexander was appointed Captain, and Tom Thompson, John Patton,
William Smith and Augustine W. Holland his assistants.

Linn Boyd having produced his certificate from the Governor, was
allowed to qualify as Paymaster of the Seventy-second Regiment of Kentucky Militia, after giving bond in penalty of $1,000.   On the 15th of
December, 1823, he was appointed Deputy Sheriff of Trigg County; and
on the 24th of May, following, on motion of George Boyd, was re-
appointed.   "What a wonderful incentive this is to young men of the
present day.   This same Linn Boyd, Deputy Sheriff of Trigg County,
served eighteen years as a member of Congress, four years as Speaker of
the House of Representatives—third in the regular line of descent from
the Presidency of the United States—and died Lieutenant-Governor of
the Commonwealth of Kentucky, mourned not only by the people of the
State, but the nation."

Hon. Linn Boyd.—The following brief sketch of this distinguished gentleman is copied from Collins' History of Kentucky: " Linn Boyd was born in Nashville, Tenn., November 22, 1800. His educational advantages were limited, but he was a man of great force of character and strong native intellect. In early manhood he removed to southern Kentucky, and settled on the Cumberland River, in what is now Trigg County. He soon engaged in politics and took an active part in the early political struggles of the county. He was a Representative in the State Legislature in 1827 from the counties of Calloway, Graves, Hickman and McCracken; in 1828, from Calloway, and in 1831, from Trigg County. He represented the First District in Congress in 1835–37, and in 1839 was again elected, serving by regular elections until 1855, in all eighteen years, during four years of which he occupied the distinguished position of Speaker of the House of Representatives—an honor never conferred oftener or longer in eighty-three years except upon Nathaniel Macon, Henry Clay and Andrew Stevenson. In 1859 he was chosen Lieutenant-Governor upon the Democratic ticket, but when the Senate met was too ill to preside over its deliberations and died at Paducah, December 17, 1859. Mr. Boyd was distinguished in politics as a strict Constitutional Democrat."

Vote on Relocation of County Seat.—The location of the seat of justice at Cadiz did not meet general approval, and in December, 1821, an act was passed by the General Assembly authorizing the citizens of the county to fix upon a place for the permanent seat of justice, the same to be decided by ballot. At the March term of court, 1822, an election was ordered for the purpose of deciding the matter, and George Street, Richard P. Dawson and Beman Fowler were appointed Judges, and William Cannon Clerk for the same. The places competing for the honor were the following, to wit: Cadiz, Boyd's Landing (now Canton), Warrington and Center. The election was held in Cadiz on the 6th day of March, 1822, the friends of the rival cities being out in full force. The vote stood as follows: Cadiz, 295; Boyd's Landing, 204; Warrington, 69; Center, 59. Thus was the matter of locating the county seat effectually decided, although the town of Canton made several strenuous efforts to have it changed in later years.

Changes in the County Boundary.—As originally surveyed, the northern boundary of the county was very irregular—a fact which gave rise to much annoyance and dissatisfaction to the citizens of both Trigg and Caldwell Counties. To adjust the matter several "curtails" were added to Trigg from the former county, the first of which was made on the 17th day of April, 1826. In June, following, a second " curtail " of sixteen miles lying between the Cumberland and Tennessee Rivers was added, and in July of the same year a tract of land extending from the mouth of Hurricane Creek six and a half miles to the northeast was also added, thus making the northern boundary a comparatively straight line.

Early Marriages.—During the first two years after the county was created there were twenty-nine marriage licenses issued, as follows: Isaac Lockhart and Polly Williams, June 10, 1820; William Bridges and Polly Thomas, Samuel Fowler and Jane Bratton, Matthew Williams and Sally Jones, Thomas Skinner and Susanna Bryant, John Beardon and Nelly Young, John Walker and Sally Tedford, Samuel McClure and Patsey Bretton, William Miller and Elizabeth Grace, Alison Williams and Sally Barndale, Larkin Gilbert and Valley Coffield, William Clark and Sophia Dawson, William Jones and Nicy Howard, Needham Coleman and Mary Tart, James Bayless and Delia Noel, Basil Holland, Jr., and Elvira Cooper, Thomas L. Baker and Malinda Cunningham. The contracting parties to the first marriage in 1821 were Perry Thomas and Elizabeth Bridges, both of whom are yet living. Then appear the names of James Tart and Polly Lawrence, Joseph McKinney and Betsey Wicker, George Bratton and Polly Bratton, Jackson Allen and Susannah Stames, William Daniel and Huldah Chapman, Aaron Collins and Susannah Watts, James Knight and Nancy Cotton, Levin Ross and Susan Anderson, Newton Davenport and Ellender Morris, Meredith Brown and Sarah Boyd, William Goode and Gincy Walker. The first license issued in 1822 was to Moses McWaters and Telitha Tanner.

Census of the County.—In 1820 the county had a population of 3,870 souls. The population in 1830 was 5,916; in 1840, 7,716; in 1850, 10,129; in 1860, 11,051; in 1870, 13,686. The following was the population in 1880 by magisterial districts: District No. 1, 1,995; No. 2, including Rock Castle, 1,603; No. 3, including Wallonia, 1,788; No. 4, 2,259; No. 5, including Canton, 1,819; No. 6, including Cadiz and Montgomery, 4,220; No. 7, 755. Total, 14,489.

Statistics.—The total amount of taxables returned by the Assessor in 1820 was $960,000. The number of tithables in the northern district that year was 422; in the southern, 397. In 1883 the legal voters in the county, distributed among the precincts, were as follows:

Cadiz	477
Canton	163
Rock Castle	134
Caledonia	104
Laura Furnace	89
Montgomery	89
Cerulean Springs	154
Linton	141
Roaring Springs	326

Bethesda...108
Ferguson Springs...134
Golden Pond...189
Wallonia.................... 116
                                                            ——
    Total...2,279

Number of children in the county between the ages of six
    and twenty-one... 3,122
Number of acres returned for taxation.......... 252,592
Assessed value of lands...............................$1,201,323
Number of town lots... 228
Value of lots... $123,608
Number of horses... 2,278
Value of horses.. $115,295
Number of mules.. 2,289
Value of mules... $138,083
Number of sheep....................... 5,400
Value of sheep.. $11,777
Number of hogs... 13,071
Value of hogs..... .... $28,573
Number of hogs over six months old.............................. 3,923
Number of cattle.. 5,206
Value of cattle.. $16,198
Number of stores...... 55
Value of stock carried by stores.................................. $81,125
Value of pleasure carriages, barouches, etc...................... $131.46
Value of gold and silverware..................................... $12,677
Total value of taxables at 47½ per cent per $100............... $1,963,667

Number of pounds of tobacco raised................................ 4,724,745
Number tons of hay.. 973
Number bushels of corn.. 626,564
Bushels of wheat.. 125,924
Tons of pig iron.. 800

County Officers.—Senators—The names of all the Senators for Trigg County were not learned, not do those that are given below appear in their regular order. In the year 1826, George L. Locker was elected State Senator for the Counties Todd, Christian and Trigg. Francis Summers represented the same counties in 1827 and 1831. After Summers, the following persons represented Trigg in the upper house of the Legislature, viz., Alfred Boyd, Isaac Burnett, George W. Barbour, Ira Ellis, T. W. Hammond, James Bryan, —— Irwin, G. A. C. Holt, James B. Garnett, J. H. Wilkinson and Robert Burnett.

Representatives.—The following are the names of the Representatives of the county and the years they served:ㆍThomas Caldwell, 1824–25; George Street, 1825–26; Abraham Boyd, 1827–28; George Venable, 1829; Lipscomb Norvell, 1830; Linn Boyd, 1831; James E. Thompson, 1832; Isaac Burnett, 1833–34–51–53; Sinco A. G. Noel, 1835;

Lisenby Nance, 1836–40; George W. Barbour, 1837; Thomas B. Redd, 1838–39; Allen T. Noe, 1841–42–43–48; Charles Humphries, 1844–53–55; John C. Whitlock, 1845; William Sorley, 1846–47; Stanley Thomas, 1849; Daniel Landes, 1850; Gordon B. Grasty, 1855–57; John Roach, 1858–59; Young A. Linn, 1859–61; John W. Gaines, 1861–62, resigned January 20, 1862, and was succeeded by John Humphries; Samuel Larkins, 1863–65; Fenton Simms, 1865–69; G. W. Quick, 1869–71; M. E. McKenzie, 1871–73; Matthew McKinney, 1873–75–76; R. A. Burnett, 1877–79; Jabez Bingham present incumbent elected in 1882. The representatives from Christian and Trigg Counties in 1820 were James Ruffin and J. C. Cravens. George Daniels represented the same counties in 1821 and 1822.

Sheriffs.—Thomas Raleigh, 1820; George Daniel, 1820–21; Abraham Boyd, 1822–23; Ferdinand Wadlington, 1824–25; William Scott, 1826–29; Presley Slaughter, 1830–31; James Daniel, 1832–33; R. S. Dawson, 1834; Levi Lancaster from June, 1834 to 1836; William Hopson, 1837; W. C. Haydon, 1838; Cullen Thomas, 1840; William McWaters, 1842–43; T. W. Hammond, 1844–47; J. J. Morrison, 1848; James Garnett, 1849; John Humphries, 1850; Stanley Thomas, 1851–52–53–54; A. B. Dyer, 1855–56–57–58–63–64–66–69–70; John L. Humphries, 1867–68; John J. Dyer, 1859–60–61–62; R. W. Major, 1871–72–73–74; W. M. Campbell, 1875–76–77; William Peal, 1879, short term. The present Sheriff is Thomas Boyd.

Circuit Judges.—Benjamin Shackelford, Henry Brown, H. J. Stites, Collins D. Bradley, George B. Cook, N. E. Gray, T. C. Dabney, R. T. Petrie and John R. Grace.

Circuit Clerks.—William Cannon, J. E. Thompson, H. C. Burnett, R. A. Burnett, B. J. Wall, Isaac Burnett and John Shaw.

County Clerks.—William Cannon, J. E. Thompson, A. S. Dabney, A. B. Dyer, Matthew McKinney, and C. C. Hook. The present incumbent is John G. Jefferson who has held the office continuously since 1869.

County Judges.—T. C. Dabney, J. E. Thompson, J. R. Grace, J. H. Wilkinson, A. B. Dyer, J. E. Kelly and Robert Crenshaw.

County Attorneys.—Matthew Mays, C. G. Bradley, J. M. Burnett, John S. Spiceland, James B. Garnett, Robert Crenshaw, J. E. Kelly, J. R. Averitt and J. C. Dabney.

Assessors.—Mayfield Johnson, Alfred M. Brown, Peter Nance, Collins D. Bradley, Perry Thomas, Jesse Cameron, C. C. Bogerd, C. Humphries, G. B. Grasty, Elliott Grace, Thomas Humphries, B. F. Caldridge, E. Wade, John Dyer, Barnett Guyer, R. H. Averitt, A. J. Cherry, J. F. Green and J. E. Edwards.

Jailers.—James Thompson, Carter T. Wood, Jonathan Smith, Parham Randall, Moses Barbour, F. Y. Lawson, John D. Searcy, Daniel Davis, John Cameron, Sydney Hopson, T. R. Russell, J. E. Edwards, W. H. Jefferson and G. J. Shoemaker.

Surveyors.—John McCaughan, Kain McCaughan, John Mabry, James Richardson, Henry Burress, B. B. Mart and E. Brandon.

School Commissioners.—Thomas C. Dabney, James B. Wallis, M. E. McKenzie, F. F. Jones, John S. Spiceland, James B. Garnett, Robert Crenshaw, J. H. Wilkinson, J. R. Averitt and C. H. Major.

First Board of Justices or Magistrates.—Abraham Boyd, Ferdinand Wadlington, John Goode, Samuel Orr, William Scott, Presley Slaughter, James Daniel, Beman Fowler and Richard Dawson. The other magistrates who served prior to 1830, were the following, to wit.: John P. Wilkinson, George Street, Lipscomb Norvell, Levin Lancaster, George H. Gordon, Stephen Landers, David Glass, John B. Hindley, Nathan Futrell, Thomas McFarlan, Philemon C. Frayser, Cullen Thomas, William C. Haydon and James J. Morrison.

Present Board.—C. C. Flora, J. W. Nunn, Blake Baker, Jr., Samuel F. Baker, John Taylor, T. G. Guthrie, W. G. Blane, Almont Dawson, Sandy Joiner, Sanford Spiceland, T. N. Ingram, F. T. Watson and Abner W. Tuttle.

Early Constables.—Robert Hawkins, Whitmill Shake, Armstrong Noe, Jonah Boyd, Richard Ricks, Starkie Thomas, A. C. Davis, John Jennings, Alfred Boyd, Samuel Northington, Thomas Thompson, Lakin Gilbert, Jonathan Cudd, David Grace, Reulen Linn, William Fowler, Charles G. Linn, Sevier Tadlock, Alfred Wimberly and Alfred Brown.

Constables for 1884.—Henry B. Wilkinson, Thomas Faulkner, W. W. Jones, J. L. Ahart, J. W. Wallace and —— Lancaster. The foregoing comprises as complete a list of county officers and representatives as it is possible to make it.

CHAPTER III.

MATERIAL PROSPERITY OF THE COUNTY—ERECTION OF PUBLIC BUILDINGS—
THE FIRST COURT HOUSE—OTHER TEMPLES OF JUSTICE—JAILS—ATTOR-
NEYS PAST AND PRESENT—MATTHEW MAYES—JUDGE BRADLEY—POLIT-
ICAL HISTORY—HOW THE COUNTY HAS VOTED FROM ITS ORGANIZATION
TO THE PRESENT TIME—ASPIRANTS WHO WERE ELECTED AND DEFEATED
—ROADS AND HIGHWAYS—TURNPIKES—SOME THAT HAVE BEEN BUILT
AND SOME THAT WILL NOT BE—RAILROAD HISTORY, WHICH IS "·SHORT
AND SWEET"—SUMMARY, ETC., ETC.

THE county grew in prosperity and developed rapidly under individual organization. Soon after the location of the seat of justice arrangements were entered into for the erection of public buildings. To
this character of internal improvement, a brief space will now be devoted.

First Court House.—Official dignity in the early days was of a home-
spun kind, and required no great expense to provide appropriate surroundings. The first building in which the Board of Justices met, or, in
other words, the first court house, if the term is not too dignified to be
applicable, was the log structure at Warrington, occupied as a residence
by Samuel Orr. This building was a rude affair, and was used by the
court but a single day. The next house, as already stated, was the dwelling of Robert Baker, at Cadiz, which was used for general court and
county purposes until the fall of 1821, at which time a temple of justice
more in keeping with the dignity and growth of the new county was
erected. The order for the first court house bears date of January 21,
1821, and the material part of it reads as follows:

"It is ordered that the building of a court house for this county be
let to the lowest bidder on the first day of the next term of this court, of
the following dimensions, to-wit: A frame building of good sound ma-
terials, with a floor paved with bricks, the whole house to be 24x36 feet,
and 12 feet pitch; two jury-rooms of 12 feet square, and the court-room
to be 22x24 feet of the pitch aforesaid; to be finished in workmanlike
manner, according to the plan then to be furnished." The original plan
of the building was subsequently changed, so as to make the length 36
instead of 24 feet.

Abraham Boyd, James Daniel, Richard Dawson and Ferdinand Wadlington were appointed commissioners to let the contract and superintend
the construction of the house. As they held out few inducements to

architects, the bidding of contractors was not very lively. William Patterson finally made satisfactory arrangements with the board, and was awarded the undertaking, he agreeing to complete the building for the sum of $1,575, the same to be paid out of money arising from the sale of the donation of land to the town of Cadiz. The building was finished and formally received by the commissioners on the 19th day of November, 1821. Three years later an addition was made to the southwest corner costing $384, and in 1824 the entire structure was painted, and the windows crossed with heavy wooden bars. From what can be learned of the building, it appears to have been illy arranged and poorly adapted for court purposes, and a few years after its completion the propriety of erecting a more commodious edifice began to be discussed. At the October term of 1831 it was decided to put up a new brick building, and William Haden, James Garnett, Thomas McFarland, Thomas W. Hammond, Philemon Frayser, Lipscomb Norvell and William Cannon were appointed commissioners with full powers to fix upon that part of the public square which they should deem most eligible, and to adopt such plans for the building as they should mutually agree upon. The plan adopted by the board was a two-story building 40 feet square containing a court-room and two jury-rooms on the second floor, and the necessary county offices below; the entire structure to be completed according to specifications by the 20th day of May, 1833. A number of proposals for the work were made by different architects, the lowest responsible bidder being David Lotspeich, who was awarded the contract for $2,445. The house was ready for use by the time specified, and immediately thereafter the old court house was ordered sold, which was done on the 8th of July, 1833, the county realizing from its sale the sum of $70.

As the business of the county continued to increase it was found that the offices were not sufficiently large, and in 1843 a clerk's office was erected, which is still standing in the rear of the new court house. The second court house served its purpose until during the civil war, when it was burned by a detachment of Confederate troops to prevent its falling into the hands of the Federals. Before its destruction, however, all the records and papers were removed to a place of safety, and aside from the building the county suffered no serious loss. The house was ordered rebuilt in June, 1865, and Thomas H. Grinter, R. A. Burnett and M. A. Smith were appointed Commissioners to let the contract and superintend the work. An *ad valorem* tax of 15 cents on each $100 worth of property was listed for the year 1866, for the purpose of securing a building fund. Messrs. Pool & Boyd were awarded the contract for $11,950, a sum which was afterward increased, and work on the building went vigorously forward until its completion in 1866. The house was 52x40 feet

in size, two stories high, and surmounted by a dome 24 feet high. Although substantially constructed it was a very indifferent building and
poorly adapted for the purposes for which it was designed. In 1881 a
Committee composed of J. F. Gentry, John G. Jefferson and Fenton
Simms was appointed to examine the condition of the building and report
the same to the County Court. After a thorough examination they reported the house to be both dangerous and inadequate for court purposes,
and recommended that steps be taken to rebuild it on a larger and more
convenient plan. At the December term of 1881 the following action
was taken concerning the matter : "*Resolved*, that our Representative
and Senator in the General Assembly are hereby requested by the Trigg
County Court of Claims to procure the passage of an act by the Legislature of Kentucky authorizing this Court to issue and sell the bonds of
Trigg County for the purpose of building new clerk's office by remodel-
ing the court house or otherwise. Said bonds not to bear a greater rate
of interest than 6 per cent, and to be redeemable at any time after ten
years from their issual—to be sold for not less than par or face value;
and also authorizing the Court to levy an *ad valorem* tax not to exceed
10 cents on the $100 worth of taxable property in the county, to pay the
interest and redeem said bonds." At the same term W. G. Blane, Fenton Simms, John G. Jefferson, J. F. Gentry and F. C. Dabney were appointed a committee for the purpose of ascertaining the best, most practical, economical and substantial plans for the work, and to that end they
were authorized to secure the services of some efficient architect and
builder.

On the 11th of February, 1882, an act was passed by the General
Assembly authorizing the county to issue and sell bonds to the amount of
$10,000 for the purpose of securing a building fund. This sum was
found to be insufficient, and a bill for an additional $2,500 was afterward
passed and work on the house commenced. The design was drawn by D.
A. McKinnon, an experienced architect of Paducah, and on the 5th of
April, 1883, Thomas E. Morgan, also of Paducah, was awarded the contract for $10,250. Mr. Morgan failing to give the necessary bond
required by the court, another contract was entered into on the 12th day
of March of the same year with Messrs. Cosby & Landrum, of Mayfield,
Ky., who agreed to complete the work according to plans and specifications for the sum of $11,400. This sum was afterward increased by the
addition of $1,000. The seating and furnishing of the court-room and
offices cost the sum of $1,600, and taken all in all the house is one of the
most convenient, beautiful and imposing structures of its size and cost in
the State. Its extreme length is ninety-five feet; extreme width, sixty-
five feet; size of court-room, 62x62 feet. On the second floor, aside

from the court room, are two jury and one consulting rooms, all of which are furnished in the most artistic manner. On the first floor are the six county offices, three on each side of a wide hall running the entire length of the building. One of the most pleasing features of the structure is the beautiful tower, in which a magnificent clock has been placed by the citizens of Cadiz at a cost of over $600. The dials, four in number, are plainly visible from every possible approach to the town, and the music of the bell tolling the hours can be heard for many, many miles. The entire building was erected under the personal superintendency of John A. Scott, of Fulton, one of the most skillful practical builders in the State, and is complete in all its parts. The following notice of the building appears in the *Old Guard* of May 6, 1884:

The carpenters' work on the new court house at this place is now completed, and the present term of the Trigg Circuit Court is being held in the magnificent court-room above. The rooms of the county officers have not been taken possession of yet, but will be in a few days, or at least so soon as the necessary furniture can be moved into them. The building is one of the most beautiful pieces of architecture in the State, and notwithstanding the work has been all done at less than one-fourth of the cost, it contains the same number of rooms as the court houses at Mayfield, Paducah, Hopkinsville and Owensboro, and the most inferior is quite superior to the best one of them.

The design of the house is sufficient of itself to make a character for Mr. McKinnon its architect, and the good wishes of the county will follow Mr. W. L. Landrum the contractor wherever he may go, for the faithful manner in which he has discharged his obligations.

Jails.—The county was supplied with a jail some time before a court house was built. At the first session of the County Court, William Husk, Samuel Orr and Abraham Boyd were appointed Commissioners to contract for and superintend the construction of a jail, and at the September term following, the contract was awarded to John Williams, who agreed to erect the building for the sum of $500. It was built of hewed logs twelve inches square, and was constructed 26x16 feet in size, ten logs high, and contained two rooms ceiled with two-inch oak plank fastened to the walls with heavy iron spikes. Its architectural plan was simply that of a tight box with one outside door, one inside door and three small windows, each of which was only nine inches square. The two apartments were known as the debtor's and criminal rooms, one leading off from the other. The doors were made of heavy timbers, the windows guarded with strong iron bars, and taken all in all it was a very secure, though quite a cramped prison pen. It stood on the northeast corner of the public square, and served its purpose until about the year 1833, when a lot was purchased where the present jail stands, and a larger and more substantial hewed-log building erected. The second jail was a square building, and contained the prison rooms, one of which was made very secure by being lined with a heavy iron cage. As the county grew in population and the criminal classes increased in numbers the place of limbo was found inadequate to accommodate the numerous guests that applied for admission, and in 1838 we find that plans and specifications were drawn up for a new stone jail to be eighteen feet square and two stories high. These plans were abandoned at the September term of 1838, and it was decided to remodel the old building by adding extra room and weatherboarding, and otherwise improving the structure. This work was done, and the building thus rendered more secure and comfortable stood until the year 1857, at which time it was agreed to erect a brick jail, and plans for the same were accordingly drawn up and submitted. The contract was awarded to John McKintry, who for the sum of $1,600 agreed to complete the building according to specifications and have it ready for use by the second Monday in September, 1857. The structure was thirty-four feet in length, fifteen feet four inches in width, one story high and contained three rooms, one of which, the dungeon, was fitted up with the old iron cage between which and the brick walls was built a "pen" of solid post oak logs reaching to the ceiling, thus rendering the apartment doubly secure. The building, though well constructed and sufficiently secure to prevent the escape of culprits confined within its walls, was found in a short time to be inadequate for prison purposes, and ten years after its completion the necessity of having a new jail began to be discussed. At the January term of 1867 it was decided by an almost unanimous vote of the Justices to erect the building, and A. B. Dyer, R. A. Burnett and M. S. Smith were appointed Commissioners to let the contract and superintend its construction. They were authorized to sell the bonds of the county to the amount of not more than $10,000, to be redeemed in not less than one year nor more than ten years, in order to secure the necessary funds for the prosecution of the anticipated work. A contract was entered into with F. W. Merz, of Louisville, to furnish the inside iron work for the sum of $4,500, and P. S. Pool being the lowest bidder for the brick and stonework was awarded the contract for the same, he agreeing to complete it for $3,520. The plans of the building were afterward changed so as to include a jailor's residence, the contractor agreeing to remodel the old building for the purpose at an additional cost of $600. According to the terms of the contract the prison was to have been completed and ready for occupancy by the 15th day of May, 1867, but owing to some cause unknown it was not received until two years later, the plans in the meantime undergoing several modifications. The building stands on the lot occupied by the old jail, and with the improvements added since its erection answers well the purposes for which it is intended.

Attorneys.—Among the list of prominent attorneys who have practiced at the bar of Trigg County may be mentioned Hon. John J. Crittenden, Daniel S. Mayes (a brother of Matthew Mayes), Joseph R. Underwood, Charles S. Morehead, Beverly S. Clark, Joseph B. Crockett, Robert A. Patterson, John W. Crockett, George W. Barbour and others. The present bar of the county is comprised of the following lawyers: Cadiz: T. C. Dabney, John R. Grace, W. F. Simms, Robert Crenshaw, J. E. Kelly, James Garnett, E. F. Dabney, Robert A. Burnett and H. B. Wayland. Linton, E. C. Spiceland. Golden Pond, Frank Oakley.

Maj. Matthew Mayes.—Prominent among the distinguished lawyers of Trigg County was Maj. Matthew Mayes, without a sketch of whom this history would be incomplete. The following sketch was prepared and kindly furnished by Mr. McKinney: Maj. Mayes was a native of Kentucky, and was born in the shadows of the past or the early dawn of the present century. His father died when he was young, and not having been designed for the legal profession his early educational advantages were somewhat neglected. He lived on his mother's plantation until he arrived at the years of maturity, when, becoming dissatisfied with the drudgery of an agriculturist, he determined to change his vocation. He taught school for a short time, and commenced the study of law in the office of his brother, Daniel Mayes of Hopkinsville. He was not long in preparing for the duties of the profession, and having received his license to practice law in the courts of this Commonwealth, removed to Cadiz on the formation of the new County of Trigg, and was admitted to the bar of this court on the 23d day of August, 1820, and here his long professional career begins. It is not in the language of hyperbole, when his friends claim that he sprang at once to the very first position in the profession. Without the brilliancy of William T. Barry or the burning eloquence of Mr. Crittenden or the two Moreheads, he was the superior of them all, not only in the technicalities, but in the broad and comprehensive principles of the common law. As a special pleader, those who were familiar with both, claim that he was the superior of his brother Daniel; and when we take into consideration the fact that the former practiced law a number of years in Lexington, and held a professorship in the Law Department of Transylvania University, and afterward, having moved to Jackson, Mississippi, where we have the testimony of Senator Foote and Sargent S. Prentiss, that he was without an equal in the whole State, some conception may be had of Maj. Mayes' perfect knowledge of that intricate branch of the profession.

As a judge of law it was conceded that he had no equal in southwestern Kentucky, and but very few in the State. As a practitioner he was a model of professional decorum, and we have often heard Judge Hise, Mr. Sharp and James F. Buckner remark that they had never sprung a point on him that seemed at all to disconcert him or take him by surprise. As a speaker he was calm, clear and concise, and never at a loss for a word to express himself, but was never ornate nor eloquent. His speeches never were tedious and generally lasted from forty minutes to an hour, and every sentence was a legal maxim. His faithfulness and devotion to his clients amounted almost to stubbornness, so much so that when they found a gentleman who was immovable in his convictions, the members of the profession frequently taunted him with the charge that he adhered to his opinions as tenaciously as Mayes would cling to a client.

He was a constant reader, but, having very little taste for poetry, history or the essays of great literary celebrities, confined himself almost exclusively to the Bible, his law books and novels; the latter he would devour by the armful. He was very decided in his political opinions, despised the very name of Democrat, but it is thought it was more from prejudice than an enlightened conviction, for he frequently confessed that he had no taste and very little knowledge of political questions. He never attempted to make a political speech, except a few in the campaigns of 1844, and never recovered from the mortification excited by the result of the contest.

In personal appearance and intellectual vigor we know of no one who reminds us so much of him as the present Speaker of the House of Federal Representatives. He had the size, carriage, complexion and every makeup of speaker Carlisle, and we can recall, at this day, but one difference in the two men. Mr. Carlisle is very calm and deliberate in social disputation, but warms up into a perfect furor of excitement the very moment he mounts the stand; while Maj. Mayes was fully as excitable in the social circle as Mr. Carlisle is upon the hustings; he was calm and as gentle when he arose to address the court or jury as if the court-room were a parlor filled with ladies.

Judge C. D. Bradley.*—The name of but few men living or dead will excite in the people of Trigg County a more pleasant remembrance than that of Judge Bradley. He settled in Cadiz soon after the formation of the county, and up to the breaking out of the war, except when he was on the bench, was the great law rival of Maj. Mayes. They were on one side or the other of all important suits, and all important cases of other courts, and if one chanced to be retained it almost insured a fee for the other on the opposite side, for notwithstanding there were better

---

* By Maj. McKinney.

speakers, for profound, comprehensive knowledge of the law it was very generally conceded that they ranked all other lawyers in this end of the State. Mr. Bradley was a great favorite in Cadiz; everybody loved and respected him, and though many differed with him very positively on questions of public policy, there was not a citizen of the town identified with the opposition who would not have risked his own life in his defense. Yet he conceived the idea that there were persons here who were devising means to have him assassinated, and the belief took such possession of his mind that he actually moved away from the town, and was never back here but once afterward. As a matter of course his apprehension was all imaginary, but no one who was at all familiar with him doubted for a moment that he honestly believed that people plotted his death. He was eccentric in all things, but withal the most delightful companion for young men in the world. One would suppose that half the object of his life was devoted to devising plans for improving the morals, the intelligence, and contributing to the pleasure of the young men of the town. He organized reading clubs, debating societies, moot courts and social games for young people, and would enter into them with all the enthusiasm and spirit of a boy of eighteen. If an old attorney was leading a young man into a snare in the trial of a case in court, you would find Bradley flying to the assistance of the young attorney, if the old one was representing the cause of one of the most intimate friends he had on earth. He would listen to the story of a school boy who had gotten into trouble with his teacher, and with too much prudence to let the boy know it, he would never lose sight of it until he arrived at the true facts of the case, then if he found the boy in error, he told him of it, and if the fault was the teacher's he was just as sure to hear it as the boy. His excitement was so intense that he took part in every dog fight that occurred upon the street, and if a social game of "seven up" was going on between the boys, he was sure to be one of the party, and would become as much interested and excited as if he had £1,000 at stake. He was very systematic and thought himself the most methodical man in the world. He had a theory for everything and arrived at all conclusions purely upon theoretical principle. He had a theory for loading a gun, the scent of a staghound, or the speed of a race-horse, and whenever one of them failed to exemplify itself in practice, he accounted for the failure by its being an exception to the general rule.

He had him a rifle made especially for target-shooting, and paid a certain man $150 for a scrub colt, because by every principle and theory of locomotion he was compelled to make the fastest running horse in the world. Yet he was always beaten at the shooting matches, and Dr. D. Maxwell, now of Paducah, upon one occasion made a bet with him to run himself a foot-race against the horse, which he did do and actually beat him. Judge Bradley took an active part in political matters, and was a stanch Union man during the war. He served a term on the bench of this district, and no man living or dead ever had a doubt of his splendid capacity and his integrity as an upright and impartial Judge.

Political History.—Much of what appears in the following pages is taken from Maj. McKinney's excellent historical sketches, and his accounts of the early elections are appropriated entire. The first recorded vote in the county was for members of Congress and for members of the Legislature at the August election of 1822. The candidates for Congress were Robert P. Henry and Dixon Given. The former received in the county 271 votes, and the latter 107. The candidates for the Legislature were Benjamin Patten, Nathan O. Haden, Thomas Raleigh and Thomas Barnett.

The vote stood as follows: Patten, 233; Haden, 202; Raleigh, 161 and Barnett, 103. Henry was elected to Congress, and Patten and Barnett were elected to represent Christian and Trigg Counties in the Legislature. In the winter of 1823 the Legislature granted to Trigg County a separate representative in the lower house. The contest at the August election for that year was hotly contested. The candidates for the Legislature were Charles Caldwell and Thomas Raleigh. Caldwell received 250 votes, and Raleigh 248; majority for Caldwell two. There were three candidates for Governor that year, and the vote in this county stood as follows: Joseph Desha, 328 votes; Christopher Thompkins, 136, and William Russell, 4. For Congress, Robert P. Henry received 477 votes.

In the year 1825 Maj. George Street, father of John L. Street, defeated Col. Caldwell for the Legislature. There were three voting precincts then, and the vote stood as follows:

	Street.	Caldwell.
Cadiz	289	30
Canton	60	84
Burnett's Precinct	6	188
	355	302

Maj. Street receiving a majority of 53 votes he was re-elected the following year over Thomas Raleigh, by a majority of 34 votes.

This last election seemed to have stirred up something of a sectional hostility in the county that has continued more or less to the present day. Maj. Street lived in the eastern portion of the county, and Col. Caldwell, near the elbow, on the opposite side of the Cumberland River. Street was therefore a Cadiz man and Caldwell a Canton man. Street had defeated Caldwell for the Legislature, and the following year defeated his friend

Raleigh for the same office. This, as was very natural, created animosity between the two sections, and hence arose the question of the removal of the county seat from Cadiz to Canton. Matters were pretty warm next year, and as both parties were marshaling for a vigorous struggle, they concluded to select from each section new men, against whom no prejudice had been aroused by previous conflicts. The Cadiz people selected George Daniel and the Canton party selected as their champion Abraham Boyd, the father of the county, and ancestor of Hon. Linn Boyd. The result was notwithstanding the great personal strength of Mr. Daniel that the Canton men were victorious. Boyd was elected by the scant majority of 46 votes.

In 1828 the contest between the two contending factions culminated in the re-election of Abraham Boyd over James Coleman, by a majority of 35 votes. But things began to show a change in 1829. The contest that year was between Dr. George Venable and Abraham Boyd. Dr. Venable was elected by only 13 votes. This ended the serious agitation of the removal of the county seat from Cadiz to Canton. The next year Lipscomb Norvell was elected over A. Samuel, by a majority of 82 votes out of the 100 cast. The next year Linn Boyd and Joseph Waddill were candidates for the Legislature, and a full vote of the county was polled, Boyd receiving 543 and Waddill 348. None of the county officers except the members of the Legislature were elected by the people. The magistrates were commissioned by the Governor, and the oldest in commission succeeded to the Sheriffalty, retaining the office for two years. William Scott by virtue of being the oldest magistrate succeeded to the office twice, the first time in 1826 and again in 1840. Dick Dawson was the Presiding Justice of the County Court up to the year 1831.

The year 1832 was the Presidential year of the great contest between Andrew Jackson and Henry Clay. It was the first year, too, that the parties were distinctly arrayed under the old familiar appellation of Whig and Democrat. No conventions were held those days, but a universal popular applause for great party leaders pointed out the candidates in the place of a convention. Still in that year, to secure a more perfect organization a congressional caucus had nominated each. Martin Van Buren was on the ticket with Gen. Jackson, as a candidate for Vice President, and John Sargent for the same place, on the ticket with Mr. Clay. The politicians of the State seemed to have selected their subordinates with a view of meeting the exigencies of the great struggle that was approaching. Among the distinguished men that appear on the electoral ticket with Mr. Clay, were E. M. Ewing, John J. Marshall, William Ousley, Ben Hardin, Theodore Chilton and M. V. Thompson. On that of Gen. Jackson were found the names of William O. Butler, John Speed, Smith-

James Guthrie, T. S. Slaughter and Matthew Lyon. The vote in Trigg County stood at the close of the polls, November 7, 1832, as follows:

	Jackson.	Clay.
Cadiz	177	301
Canton	104	20
Roaring Springs	98	53
Totals	439	374

Majority in the county for Jackson, 65 votes. The candidates for the Legislature that year were Judge James E. Thompson and Dr. Isaac Burnett. It was a strictly a political canvass with just enough personal matters thrown in to enable Judge Thompson's great personal popularity to bear him triumphantly through. He was elected by a majority of 52 votes. The next year Burnett was elected by a majority of 159 votes, over two competitors, Robert Baker and Col. T. W. Hammond.

In the Presidential campaign of 1836 Harrison and Granger were the candidates of the Whig party, and Martin Van Buren and Richard M. Johnson were candidates of the Democratic party. Van Buren carried the county by a majority of eighty-eight votes.

The year 1840 was one of the most notable epochs in the history of Kentucky, or perhaps in American annals. The political canvasses were vigorous, impressive, and very aggressive. Public meetings were held in various portions of the county, and clubs were formed, and more than one canoe or log-cabin was placed upon wheels and hauled around, and more than one barrel of hard cider was tapped to elevate the spirits of the enthusiastic Whigs. John L. Murray and Robert Patterson were the Democratic and Whig electors for the First District that year. Mr. Murray, whose health had already begun to fail, did not participate very actively in the canvass, but Patterson was everywhere, addressing the large audiences, giving free rein to acrimonious invective, the effect of which was said to have been wonderful. The result was, at the November election the county showed only a majority of nineteen votes for Van Buren and Johnson over Harrison and Tyler. The latter carried the State by a large majority, and were overwhelmingly elected to the Presidency and Vice-Presidency of the United States. This was the first Whig ticket that had ever been elected since the formation of the party, and unless we claim Gen. Taylor, who was voted for by the Whigs as a "no party man," it was destined to be the last.

But few persons living then will fail to recollect the exciting political events of 1844. It was about this time that the question of an increase of slave territory began to warmly interest the citizens of the country, and a limited abolition sentiment began manifesting itself in many of the Northern States. Early in 1844 it was well known that the efforts of the

Democracy would be directed in the coming campaign toward the election of a President who favored the admission of Texas into the Union, and thereby an increase of slave territory; while the Whigs on the contrary took an opposite stand, opposing the admission of Texas, in order to limit the domain of slavery, and they accordingly nominated Henry Clay, while the Democrats selected James K. Polk. These were the principal tickets, though not the only ones. The Liberty party placed in the field Birney and Morris, the platform differing somewhat from that of the Whigs, but resembling it in opposing an increase of slave territory. The vote stood in Trigg County as follows:

	Polk.	Clay.
Cadiz	265	397
Canton	212	96
Roaring Springs	174	64
Totals	651	557

A majority for Polk of 94 votes.

In the Presidential campaign of 1848 the first extensive Free-Soil movement was made. The violent debates in Congress on questions growing out of slavery attracted universal attention and interest. In 1846 David Wilmot, of Pennsylvania, had introduced in Congress what became known as the Wilmot Proviso, which prohibited slavery in any territory which might be acquired from Mexico or elsewhere. Though the measure was defeated finally, some of the most eloquent and passionate speeches in American history were delivered in Congress while it was pending. The interest in Trigg County led to the partial organization of a Free-Soil party, many citizens who had formerly figured prominently in both old parties joining its ranks. The Whig candidates were Zachary Taylor and Millard Fillmore. The Democrats nominated Lewis Cass and William O. Butler, while the Free-Soilers put in nomination Martin Van Buren. Unfortunately no record of the vote of Trigg County for that year was obtained, the poll book having by some means become misplaced.

In the year 1850 the present Constitution of Kentucky was adopted, and on Monday, the 12th of May, an election was appointed for the purpose of selecting persons to fill all the civil offices of the State. Previous to this time there had been no election of such officers by the popular voice of the people. The Judges of the Court of Appeals, Circuit Judges, Commonwealth Attorneys, Justices, etc., were all appointed by the Governor; the Clerk of the Court of Appeals by the Judges of that court; the Circuit Clerks by the Circuit Judges; the County Clerk by the Justices comprising that court, and the Jailor, Assessor, Constables, etc., by the same.

No elections were held by the people except for President, Vice-President, Governor, Lieutenant-Governor, Members of Congress, and of the

Senate and Legislature. The following candidates were before the people at the first election under the new Constitution :

Thomas Towles, Fay Henry and J. W. Waddill, for Commonwealth's Attorney; Towles was elected.

Thomas C. Dabney, Mark M. Tyler and T. W. Hammond, candidates for County Judge; Dabney elected.

The candidates for Circuit Clerk were Henry C. Burnett and James E. Thompson. Burnett was elected, and before the expiration of his term of office resigned the position, and was elected to Congress from this district.

A. S. Dabney and E. Vinson, Jr., were opposing candidates for County Clerk; Dabney elected.

Candidates for Sheriff were Stanley Thomas, B. J. Wall, John Humphries, Thomas Ingram and Ira Ellis; Thomas elected. Otley Grace, John J. Dyer, Thomas Rogers, —— Adams and —— Layton were candidates for Assessor; Grace elected. James Richardson, A. Thomas, B. B. Mart and Kinchen Battoe for Surveyor; Richardson elected. Daniel Landes was elected to the Legislature, and George W. Barbour to the Senate.

After the Presidential election of 1848, there was no abatement of interest throughout the country until the passage of the celebrated "Omnibus Bill" in 1850. The question of the admission of California into the Union had come up, and had stirred to intense bitterness the sentiments of both parties in Congress, and in all portions of the country. And when Henry Clay came forward with his celebrated compromise, which provided among other things for the admission of California as a free State, and for the return of fugitive slaves to their masters, both Clay and his compromise were hailed by all except the Abolitionists with universal joy. The Free-Soil party was determined, and kept the South violently nettled. The Whigs nominated Gen. Winfield Scott, and the Democratic standard-bearer was Franklin Pierce. The vote in this county was as follows: Pierce and King, 629 votes; Scott and Graham, 560; Pierce's majority, 69 votes. This was the last political struggle of the old Whig party. The agitation of the great principles for which Mr. Clay had so aggressively contended tranquilly subsided, its organization was broken up, and the record of its achievements glided peacefully away into history.

The year 1856 was the first year the Abolitionists had ever attempted seriously to extend their views touching slavery into anything like national proportions. The fugitive slave law was intensely odious to all the North except a few who were in sentiment favorably disposed toward slavery. The Republican party sprang into life and conducted one of the most exciting campaigns in the history of the nation. They called a national convention, which had a full representation from the Northern and Western States, and nominated Fremont and Dayton for President and Vice-President.

Buchanan and Breckinridge were the names presented by the Democratic, and Fillmore and Donaldson by the American party. "The most prominent candidate for the office of Vice-President this year was a distinguished citizen of Trigg County, and its old Representative in Congress, the Hon. Linn Boyd. Mr. Boyd would surely have been the nominee but for a successful ruse upon the part of the delegation from Virginia. It was pretty well conceded that Mr. Boyd was the strongest man whose name had been mentioned in connection with the office, and unless something was done to arrest the tide in his favor, would most likely receive the nomination on the second or third ballot. Just then the name of John C. Breckinridge was proposed; and after a number of ineffectual attempts to have his name withdrawn, with the purest motives, the gentleman himself, who was present, was called upon the stand for the purpose of withdrawing his name in person, which he did, but the fine appearance of the man, the dignity and elegance of his style and the pure disinterestedness of his patriotism and devotion to his party electrified the whole body, and each individual member appearing to rise at once to his feet, he was nominated by acclamation. This was the last election in which all the conflicting elements of the Democratic party have been thoroughly united." The vote of Trigg County was as follows:

	Votes.
Buchanan and Breckinridge	859
Fillmore and Donaldson	581
Fremont and Dayton	0

The Presidential canvass of 1860 was contemplated from the beginning by all men of reflection with the most profound solicitude. For a few years preceding 1860 the sentiment on both sides had become so bitter, and the North, and especially the Republican party, had been so outspoken against slavery that the South instinctively felt that the election of the Republican candidate, Mr. Lincoln, meant serious interference with that institution. The November election was scarcely over ere ordinances of secession were passed, and preparations for war began on both sides. The war came, and the Republic was preserved in a modified form. The vote of the county is given as follows by districts:

	Breckinridge.	Douglas.	Bell.	Lincoln.
Cadiz	182	3	215	0
Canton	65	39	82	0
Roaring Springs	120	95	78	1
Ferguson Springs	51	23	58	0
Wallonia	104	1	75	0
Bethesda	90	0	61	0
Futrell's	66	16	31	0

It will thus be perceived that Breckinridge received 675 votes; Bell, 600; Douglas, 175; and Lincoln but 1.

In 1864 the contest was really upon the question of continuing the war. As the Confederate States were out of the contest, the question was decided wholly by the Northern States. Lincoln's re-election developed the fact that the North was in favor of continuing the war, and the struggle for supremacy was vigorously renewed. The vote of this county, if any at that election, is not accessible.

The Presidential election of 1868 placed Gen. Grant at the head of the nation. The election returns for Trigg show the following vote: Seymour and Blair, 1,199; Grant and Colfax, 108. In 1872, Grant came up for re-election. The Republicans who opposed him united with the mass of the Democracy and placed Horace Greeley in the field. The straight-out Democrats nominated Charles O'Conor. Trigg County voted as follows: Greeley and Blair, 977; Grant and Wilson, 928; O'Conor, 71. In 1876 Tilden and Hendricks were the nominees of the Democratic party, and Hayes and Wheeler were selected as standard-bearers by the Republicans. The events of that celebrated campaign have gone into history and need not be repeated here. The following result shows how Trigg County's vote was divided between the two tickets: Tilden and Hendricks, 1,508 votes; Hayes and Wheeler, 994 votes.

In 1880 three national tickets were put in the field—Hancock and English by the Democrats, Garfield and Arthur by the Republicans, and Weaver and Chambers by the Greenback party. The election in Trigg County gave the following return: Hancock, 1,262; Garfield, 873; Weaver, 48. Thus it will be seen that the county has been from the first Democratic, and that, too, by a majority which numerous disasters have been unable to overcome.

Roads and Trails.—The early lines of travel through this part of Kentucky were along the Indian trails. These were clearly defined paths about eighteen inches wide and worn into the ground, sometimes to the depth of eight or ten inches. They traversed the country in almost every direction, but no traces of them are to be found at the present time. An early trail known as the Buffalo trace, so called from its having been used by buffaloes as well as by the Indians, led from the Cumberland River to Cerulean Springs, passing through the intervening section of country in a northwesterly and southeasterly direction. This trace was well defined as early as 1790, and was used as a road by the first settlers in traveling to and from the points connected. As the country became more thickly populated and roads a necessity, it was legally established, and was one of the earliest prominent thoroughfares in Trigg County. Only portions of the original route are used at the present time, the greater part having been abandoned many years ago. Another early road, and one that was quite extensively traveled, led from Hopkinsville to the Saline Salt works in Illinois. It passed in a northwesterly course through the northern part of Trigg County, and for many years was one of the principal highways of this section of the State.

The most important highway in Trigg County is the Columbus & Bowling Green State road, better known in this part of the country as the Canton & Hopkinsville road, established by an act of the State Legislature about the year 1819 or 1820. It leads from Bowling Green to the Mississippi River, passing through this county in a northwesterly direction, and was for many years the principal stage and mail route for Trigg and Christian Counties. The most important section of the road is the part lying between the towns of Canton and Hopkinsville, over which all the merchandise for the two counties was freighted until the construction of the railroad to the latter place.

Prior to 1860 Canton was the distributing point for a large area of territory, and on this road could be seen, almost any day, lines of freight wagons, extending a mile or more in length. In the year 1858–59 a stock company, composed of the leading business men of Cadiz and a few from Christian County was organized, for the purpose of constructing a turnpike from the landing to Hopkinsville, and a charter for the road was accordingly obtained. The stock was placed upon the market in shares of $100 each, and work on the road went briskly forward until a section fourteen miles in length was completed. The part finished extends from the landing to within a few miles of Montgomery Village, and cost the sum of $60,000. The road proved a paying investment, and returned a handsome profit until the completion of the railway to Hopkinsville, when, owing to the serious interference with the freighting interests, the stock began rapidly to decline. The present board of managers consists of the following gentlemen, to wit : J. S. Wharton, President and Collector ; Thomas H. Grinter, Secretary and Treasurer ; John L. Street, M. S. Thompson, W. J. Fuqua and R. Wilford.

"The same year the charter was obtained of the Kentucky Legislature to build the Hopkinsville, Cadiz & Canton Turnpike; one was also obtained to build a pike from a point on the Cumberland River, from what was then known as the Old Kelley Furnace Landing to Hopkinsville, and a town was chartered at the latter point. It being near Lineport, Tenn., a village through which the line dividing the States of Kentucky and Tennessee ran, the new town being near the old one, and also near the line of the two States, was consequently called Linetown on Linton. Subscription books for stock began to be circulated, not until some time after the Cadiz & Canton pike had been put under contract, but was prosecuted with so much more energy that the two pikes were built and completed to the Christian County line about the same time; Hopkinsville and Christian County refusing to give any assistance to continue the road through that county, the work was discontinued at the line between the two counties, nor has it ever been resumed. Dr. John C. Whitlock was the President, and it may be said of a truth that he built and established both the pike and the town." The road never proved a paying venture, and has not been kept up for several years.

Railroad.—Hopes of securing a railroad have been entertained by the citizens of Trigg County for a number of years, and several projected lines have been run through the country at different times. The Indiana, Tennessee & Alabama road was surveyed in 1879, and is likely to be completed within the next year. The projected route passes through the northeast corner of the county, and crosses the boundary at the Hopkinsville road, near Henry Bryant's farm in Montgomery Precinct. This road, when completed, will be of great benefit to the country through which it passes, by affording markets within the easy reach of the citizens of eastern Trigg. It will also enhance the value of the lands lying contiguous.

To sum up, Trigg County needs railroads to properly develop its rich mines of wealth. With the requisite railroad facilities added to the water highways, Trigg would be fortunate above most of her neighbors. With all her tobacco, grain, stock, timber, rich ores, etc., railroads would soon make Trigg one of the richest counties in southwestern Kentucky.

CHAPTER IV.

RELIGIOUS—SYNOPSIS OF THE CHURCH HISTORY OF TRIGG COUNTY—SOME
OF THE PIONEER PREACHERS OF SOUTHERN KENTUCKY—THEIR PECUL-
IAR CHARACTERISTICS — DUDLEY WILLIAMS — REUBEN ROSS AND
OTHERS—NUMBER OF CHURCHES IN THE COUNTY—SCHOOLS—PAST AND
PRESENT INSTITUTIONS OF LEARNING—TEACHERS—STATISTICS—THE
PRESS—CANTON OBSERVER—YEOMAN—CADIZ ORGAN—THE TELEPHONE
AND OLD GUARD—STANDING UPON A SOLID FOUNDATION—CRIME AND
LAWLESSNESS—CONVICTIONS AND EXECUTIONS—"OBEY THE LAWS"—
TRIGG COUNTY MEDICAL SOCIETY, ETC., ETC.

IN the early history of southern Kentucky it was not thought necessary
that preachers should be educated men. It was sufficient for them to
preach the Gospel from their simple understanding of the Bible alone.
They have passed away, but they have left behind them the record of a
mission well and faithfully performed, and may their sacred ashes repose
in peace, in the quietude of their lonely graves until awakened by the
archangel's trump in the last great day.

Among the earliest preachers in the county, of whom there is any
record or knowledge, was Elder Dudley Williams, a member of the Baptist Church. He was one of the self-appointed missionaries of the frontier who went from place to place, intent only to show men the way to life
everlasting. Elders Dorris, Brown and Thomas Ross were also early
preachers in the county. They were Baptists, and held religious services
from house to house during the early days of the county's history. Elder
Reuben Ross was a distinguished preacher of the Baptist Church also,
and a man of more than ordinary intellectual acquirements and eloquence.
He was a man of generous mind, and co-operated freely with ministers of
other denominations. He believed that in "things essential there should
be unity," and in things not essential there should be liberty, and in all
things charity. He was one of the founders of the Dry Creek Church,
near Linton, one of the oldest church organizations in the county, and
assisted in the establishment of the Donaldson Creek Church as early as
1814. Another Baptist Church, thought by some to be the first in the
county, was formed in the year 1806, at Cerulean Springs. Elders Fielding Wolfe, Reuben Rowland and Peyton Nance, zealous workers in the
cause of the Master, ministered to this church for many years during its
early history.

Following close in the wake of the Baptists came pioneer missionaries of the Methodist Church, and established flourishing societies in various parts of the county. Later the Christians, or Disciples, as they are more familiarly known, obtained firm footing in the southern part of the State, and in Trigg are several of their oldest and most influential organizations. Thus a population increased, churches sprang up in all the different settlements of the county. At the present time every village and hamlet, and nearly every neighborhood has its church and Sunday-school. There is no lack of religious facilities, and if the people do not walk in the "straight and narrow way" they have but themselves to blame for any short-comings laid up against them. There are in the county at the present time fifteen Baptist Churches, and about the same number of Methodist. The Christians have five organizations; the Christian Union three; the Presbyterians one, and the Catholics one. The above are all white churches. The colored people have several flourishing societies, principally Methodist and Baptist.

Schools.—Scarcely second of the active forces that influence the development of society is the public school; nothing adds so much to the prosperity of a community, or to its civilization and enlightenment as a thorough system of public instruction, and the cause of education should enlist the hearty support of every citizen irrespective of party affiliations. " The statutes of Kentucky show that the first experiments to extend the fostering aid and care of State patronage to the interests of general education were made nearly three-quarters of a century ago. An act of the Legislature, approved February 10, 1798, donated and set apart of the public lands of the Commonwealth 6,000 acres, for the support and benefit of Franklin, Salem and Kentucky Academies, and for Jefferson and Lexington Seminaries. Similar acts were approved December 21, 1805, and January 27, 1808, embracing like provisions, and extending them to all existing counties of the State."*

It would be impossible within reasonable space to trace the course of legislation upon this most important subject of public schools. Almost every session of the Legislature has witnessed the passage of some special or general law in relation to the school interests of the State. The difficulties in the way of the early progress of the system were numerous, and for a time insurmountable. Funds for the pay of teachers and for the erection of schoolhouses were lacking, qualified teachers could not be found, the school districts were sparsely settled, much of the legislation was impracticable, the funds were mismanaged, and more fatal than all, was the strange prejudice entertained by many against popular education under the name of " free schools." Against the various hindrances, how-

* From Collins' History.

ever, the system has slowly made its way in spite of hostile judicial decisions, until now, though far from being perfect, and much inferior to the systems of other and newer States, it is accomplishing the great objects for which it was intended.

The early schools of Trigg County, like the whole of Kentucky, were of the commonest kind, and the cause of education for more than a generation was in anything but a flourishing condition. For half a century or more the schoolhouses, books, teachers and manner of instruction were of the most primitive character, and very different from what they are at the present day. The buildings, as a general thing, were very small log structures, with puncheon or dirt floors, and furnished with rude benches made of the split trunks of trees. A wide board fastened to the walls by wooden pins extended around the room, and answered the purpose of a writing desk during certain hours of the day. The apartment was heated by a large fireplace which occupied almost an entire end of the building, and light was admitted through greased paper windows fitted into an opening in the wall. A few of these humble temples of learning—time-worn relics of the early days, are yet to be found in many portions of southern Kentucky—eloquent of an age forever past. The majority of the pioneer schools was maintained altogether by subscription, and it was not until within a comparatively recent period that any substantial good began to be realized from the general system of public instruction. The county is still somewhat backward in the cause of education, and has not made that progress that it should have done, although much has been accomplished during the last decade toward bringing the common schools up to a higher degree of excellence. New and commodious houses have been erected, old houses have been repaired and refitted, better teachers employed, more liberal salaries paid, and many other needed improvements added.

There are in the county at the present time fifty-six public schoolhouses, only eighteen of which are framed, the others being log, and the majority of them very indifferent structures. During the school year of 1882 and 1883, 3,543 white and 1,395 colored pupils attended the public schools. Sixty-three teachers were employed, and the sum of $7,500 paid them for their services.

In addition to the public schools there are several private institutions of learning in the county, where the most thorough and systematic instruction is given by competent teachers. The most important of these schools is the Wallonia Institute. There are also excellent private schools at Cadiz, which are more appropriately mentioned in the history of that town.

The Press.—The newspaper is an important factor in American society, and its establishment marks an epoch in the history of a community. In the main, it reflects the character of its constituency; it leads to a union of sentiment and purpose, and thus renders the moral force of society more effective. Hand in hand with the church and the school, it comes in the van of civilization, and society in this age cannot afford to dispense with its power.

Ezekiel Vinson was the first man that had nerve to start a newspaper in this county away back in the fifties. This was a modest six-column long primer independent local sheet called the *Canton Observer*, from its having been published at that place. After issuing the paper one year at Canton, Mr. Vinson moved his office to Cadiz, and changed the name of his paper to the *Cadiz Weekly Observer*, under which head it made its regular appearance for about two years, at the end of which time T. N. Ingram & Co. became proprietors. Under their management the office was removed to Canton, and J. S. Spiceland secured as editor. Spiceland afterward purchased the office, which was again brought to Cadiz, and the paper in 1857 was merged into the *Cadiz Organ*.

Canton Yeoman.—This was venture number two in the way of newspaper enterprises in Canton. The *Yeoman* was Democratic in politics, and first made its appearance in 1857 under the editorial management of J. T. Ingram. Not meeting with sufficient patronage at Canton, Mr. Ingram, at the breaking out of the war, moved his paper to Mayfield, where it was afterward suppressed for its outspoken Southern senti ments.

The *Cadiz Organ* was published by John S. Spiceland, and was established about the year 1857-58—a seven-column weekly Democratic paper. Spiceland carried it on about two years, at the end of which time he sold out to J. W. Gobin, who several years later merged it into the *Trigg County Democrat*. Mr. Gobin published the *Democrat* about nine months, when he sold to C. T. Wilkinson, under whose management it was regularly issued until April, 1882, at which time it suspended. When Wilkinson became proprietor he secured the services of Judge J. H. Wilkinson as editor, who made it the strongest and ablest paper the county had had up to that time. Judge Wilkinson wrote and published a great deal of matter. His facile pen ran smoothly over the paper, and when he cared he could invest his subject in strong and glowing language. He died in 1882, and in his death the editorial fraternity lost an able and valued member.

A small sheet called the *Union Democrat* was started at Canton in 1861 by E. C. Spiceland. This paper was radical in its adherence to the Federal cause, and met with but little patronage in consequence thereof. Mr. Spiceland published the *Democrat* but a few months, when it died a natural and easy death.

*The Kentucky Telephone.**—The first number of the Kentucky *Telephone* was issued January 4, 1882. It was established by A. T. Wimberly, one of the present proprietors. It was a seven-column folio until October 27, 1882, when it was enlarged to eight columns, its patronage being such as to demand it. It is a weekly, and in politics Democratic. Matthew McKinney and A. T. Wimberly were the editors, the former being the principal editor until September 7, 1883, when he resigned. A. T. Wimberly then took charge of the editorial department, and was sole editor and proprietor until January 1, 1884, when he sold a half interest in the office to Webb Watkins, who was at that time foreman of the printing department. It is now published under the firm name of Wimberly & Watkins, with A. T. Wimberly as editor and Webb Watkins as associate. The business of the paper has been very successfully managed. Its circulation has not been less than 950 since the end of the first year's existence, and it has reached 1,300. It now has a circulation of 1,200. Its advertising patronage is liberal, and everything considered, there is not a county paper in southern or western Kentucky that receives a more liberal patronage than the *Telephone.*

Old Guard.—This publication, the latest newspaper venture in Trigg County, was established January, 1884, by G. B. Bingham and Matthew McKinney. It is a seven-column folio, Democratic in politics, and under the able editorial management of Major McKinney has already acquired an extensive circulation, which is constantly increasing.

The business of the paper is successfully conducted by Mr. Bingham, while as a writer Maj. McKinney is the peer of any newspaper man in Kentucky. The outlook of the *Old Guard* is very promising, and its friends predict for it a brilliant future.

Trigg County has an able press, and should appreciate it as it deserves. Few counties have two better or more sprightly newspapers. They have prospered through the energy of their owners, and are now upon a solid foundation; their patrons should see that they continue so, by supporting them liberally.

Crime.†—Notwithstanding the history of Trigg County has been proverbial for its good order and the peacefulness of its population, if we take some other counties as examples her record has been rather a bloody one. It is pretty well conceded now that in most of the counties of Kentucky if a criminal is found guilty and the death penalty affixed, that public sentiment has driven the jury to the finding of the verdict; but if malefactors will take upon themselves the trouble to look into the county records of Trigg, we think they will come to the conclusion that it is not a very favorable location for the perpetration of their murderous designs.

* Prepared by A. T. Wimberly.
† From McKinney's Sketches.

The death sentence has been pronounced seven times since the county has been organized, and there have been five executions. The first was Jerry, a slave of Starkie Thomas, who was arraigned for trial in the Trigg Circuit Court the 7th day of July, 1841. The jury was composed of a lot of stanch old gentlemen, among whom are remembered the following: John H. Prescott, George Grace, John Wallis, Sam Stanrod, Thomas H. Young, Alex Wilson, Robert Hawkins, William H. Martin, Z. E. F. Mitchison and William Waldin.

He was prosecuted by Iredel Hart and defended by Cormenius Burnett. He was found guilty, and executed on the 30th day of July, 1841. The day of Jerry's execution drew the largest crowd to Cadiz that has ever been there from that day to this. The bulk of the population not only of this county but most of the adjoining counties all seemed to have been there. Not only the gentlemen but the ladies turned out in full force, and the most refined and cultivated ladies in the county at that. There was considerable sympathy manifested for Jerry, and most likely if such a case had occurred during Gov. Blackburn's administration, he would have been called upon for an interposition of executive clemency. The proof was positive, but there were mitigating circumstances, the introduction of which the law forbade, that gave the finding of the jury somewhat the appearance of a harsh verdict.

The second execution was Minerva, a servant, the property of Mrs. Martha Mayes. Herself and husband, the property of Jane Miller, were tried for arson—the burning of the storehouse of Messrs. Gardner & Ragon. It seems to have been the generally received opinion that George. was guilty, but there was always a doubt in the minds of the people as to the guilt of Minerva, except perhaps the knowledge of her husband's intention to commit the offense. Public sentiment, however, was wrought up to a high pitch, and notwithstanding the testimony was all circumstantial, they were both found guilty. George committed suicide in jail before the day of execution, and Minerva suffered the extreme penalty of the law on the 9th day of February, 1856.

Sol Younce was tried and found guilty by a Committee of Vigilance as being a leader in a proposed insurrection of the negroes, and a plot to murder the whites—found guilty, and was executed some time in the spring of 1856. There being no record of this matter kept, we are consequently unable to give the precise date.

Anthony, a slave, the property of R. V. Grinter, was regularly indicted by the Grand Jury and tried for a similar offense, found guilty, and was executed on the 6th day of February, 1857. Anthony had been tried for his life on one occasion previous to this. The first offense was the breaking open and robbing the house of Mrs. Kelly.

The next conviction and sentence was Austin Bingham for murder. He was sentenced to be hung, and the day of execution fixed for the 4th of November, 1859. There was a great effort made both in the trial and after judgment by his attorneys to save his life, and finally Gov. Magoffin was prevailed upon to commute his punishment to imprisonment for life. He died in the penitentiary a few years after.

Andrew Jackson was tried and found guilty of murder, condemned, and executed on April 12, 1860.

John Bridges was tried for murder, and executed on the 30th day of June, 1882.

"Let justice be done though the heavens fall," is the motto of our people, but they very much hope at the same time that long years may elapse before another crime will be committed in the county that will demand so severe a penalty.

Trigg County Medical Society.—The medical fraternity of the county have formed themselves into an organization known as the Trigg County Medical Society. The society was organized in 1872, any graduate of medicine from a respectable medical college being eligible to membership.

The first officers were Dr. Thomas Jefferson, President; J. S. Lackey, Secretary; and J. W. Crenshaw, Treasurer. Many of the physicians of the county have since joined the society. Dr. J. W. Johnson is President of the organization at this time; J. L. Trice, Vice-President; and J. W. Crenshaw, Secretary and Treasurer. The present membership consists of the following physicians: J. W. Johnson, J. L. Trice, Levi Lindsay, J. W. Crenshaw, T. L. Bacon, A. G. P. Good, William Lindsay, J. W. Cullom, Henry Blane, —— Roscoe and J. H. Lackey. The society is yearly growing in interest, and its meetings are productive of much good to the profession in the county.

CHAPTER V.

War History—The Revolutionary Patriots—Some Who Settled in Trigg County—Our Second Misunderstanding with England—Battle of New Orleans—War with Mexico—Trigg County's Part in It—The Late Civil War—Company G of the Fourth Infantry—A Sketch of Their Service—The Handful Who Survived the War—Companies B and D of the Eighth—Their Exploits and Achievements—Company B of the Second Cavalry—Company D of the Same Regiment—The Federal Side—It is Rather Brief--The Forty-eighth—Other Volunteers—Burning the Cadiz Court House—Murder of a Negro Soldier—A Few Incidents—Peace, etc., etc.

BUCKLE, in his History of Civilization in England, startles the world with the announcement that the invention of gunpowder, "though a warlike contrivance, has in its results been eminently serviceable to the interests of peace." His argument is about as follows: 1. Its invention has made war more destructive to human life, thereby exciting the fears of would-be belligerents, and causing them to dread its issues; therefore it has been " eminently serviceable to the interests of peace." 2. Its invention has made war more expensive, thereby putting it out of reach as an everyday luxury, and making it only possible to the wealthier nations; therefore in this respect also it has been " eminently serviceable to the interests of peace."

By the same process of reasoning the invention of dynamite should have precipitated the millennium. Its greater destructiveness should have shocked the world into a paralysis of fear, and its greater expensiveness should have made war forever impossible to the richest.

No; the true solution of the problem of modern civilization lies elsewhere than in the invention of improved agencies and implements of destruction. We must go beyond and deeper. War is the outgrowth of human passion and pride, and the true conservators of peace must be sought for and found in those influences and agencies that correct and control these. The Christian religion, reaching down to the very fountain-source of man's being, and turning hate to love, covetousness to alms-giving, and selfishness to self-sacrifice, is alone such principle. In its enlightening and ennobling influences are to be found the prime factors of the present civilizations. Its very germ-life is to be found imbedded in the injunction, "Therefore, all things whatsoever ye would that men should do to you, do ye even so to them." The life and teachings of the Son of Mary are the very incarnation of peace, and under the benign influence of such example and teaching the moral conscience of the world has been educated to look upon war as an unmitigated evil, and its instigators as heartless tyrants and oppressors of the race.

War is always an aggression upon one side or the other; the stronger, from motives of cupidity and power, making encroachments upon the rights and privileges of the weaker, or the weaker seeking to revenge themselves upon the stronger.

In the war between the mother country and her colonies she was the aggressor. The King, backed by a venal Parliament, sought to impose onerous burthens of taxation upon the struggling colonists, while at the same time persistently refusing to concede to them the just and inalienable right of representation. The colonies insisted that taxation and representation were inseparable and should go together, and therefore that " taxes or subsidies of every sort for the support of Government should be the voluntary tribute of the people through their representatives." The insistance upon this principle of taxation without representation by Parliament on the one hand, and its resistance by the colonies on the other, soon brought about the heroic struggle which finally resulted in the complete independence of the latter.

It is not the present purpose to recount any part of that eventful period—it was over and almost forgotten before this part of " the dark and bloody ground " was thought of as a possible habitation—but to preserve to the pages of history the names of some of those who were participants in its fortunes. After the war was over and the people had again settled down to the more peaceful vocations of life, the growing importance of this portion of Kentucky began to attract the attention of many of the more adventurous spirits of Virginia, Georgia and the Carolinas. Many of the war-worn veterans of these and other States, by themselves or in groups, began to make their way to this, then a part of Christian County, and the contiguous portions of southwestern Kentucky. A few of these names have been preserved, and it is the pleasure of the historian to spread them upon these pages.

In the year 1792, Thomas Wadlington, of North Carolina, who had been a soldier under Gen. Nathaniel Greene, came West with his family and settled near Kent's Bridge on Little River, about five miles from the present site of Cadiz. All that is known of his war record, beside the mere fact that he was one of Greene's men, is that he participated in the battle of Guilford Court House under that distinguished officer. No doubt he was in the subsequent engagements at Camden, Ninety-six and Eutaw Springs, but there is no record remaining of the fact, and none living able to decide.

Another of Gen. Greene's veterans in the campaigns of North and South Carolina, and who came to the county in 1806, was James Thomas, father of Perry Thomas, now in his eighty-eighth year. James Thomas, beside being a good farmer, was an excellent citizen and full of "the milk of human kindness." He settled on the place adjoining that on which his son Perry now resides, and continued to live there till the year 1832, when he died full of years, and was gathered to his fathers.

In 1811 Capt. Thomas Humphries, of Virginia, came to the county with his brother Absalom. He and Absalom and three other brothers had been in the patriot army, and had distinguished themselves on many a hard-fought field. Thomas was a Methodist preacher of much force and eloquence, and perhaps the most cultivated and accomplished scholar in the county at that day. Only one of the veterans who followed the fortunes of Gen. Francis Marion, "the Swamp Fox," is now recalled. John Grasty, of South Carolina, came to Christian in 1790, and settled in that portion now comprehended within the boundaries of Trigg County. Besides being a scarred and war-worn veteran of the Continental army, like Humphries he was a man of education and refinement, and for a long time taught one of the early schools.

The name of but one Revolutionary soldier appears as such upon the Trigg County records. In 1820, June 19, Thomas Owsley (indexed Woosley) made application for a pension, and produced in open court the following schedule of his property: "An old horse, one cow, one calf, two two-year-old heifers, fourteen sheep, two sows and seventeen pigs, six old pewter plates, five knives, as many forks, and some wooden utensils of little or no value."

Besides these, the names simply of James Barnum, Miles Hollowell, John Mayberry and Balaam Ezell, an old Baptist preacher, have been preserved. They were among the earlier settlers of Trigg, and were doubtless as gallant in war as they were afterward adventurous and enterprising in peace.

The War of 1812.—The humiliation and defeat of "the mother country" by her rebellious colonies left a bitter sting in her proud, imperious heart. Though acknowledging their independence, and outwardly maintaining a show of amity and good-fellowship, within their rankled feelings of wounded pride and deep resentment. These exhibited themselves from time to time in overt acts of aggression upon the high seas and elsewhere. In June, 1807, the British man-of-war Leopard fired into the United States frigate Chesapeake, killing three men and wounding eighteen more. This act of unprovoked hostility was, it is true, disavowed by the British Government, but again in 1811 the Little Belt, a British sloop-of-war, fired into the United States frigate President.

This time they did not fare so well, for the doughty Commodore (Rogers) replied by a broadside, and soon placed his antagonist *hors de combat*. About this time also the feeling of hostility toward England in this country was much aggravated by the Indian outbreaks in the Northwest, which were attributed directly to her instigation. Gen. William Henry Harrison promptly met and suppressed them for the time, but there was every indication of further trouble in the future, and much uneasiness was felt. At last the emissaries of the British Government became so bold as to seek to corrupt our own citizens, and one John Henry was found trying to foment sedition among certain disaffected classes in New England. The fact was communicated by President Madison to Congress in a special message, and taken in conjunction with the other acts of unfriendliness and aggression, and the frequent and forcible impressment of American seamen upon the high seas, finally led to a declaration of war upon the part of the United States Government. The people were much exasperated against the English, and everywhere the declaration of hostilities was received with demonstrations of hearty approval. In Kentucky much enthusiasm was manifested. The war spirit blazed forth, and over seven thousand volunteers at once tendered their services to the Government. In answer to a call for 1,500 by the Governor to join Gen. Hopkins at Louisville, over 2,000 responded. Among those from Trigg County, then a part of Christian, were Lieut. Hampton Wade (grandfather of Lieut. Robert Major of the late war), James Baradill and Jonas Mitchell, uncles to Perry Thomas, Stephen Boren, William Campbell and Asa Reddick. These gallant spirits,· or the most of them, followed the fortunes of Hopkins in his expeditions against the Kickapoos in Illinois, and the following November moved against the Indian villages on the Wabash in Indiana. It is not the present purpose to follow the varying fortunes of our arms in this war, though Kentucky perhaps contributed to its success more than any other State in the Union. Suffice it to say that, in the main, both on land and sea they were crowned with success, and in December, 1814, a treaty of peace was signed at Ghent, conceding to us all the points involved in the controversy. But the news of the treaty did not reach our shores till fifteen days after the battle of New Orleans had been fought and won.

On the 8th of January, 1815, Sir Edward Pakenham with some 12,000 soldiers and marines attacked Gen. Jackson, who was entrenched behind cotton bales at New Orleans. The result was a most brilliant victory for our arms. "Two thousand British soldiers led in a charge on Jackson's breastworks were left dead or wounded on the field. Pakenham himself was killed; Maj.-Gens. Gibbs and Keane, the two officers next in command, were both wounded, the former mortally; while Jackson's loss was only seven killed and six wounded."*

Here also Trigg County was well represented. Among those of her sons who participated in the fight, under Col. Posey it is thought, were James Wade, a cousin of Hampton Wade; George Newton, familiarly known as " King Newton;" James Saltzgiven; John Jones, an uncle by marriage of John L. Miller; James, father of Wimberly Thomas, who was wounded and subsequently, on his return home, died of his wounds; T. W. Hammond; Barnes and Henry Jones, brothers; Jerry Saunders, Jack Cotton, Winborn Futrell, William Ramey, David Cahoon, or Calhoun, Warren Clark, William Pitts, Robert Coleman, Henry Vinson, Christopher Brandon and William Rushing. Sergt. Lunsford Lindsay, father of Dr. Lev Lindsay, went from Orange County, Va., under Capt. William Stevens, and served in the war, but where and under what circumstances is not known. He moved to Trigg a few years after, 1819, and was long identified with her best interests as a good and useful citizen.

The Mexican War.—After the termination of this second war with England a long and restful peace smiled upon the country, only interrupted from time to time by the fitful outbreaks of the Seminoles in Florida, and in 1832 of the Black Hawk war in the Northwest. Gen. Winfield Scott speedily put down the Winnebagoes under Black Hawk, and in 1837 Col. Zachary Taylor succeeded in bringing the Seminoles to terms.

In this latter war with the Florida Indians Trigg County had one representative at least, in the person of Harrison Frizzell, who was also afterward in the war with Mexico.

The difference with Mexico had its origin in the openly-expressed sympathy, if not active aid, of the Americans with Texas in her struggle for independence. On the 12th of November, 1835, the latter, through her representatives at San Philipe de Austin, declared her independence of Mexico, and set up a regular State government for herself. This brought on an engagement, first at Bexar, and then at Goliad, in both of which the Mexicans under Gen. Cos were beaten. Gen. Santa Anna, President or Dictator of Mexico, then moved on the Alamo with 7,500 men, and late in February, 1836, attacked the garrison. Col. Travis with 140 brave Texans defended the place, and for eleven days, in which Santa Anna lost 1,600 killed and wounded, succeeded in keeping them at bay. The defense was unprecedented in the annals of war, and at the time thrilled the whole nation with wonder and admiration. The place was finally carried by storm, and on the 16th of March the entire garrison was cruelly put to the sword by their cowardly captors. Among

* History of the United States: By Alexander H. Stephens.

B5

those who perished at Alamo were " the brave, eccentric and famous David Crockett, of Tennessee," and one of Trigg County's gallant sons, Jesse Humphries, a descendant of the brothers Thomas and Absalom Humphries, of Revolutionary fame.

A second butchery followed shortly afterward at Goliad, where Col. Fanning and 300 of his men were cruelly put to death. These enormities upon the part of the Mexicans exasperated the American people to the very highest pitch of indignation. Texas, nothing daunted, and perhaps secretly instigated by the Americans, proceeded to adopt a Constitution for an independent republic, and elected David G. Burnett as President. Commissioners were sent to this and other countries, asking for recognition. In 1837 the United States recognized her independence, and in August of the same year she proposed to annex herself to the United States, but it was not till the 29th of December, 1845, that Congress acceded to her request. The Mexican Minister called for his passport and withdrew from the country, and Gen. Zachary Taylor was sent to the Rio Grande. Here on the 26th of April, 1846, hostilities began with the killing and capturing of Capt. Thornton and sixty-three men. A series of brilliant engagements began under Taylor at Palo Alto and Resaca de la Palma, and later on under Scott at Vera Cruz, Cerro Gordo and other places, resulting in the capture of the city of Mexico on the 12th of September, 1847, and the subsequent submission of the Mexican Government to the forces of the United States.

In this war, through her Taylors, Clays, Crittendens, Prestons, Breckinridges, Butlers, Marshalls and others, Kentucky covered herself with glory. More than 13,700 men offered themselves as volunteers, though only about 5,000 or less had been called for as Kentucky's quota and could be accepted. Trigg County tendered one or more companies, but the quota being already made up they were declined. The companies were disbanded, but quite a number of the more adventurous spirits who had composed them hurried off to different points to seek enlistment in other commands. The first man to go was Lycurgus Edrington, now of Missouri, and he is said to have been the first man to volunteer from this Congressional District in any command. He was a man of fine physique, and made a brave and efficient soldier.

Shortly after Wiley Futrell, also in the late war under Col. Suggs of the Fiftieth Tennessee; James Thomas, Fifer; Alfred Boyd, Quartermaster, George Boyd, his son; Reuben Nance, Commissary; Owen McGinness, Gilliam M. Ezell, Alfred Martin, Robert and Frank Husk, Ezekiel Beard, George Orr, Griffin Lackman and Archie Bowie made application and were accepted in Company E, Fourth Kentucky Infantry, then being organized at Hickman, Ky. The officers of this company were George Cook, Captain; John Snyder, First Lieutenant; Edward Barbour, Second Lieutenant; Benjamin Egan, Third Lieutenant.

Six others, Edward Spiceland, Linn Bell, Alfred Sumner, Harrison Frizzell, John Ward and John Farleigh, arriving shortly afterward and finding the company full, engaged as wagoners, and in this capacity accompanied Gen. Taylor on his campaign into the interior of Mexico.

The organization of Capt. Cook's company being complete in October, 1847, it embarked with Company C, of Caldwell County, on board a steamer and proceeded to join Col. John S. Williams, Fourth Regiment of Kentucky Infantry at New Orleans. The officers of the Fourth were John S. Williams, Colonel; William Preston, Lieutenant-Colonel; and William T. Ward, Major. From New Orleans without delay, the regiment was embarked on a fast-sailing ship for Vera Cruz, where on their arrival they were assigned to duty in the brigade under Gen. William O. Butler. Gen. Butler began his march to the City of Mexico in November, but before they could reach that point it had surrendered to the forces under Gen. Scott. With the fall of the city the war closed, and after a few days the troops were disbanded and returned home.

Though not in any engagement the company lost heavily from measles, dysentery and other "camp" diseases. Griffin Lackman died and was buried at Jalapa, Alfred Martin and Ezekiel Beard died on their return to Vera Cruz, George Orr died and was buried at the head of Wolf Island, and Robert Husk died at Smithland. The body of the latter was brought on to Trigg, where it was buried with appropriate honors by his comrades and a large concourse of sorrowing citizens. The balance of the company was mustered out at Louisville, August, 1848, and on its return was welcomed home with a splendid banquet spread in a grove near the town of Cadiz.

The Great Civil War Between the States.—It would be interesting to go back to the beginning and trace out step by step the cause or causes that led up to this great struggle, but this has been done by abler pens, and the reader is referred to Alexander Stephens' History of the United States as a fair and impartial view of the subject. Though there were many secondary causes, the war had its origin primarily in the introduction of African slavery into the Colonies. Slavery was the germseed of the deadly upas that, planted in the virgin soil of the Colonies, grew with the growth of years and finally spread its blighting shadows over the whole continent. It was the infectious virus that, injected into the veins of that youthful people, ultimately resulted in the poisoning of the whole body politic of the full-grown nation. Nor is it a question of responsibility as to its introduction, nor yet as to its agitation by the friends and champions of either side. The future historian must and will decide that both were wrong; the North in making war on the reserved rights and constitutional prerogatives of the Southern slave-owner, and the South in resorting to questionable and suicidal methods of redress in secession and revolution. It was a fatal mistake on both sides, and entailed great loss and much woe and misery upon the whole race. The years of heated agitation of the subject of slavery both in and out of Congress finally brought matters to the culminating point, when, in 1860, Abraham Lincoln, of Illinois, and Hannibal Hamlin, of Maine, as representatives of the Anti-slavery party of the North, were elected President and Vice-President. The South looked on it as an open declaration of hostilities upon the part of the North, and in the following December the State of South Carolina met in Convention at Charleston and passed an ordinance of secession. This ordinance cited as reasons for the act the fact that " the States of Maine, New Hampshire, Vermont, Massachusetts, Connecticut, Rhode Island, New York, Pennsylvania, Illinois, Indiana, Michigan, Wisconsin and Iowa " (all of which had voted for Lincoln and Hamlin) " had enacted laws which either nullified the acts of Congress for the rendition of fugitives from service or rendered useless any attempt to execute them, and that Iowa and Ohio had refused to surrender fugitives from justice charged with murder, and with inciting servile insurrection in the John Brown raid, as well as the danger to be apprehended from the centralizing doctrines and principles of the party soon to come into power in the Executive Department of the Federal Government."

This act of secession upon the part of South Carolina was soon followed by similar acts upon the part of Florida, Alabama, Georgia, Louisiana and Texas. A Congress of Southern States was called to meet at Montgomery, Ala., on the 4th day of February, 1861, and on the same day a Peace Congress in Washington City, by the friends of peace in both North and South.

In the latter many notable speeches were made by representative men of both sections, but that which produced the profoundest sensation was made by the Hon. Salmon P. Chase, of Ohio, the accredited Secretary of the Treasury of the incoming administration. Speaking for the party that had just elected Mr. Lincoln, he declared that the North would never consent to the decision of the Supreme Court in reference to the extension of slavery into the Territories, nor yet to the constitutional provision for the rendition of "fugitives from service" where such fugitives sought asylum within their jurisdiction. The effect of this declaration was a confirmation of the fears of the more moderate slave-holding States, and measures were accordingly taken by all of them except Kentucky to follow the example of South Carolina and the other seceding States.

The Congress was held at Montgomery also, and a Constitution for one year adopted, with Jefferson Davis, of Mississippi, as President, and Alexander H. Stephens, of Georgia, as Vice-President of the new Confederation. The State of Kentucky was rent and torn by conflicting opinions. Three parties sprang up—the Southern, favoring secession, the Northern, favoring union at all hazards, and the Neutrality party, opposing both. The latter were in power, and dictated the policy of the States. But when once hostilities were fairly begun, they found themselves unable to prevent the invasion of the State by the armies of either side. Intense excitement prevailed everywhere; towns, cities, communities, churches, and even families were divided in sentiment. Both Northern and Southern sympathizers rushed to arms, the former establishing their camps of instruction and rendezvous at "Camp Dick Robinson," Kentucky, and "Camp Joe Holt," near Jefferson, Ind., and the latter at "Camps Boone" and "Burnett" near Clarksville, Tenn.

The people of Trigg partook largely of the general excitement, and being mostly Southern, such of them as designed taking part in the coming struggle repaired at once to the Southern camps. On the 1st day of July, 1861, a company composed of some of the best young men of Trigg County, rendezvoused at Canton, on the Cumberland River, under the following officers: Dr. J. L. Price, Captain; John Cunningham, First Lieutenant; John T. Baker, Second Lieutenant, and Francis M. Baker, Third Lieutenant. Thus organized the company numbered about ninety-three men rank and file. Among them were the following-named non-commissioned officers and privates: Robert W. Major, G. M. Ezell, A. L. Wallace, Z. Hughes, A. W. Wadlington, H. D. Wallace, Robert Dew, W. W. Dew, W. L. Durrett, W. H. Anderson, W. A. Atwood, Tandy Battoe, W. H. Braberry, J. W. Bell, J. F. Baker, J. G. Baynham, Linn Boyd, W. T. Boyd, Franc M. Bounds, J. T. Batt, R. A. Batt, William Bridges, M. C. Cunningham, Sr., M. C. Cunningham, Jr., E. A. Cunningham, G. G. Cunningham, Robert Calhoun. D. Cannon, W. F. Dew, W. B. Eidson, Franc M. Ferguson, J. O. Ferguson, F. M. Ferguson, J. Q. Foster, S. P. B. Faughen, J. V. Gant, M. Gresham, G. E. Grace, Richard Grace, S. Hodge, F. M. Hughes, H. Hughes, D. Hale, Riley Herald, F. P. Ingram, G. Johnson, S. A. Jefferson, N. Lyon, J. T. Lancaster, Richard Mayberry, William Meredith, G. W. Mitchell, J. F. Pritchard, Richard Pogue, H. Pister, W. W. Ryan, M. Rogers, A. P. Rutledge, D. Ray, R. P. Sanford, Monroe Sears, A. Smith, William Sills, T. R. Tyer, E. Timmons, A. C. Thomas, W. S. Williams, H. Williamson, J. B. Winn, W. K. Wallis, Walter Watkins and S. A. Yarbrough.

Both officers and men in physique and intelligence were far above the average, and when uniformed and under arms were as fine a looking body of men as ever went on dress parade. As to their prowess in battle the following recital will suffice to show:

On the 2d of July, 1861, they took up the line of march to "Camp Burnett," Tenn., where, on August 15, they were mustered into the Confederate service for a period of one year. Here, as Company G, they were assigned to duty in the Fourth Regiment Kentucky Infantry, with Robert P. Trabue, Colonel; Andrew R. Hynes, Lieutenant-Colonel, and Thomas B. Monroe, Major.

About the 20th of September, the Fourth moved into Kentucky, and went into camp at Bowling Green where, with the Second, Third, Fifth (afterward Ninth) and Sixth Infantry, Helm's First Regiment of Cavalry, and the batteries of Graves and Cobb, they were brigaded under Gen. Simon Bolivar Buckner.

At this point, during the several months of their stay, nothing of consequence occurred beyond the usual daily routine of camp-life, guard, drill and picket duty. On the 16th of November Gen. Buckner was promoted to the command of a division, and Brig.-Gen. John C. Breckinridge took command of the brigade. On the 20th of January, 1862, the Second Regiment, under Col. Roger Hanson, with Graves' Battery of Light Artillery, was detached and sent under Buckner to re-inforce the threatened garrison at Fort Donelson. Here on the 13th of February, 1862, Gen. Grant made his first attack by land and water, and after three days of stubborn resistance, being entirely surrounded, Gen. Buckner surrendered the forces under his command.

In the meantime, about the first of the month, the disastrous battle of Fishing Creek had occurred, resulting in the defeat of Crittenden and the killing of Zollicoffer, and Kentucky being no longer tenable, on the 11th of February Gen. Johnston began his retreat on Nashville. At Nashville news of the surrender of Forts Donelson and Henry first reached the command, and with bowed heads and heavy hearts they continued their retreat to Burnsville, in northern Mississippi. At Corinth a re-organization of the army took place: Breckinridge was promoted to the command of a division consisting of the "Kentucky Brigade," Statham's Brigade, Bowen's Brigade, Forrest's Regiment of Cavalry, Morgan's Squadron, a company of cavalry under Capt. Phil B. Thompson, which had reported to Gen. Breckinridge as a body guard, or headquarter scouts, and the light artillery pertaining to each organization. It was styled the "Reserve Corps," and as such was to support Gen. Leonidas Polk in the coming fight. Moving out from camp on Sunday morning, the 6th of April, the enemy were encountered at Shiloh, near Pittsburg Landing. And here for the first time, this part of the brigade went under fire. They received their "baptism" with all the coolness and self-possession of trained veterans, and it is no exaggeration to say, from the first shock to the last their united charge was never withstood. Early in the action Breckinridge assigned the command of the brigade to Col. Trabue, and himself superintended the movements of the corps on the right. At half-past 9 o'clock A. M., they came under the enemy's fire in an open field one and a half miles from Pittsburg Landing. The enemy were deploying into line and while so doing the brigade opened upon them. At this point the combat raged with varying success for one hour and a quarter, when Stewart's and a part of Anderson's Brigades coming up to support, Trabue made a charge completely routing the enemy from his position. The loss of the brigade here in officers and men was very heavy, but that of the enemy was far greater. The command encountered was composed of two Ohio, one Missouri and an Iowa regiment, and their loss in killed, wounded and prisoners was fearful. One regiment alone, the Forty-sixth Ohio, lost in killed and wounded four or five hundred. About four or five hundred yards on a Missouri regiment was encountered, charged and dispersed, and a full battery of guns captured. Pressing on through the dense under-growth they soon encountered Prentiss, who was being pressed on the right by that portion of the corps under Breckinridge, and charging, they both entered his camps about the same time. Completely beaten and hemmed in on all sides, after a desperate struggle the gallant Prentiss surrendered his sword. This action occurred near nightfall, and darkness coming on the brigade returned and occupied his camps. Tired, worn and hungry the men here found plenty to eat and drink, and after much "looting" lay down to rest. In this day's fight seventy-five were killed and about three hundred and fifty wounded. Early the next morning (Monday) the fight was renewed. Moving to the front beyond Shiloh Church, the Fourth together with the Fourth Alabama were ordered by Gen. Bragg to charge the enemy who were in and near a house used as a forage-depot. Four times back and forth was the ground crossed and re-crossed, but all in vain. The enemy were too strong for them, and failing to receive support they were compelled to fall back a short distance to the rear. Reunited to the rest of the command and the enemy moving to the right, they were marched in pursuit, and again engaged them near the Shiloh Church, and about one hundred and fifty yards to the right. And here Col. Trabue in his report says: "The fragmentary forces of both armies had concentrated at this time around Shiloh Church, and worn out as were our troops the field was here successfully contested for two hours, when as if by mutual consent both sides desisted from the struggle."

This as recounted was the part taken by the Trigg County boys in their first battle. Their loss in the two days' fight was nine men killed and fourteen wounded. Capt. Trice was injured by the explosion of a shell, and received a minie in his leg, and later on was captured by Capt. Jeffries, of the Fourth Kentucky, Federal. He was carried to Indianapolis, and after to Johnson Island, where he remained till exchanged at Vicksburg in the fall of 1862. After the war, Capt. Jeffries magnanimously returned him his sword, having advertised in the *Courier-Journal* to find his whereabouts.

Re-inforcements for the Federals coming up under Gen. Buell, the Confederates drew off the next day and returned to Corinth. Breckinridge remained behind with his corps and successfully protected the retreat. After the battle, Lieut. Cunningham resigned, and the company having been so fearfully decimated, was consolidated with Companies K and I of the same regiment.

From Corinth the brigade marched to Tupelo, Miss., and thence with the balance of the corps to Vicksburg. Here for two months, exposed to heavy and frequent bombardments, the corps successfully defended the city from the combined attack of both army and fleet. On the 27th of July the enemy disappeared, and after a short rest, Breckinridge, with about 6,000 men, the ram "Arkansas" to co-operate by river, was sent against Baton Rouge. Brig.-Gen. Ben Hardin Helm was placed in command of the brigade, but receiving a severe fall from his horse which disabled him, the command devolved upon Col. Thomas H. Hunt of the Ninth. Early in the fight Col. Hunt received a severe wound through both thighs and from this on to the close of the action Capt. Buckner, of Breckinridge's staff, was in command. The Fourth was on the right, and encountering the Fourteenth Maine, drove them under the river bank to the protection of the gun-boats. In this charge one of Trigg's gallant boys, Douglas Cannon, was killed and several others wounded. The "Arkansas" failed to co-operate, having broken some part of her machinery on the way down, and thus, though the land attack was successful, Breckinridge was compelled to draw off.

The corps was then moved to Port Hudson, which they commenced to fortify, but in a short time were ordered to Jackson, Miss. Here the sick and wounded who had been left at Vicksburg and elsewhere rejoined the command. The division moved by rail up the Mississippi Central to Cold Water Creek, above Holly Springs, and disembarked at that point on the morning of the 11th of September. From here, by order of President Davis, Breckinridge, leaving all but the Fourth, Sixth and Ninth Regiments, a Tennessee brigade, a company or two of cavalry, and the batteries of Cobb and McClung, started on the 19th of September to overtake Bragg in Kentucky. The Kentucky Brigade was again temporarily assigned to the command of Col. Trabue, in the absence of Gen. Helm. Reaching Knoxville on the 3d of October they found the Second Regiment and Graves' Battery, which had been exchanged, awaiting them. Hanson, being the senior Colonel, took command, and at once pushed on in the direction of the Gap, but when near Maynardsville received intelligence of Bragg's retreat, and at once returned to Knoxville. On the 23d they were moved by rail to Shell Mound, and from thence on the 28th to Murfreesboro, where they went into camp. The next movement of the brigade was on Nashville to co-operate with Morgan, who was to destroy the depots, cars and other structures at Edgefield. Morgan was only partially successful, and the force returned.

In December the brigade was marched to Baird's Mills on the road to Hartsville, and the Second and Ninth detached and sent with Morgan to attack Hartsville. The movement was successful, the enemy were completely surprised, and more than 2,000 officers and men captured. Returning with these to Baird's Mills, the Fourth was put in charge of the prisoners, and conducted them back to Murfreesboro.

Here the company was again re-organized with Trice as Captain, J. F. Baker, First Lieutenant, Robert W. Major, Second Lieutenant, and Gilliam M. Ezell, Brevet Second Lieutenant.

On Sunday, the 28th of December, Bragg moved out to the crossing of Stone River to confront Rosecrans. The Kentucky Brigade was thrown forward to take position on a commanding eminence with its left resting on the river. The Fourth reached down to the river's edge, and the other regiments were formed on the right. Company G was sent out in front as skirmishers, and on the day of the general battle (Wednesday) brought on the engagement. Two days after, at the same point, and just before the Kentucky Brigade was ordered forward into the memorable "Slaughter Pen," Lieut. Major was ordered to take a portion of his company and dislodge the enemy from a house in front near the river bank. Taking H. D. Wallace and William Brayberry with him, he crept along under the bank till within a short distance of the house, and then at a given signal (the firing of a shell into the building), he rushed with his comrades to the house. At the same time Captain Trice with the balance of the company, and Captain Utterback's Company of the Sixth dashed forward upon the building from the front. The enemy were quickly driven out and Major rushed in and set fire to it. Their object accomplished the company returned to the skirmish line through a perfect hail of bullets. In the charge on the house the gallant Utterback of the Sixth was killed.

The next fight in which the brigade participated was at Jackson, Miss., whither, the following spring, Breckinridge had been sent to re-inforce Joe Johnston. After the fall of Vicksburg, Johnston returned to Jackson, and awaited the coming of the enemy. On the 10th he came up, and invested the place, and on the 12th, after more or less desultory fighting, he made a serious charge on Breckinridge's position near Pearl River. The charge was received by the brigade, supported by Stovalt's Brigade and Cobb's Battery, and after a short, sharp fight, in which the enemy were roughly handled, they retired with the loss of 200 killed and 250 wounded and prisoners.

On the 18th Johnston retired to Camp Hurricane, about eight miles from Morton. Here the command rested till the 26th of August, when they were ordered to proceed by way of Mobile to Tyner's Station, near the Chickamauga. On the 18th of September they bivouacked on the Chickamauga, and on the next day were led into the fight on the left. Company G here had the honor of assisting in capturing a battery which they charged from the skirmish line. That night they were moved to the right to the support of Gen. Polk, and at daylight went into the fight. The battle raged all day with varying results, but at night it was terminated by the complete route of the enemy. Had there been one hour more of daylight for the pursuit, there is no doubt but the entire army would have been captured. But the victory was not without heavy loss on the part of the brigade. Of 1,300 who went in, sixty-three were killed and 408 wounded. Gen. Helm fell early in the action on the second day, and Col. Joe Lewis of the Sixth took his place. Company G lost two killed and fourteen wounded. In the battle of Missionary Ridge, which soon followed, the brigade was in the center near Bragg's headquarters on the first day, but moved to the support of Cleburn on the right. On the second day it assisted in the repulse of the enemy, but without much loss.

Only one man fell in Company G, W. D. Wallace, but that one was a "host within himself." He fell, where he was ever to be found, at his post.

On the retreat to Dalton, the brigade, with Cleburn's Division, protected the flying columns of Bragg, and finally succeeded in checking the enemy at Ringgold Gap. At Dalton, Bragg was relieved by Johnston, and the whole army went into winter quarters. The brigade, though much rejoiced, as was, indeed, all the rest of the army, at the exchange of general officers, were much grieved at the loss of their gallant division-commander, John C. Breckinridge, who was transferred to another department. Gen. William B. Bate (Old Grits), of Tennessee, was assigned to the command of the division, and Col. Joe Lewis promoted to the command of the brigade. On the 6th of May, 1864, the campaign opened at Rocky Face Gap, and Sherman began his series of flanking movements.

After a few days' skirmishing and maneuvering in front of the Gap, he attempted to turn Johnston's left, but the wily Confederate was in his front awaiting him at Resaca. Here Lewis' brigade received the brunt of the fight, repelling two gallant charges in handsome style, and standing firm under a furious cannonading. The Second and Fourth were principally engaged and lost heavily. The Trigg boys were among the sufferers. Lieut. Major was wounded on the chin by a fragment of shell, two men—Mike Rogers and Francis M. Forguson—killed, and five or six wounded. Forguson was a brave man, and accounted one of the best shots in the division. He was a sharpshooter, and from the Gap to Resaca is said to have killed twenty-five officers, principally mounted. He had been on the skirmish line sharpshooting, and was returning over the works when shot through the head. He was a cousin of the present Judge J. R. Grace. Major, who had been in command of the company, was sent to the hospital at Newnan, Ga., and Second Lieut. A. L. Wallace took command. He was killed in the next battle, 28th, at Dallas, leading a charge on the enemy's works. After his fall the command devolved on Orderly-Sergt. W. A. Atwood, who had charge of the company to Kenesaw Mountain. Here both Baker and Major returned from hospital and took their respective places in the company. The company participated in all or most of the engagements of this campaign from Dalton to Atlanta and Jonesboro, Ga., where on the first day Capt. Baker was wounded, and on the second, Major both wounded and taken prisoner. The same ball that wounded Major also wounded Sergt. Wallace, and both fell into the hands of the enemy. Besides several others slightly wounded here, William Meredith was killed. Major made his escape from the cars between Wartrace and Murfreesboro, Tenn., and after many perils and hardships returned to the command at Newnan, Ga.

After Jonesboro the brigade, which had been exchanged at Rough-and-Ready, under special cartel, was mounted, and when Sherman started on his "march to the sea," disputed every inch of the way to Savannah, and then through South Carolina, till the final surrender of Lee and Johnston. They were paroled at Washington, Ga., May 7, 1865. Only thirty-seven out of seventy-five—less than half—remained to be paroled, and not a single man of these but had from one to five wounds on his person.

Dr. Trice, who had been compelled to resign on account of blindness, superinduced by the shock of the shell at Shiloh, and other causes, had joined his father at Marion, Ala., where he remained till 1866, when he returned to Canton.

Companies B and D, Eighth Regiment Kentucky Infantry.—About the beginning of September, 1861, two other Confederate companies were organized in the county, one at Noah's Spring, Montgomery Co., Tenn., under the following officers: A. C. Buckner, Captain; William Henry, First Lieutenant; Preston H. Davis, Second Lieutenant; F. G. Terry, Third Lieutenant, and numbering eighty-five men, rank and file; the other at Wallonia, under Jabez Bingham, Captain; J. S. Wall, First Lieutenant; E. S. Pool, Second Lieutenant; and William Miller, Third Lieutenant, and numbering 104 men. After remaining at Noah's Spring some two weeks the one under Buckner moved to Hopkinsville and went into camp at the fair grounds, where they were assigned to the Eighth Regiment of Kentucky Infantry as Company D. The other company remained at Wallonia till about the 23d of October, when they also moved to Hopkinsville and joined the Eighth Regiment as Company B.

Shortly after the arrival of these two companies the Eighth was re-organized with Henry C. Burnett as Colonel, Reuben Ross Lieutenant-Colonel, and First Lieutenant William Henry of Company D promoted to Major. On the promotion of Henry, Lieutenants Davis and Terry were promoted in turn, and George Wilford elected Brevet Second Lieutenant. Another change in the regiment took place in a short while. Lieut.-Col. Ross resigned and H. P. Lyon was promoted from Captain of Artillery to fill the vacancy. He joined the regiment at Providence, Tenn., January, 1862, while en route for Fort Donelson, where they were ordered to join the brigade under Gen. Clark. Before reaching Fort Donelson First Lieut. Wall, of Company B, died, and J. W. Brown was elected to fill the vacancy. The brigade under Clark was assigned to a position on the left of the "Winne Ferry" road, and for two days were under a heavy and galling fire from the shore batteries. On the morning of the third day, Saturday, they were sent to relieve Floyd's Brigade which had been detached and sent to another part of the field to make a flank movement. The brigade were not long in their new position before they were charged by the enemy in heavy force. Though for the first time face to face with an enemy the men deported themselves with the steadiness of veterans. The charge was gallantly repulsed, and a countercharge made in turn in which the enemy were driven, the famous Swartz's battery captured, and a number of prisoners taken. Among others in this day's fight Lieut. Terry was wounded and sent back to the hospital at Nashville. On Sunday morning before the surrender Capt. Buckner and Lieut. Davis and some eight or ten men made their escape from the fort, and with Terry fell in with Johnston's army as they retreated through Tennessee. The rest of the command were sent to prison at Camps Morton and Chase, where they remained till the following September, when they were exchanged at Vicksburg. At Jackson, Miss., shortly after being exchanged, the Eighth was re-organized with Lyon, Colonel;

A. R. Shacklett, Lieutenant-Colonel; Jabez Bingham, Major; and John Couch, Adjutant. The companies were re-organized as follows: Company D, F. G. Terry, Captain; George Wilford, First Lieutenant; Lee Turner, Second Lieutenant; W. D. Smith, Brevet Lieutenant; and Joseph H. Mitchell, Orderly Sergeant; Company B, J. W. Brown, Captain; W. L. Dunning, First Lieutenant; J. E. Kelly, Second Lieutenant; and J. R. Gilfoy, Brevet Second Lieutenant. From Jackson the regiment was ordered to Holly Springs under Gen. Baldwin, Tilghman's Division, to intercept Grant. Grant coming up, Tilghman retreated to Coffeeville, Miss., where he encountered and repulsed the enemy under Gen. Lee. After this the command went into winter quarters at Grenada. In the spring of 1863 they were sent to re-inforce the garrison at Fort Pemberton, at the head of the Yazoo River, where, in about a month, the enemy withdrawing, were sent to the assistance of Gen. Bowen at Grand Gulf. On the march to Grand Gulf the Eighth was assigned to Buford's Brigade of Loring's Division, and on reaching Big Black River found Gen. Bowen, who had been compelled to retreat.

Captain Terry's company were mounted at Big Black Bridge, where they had been sent to intercept the enemy's cavalry, and here, until Pemberton had gathered his forces in hand, defended this important crossing.

In the general battle which ensued at Champion Hill, the Eighth took an active part, and here Lieut. Kelly of Company B was severely wounded. Pemberton was defeated and fell back on the Big Black. The enemy pursued with vigor, and Pemberton continued his retreat to Vicksburg. At the "bridge" Col. Lyon got possession of a battery, and being an experienced artillerist succeeded in holding the Federals in check till the rest of the army were safely drawn off. This accomplished, he turned and contested the balance of the way to the works at Vicksburg. The Eighth remained in Vicksburg only about a week, when being mounted Col. Lyon was ordered to make his way through to Grant's rear. This perilous mission was successfully accomplished in the night, and an immediate dash made on Raymond, where a lot of disabled Federals were captured who had been wounded in a recent fight betwen Gens. Lew Wallace and Gregg. Lyon operated on the enemy's rear with much success till Gen. Johnston came up with his forces to relieve the siege of Vicksburg, when he reported to that officer. On the latter's advance from Jackson, the Eighth was again dismounted and assigned to Buford's Brigade. At the Big Black, news of the surrender being received, the Confederates fell back on Jackson and awaited the coming of Sherman. Here the command participated in all the engagements pending the investment of the place, and after, near the "Fair Grounds," with two other regiments of the brigade, made a stand against a much larger force, that elicited the praise of the Commanding General. General Johnston, who witnessed the fight, is said to have pronounced it the most gallant and stubborn resistance he had witnessed during the war. Many of the enemy fell within ten or twenty feet of the Confederate lines. After the evacuation of Jackson, the brigade fell back with the army to Forrest's Station, where they remained inactive till September, when with Gen. Loring they moved to Canton, and afterward, in February, to Demopolis, Ala., to intercept Sherman, who was moving on Meridian. Here the three Kentucky regiments of Buford's Brigade were mounted and sent to Forrest at Gainesville, and Buford being promoted to the Second Division, Col. A. P. Thompson took command; and here, also, companies D, C, and F, were consolidated, with the following officers: J. W. Brown, Captain; Logan Field, First Lieutenant; W. L. Dunning, Second Lieutenant; — Rowland, Third Lieutenant. Capt. Terry was assigned to duty as Ordnance Officer of the brigade. Thus organized, the command moved to join the rest of Forrest's forces at Tupelo, Miss., preparatory to a raid into Kentucky and west Tennessee. On this raid, at Paducah, through some mistake Thompson made an unsupported attack upon the fort with his brigade alone. In the charge, Col. Thompson was killed by a shell, and some 100 were killed and wounded. The fatal shell also killed a horse ridden by Capt. Al. McGoodwin of the Third Kentucky, who was riding on one side of the Colonel, while the Colonel's flesh and blood were scattered over Capt. Terry, who rode on the other. The charge on the fort was repulsed, but Lieut. Logan Field, with a portion of his company, charged and took the Marine Hospital on the right, from which they fired a plunging shot into the fort, till dislodged by the enemy's gunboats. Night coming on, after supplying themselves plentifully with commissaries', quartermaster's and hospital stores, the brigade drew off with Forrest into western Kentucky. Here the Kentuckians were permitted to return to their homes to rest, recruit for a time, and afterward rendezvous at Trenton, Tenn. From this point, designing to attack Fort Pillow, Forrest, about the 10th or 12th of April, sent them to make a feint on Paducah. Arriving in front of the town, they made a dash in, capturing a few prisoners and about 100 head of horses and mules, and then rejoined Forrest at Jackson, Tenn. From here, after a short rest, Forrest moved to Tupelo, Miss., and was again about to return into Tennessee, when he learned of Sturgis' raid into that part of the State. Turning, he met him at Guntown or Bryce's Cross-Roads, and with his usual impetuosity charged at the head of his columns. Here Lyon, who had been on detached service and was promoted, returned in time to command the brigade in the fight. He was the first to strike the enemy's advance, driving them back on the main body, and holding them for six or eight hours till the other commands came up. About 1 P. M. the fight became general and the enemy gave way. Brown's company of Trigg boys had the honor of capturing a piece of artillery in their first charge; also two or three ordnance wagons, which supplied them with necessary ammunition. Capt. Terry, Acting Inspector-General on Buford's staff, and one other were the only staff officers on the field. Sturgis, driven at all points, was soon in complete rout, losing not less than 3,000 killed, wounded and captured, seventeen cannon and eighteen caissons, 450,000 rounds of cartridges, 350 wagons and ambulances, more than 1,000 horses and mules, six months' medical supplies, forty days' rations, and two wagon loads of "John Barleycorn." The latter it is supposed was carried along as a kind of "*spiritual defense*" against the more formidable enemy of that section—malaria.

The subsequent operations of the Eighth under Forrest in Mississippi were at Pontotoc, Old Harrisburg and Town Creek, in July. On the 4th October, 1864, they were detached and sent into west Tennessee to gather up the troops under Col. L. A. Sypert, who had been operating in Kentucky, and was then at Paris, Tenn. After this they reported to Forrest at Mt. Pleasant, Tenn., and were permitted by him to return with Col. Lyon into southwestern Kentucky, to rest and recruit. While on this visit, Lyon made an attack on the garrison at Hopkinsville, commanded by Col. Sam Johnson, and captured, with the loss of one man killed, thirty or forty prisoners, and seventy-five or eighty horses and mules. He next attacked and captured the garrison at Eddyville, and then without interruption crossed the Cumberland above Clarksville, and rejoined Forrest at Paris, Tenn. The next move was on Fort Heiman, where four steamboats, one gun and about two companies of furloughed men were captured. Next at Johnsonville, on the Tennessee River, where were captured and destroyed four gun-boats, fifteen steamboats, twenty-three barges, and two warehouses, supposed to contain over two and a half million dollars' worth of army supplies.

In November Lyon with a portion of the Eighth was detached and sent into southwestern Kentucky to collect up stragglers and create a divertisement in favor of Hood, who was approaching to the attack of Nashville. During his absence Col. Ed Crossland took command of the balance of the brigade, with Capt. Terry Acting Assistant Adjutant-General on his staff. Hood starting on the march to Nashville, Forrest moved to join him at Florence, Ala. On this campaign they took part in the following engagements: Lawrenceburg, Butler's Creek, where Col. Crossland was wounded and the command devolved on Col. W. W. Faulkner, of the Twelfth Kentucky, Campbellsville, Columbia, Maury's Mills,

Spring Hill, Franklin, Nashville, Smyrna, Murfreesboro and all the subsequent encounters on the retreat.   At Corinth, Miss., Forrest halted to
rest both men and horses, and the Kentucky Brigade went into camp near
Okolona at the same time.   Here they remained from January to March,
1865, when they rendezvoused at West Point, Miss., and thence moved to
intercept the raid of Wilson on Selma and Demopolis, Ala.   At Monte-
vallo the enemy were encountered and a three-days' running fight ensued, in which nearly one-half of the Eighth were either killed, wounded
or captured.   The balance escaping, returned to West Point, Miss., where
news of the surrender of Lee and Johnston being received, Forrest sent
the Eighth to Columbus to guard stores.   And here, on the 15th of May,
1865, the Eighth, decimated by disease, capture and death to a mere
skeleton, surrendered to the enemy and were paroled.   Of the Trigg boys
there remained F. G. Terry, Joseph H. Mitchell, Taylor Ethridge, A.
B. Crawley, Joseph Dabney, Zenas Alexander, Reuben Stallions and
Richard Lester.   The rest were either killed, wounded, captured, or deserted.

Company B, Second Regiment of Kentucky Cavalry.—The next
company to organize in Trigg for the Confederate service was at Wallonia,
August 1, 1862.   This company was composed of about eighty-four men,
rank and file, and was officered as follows: G. G. Goodwin, Captain;
James Mitchell, First Lieutenant; Samuel Martin, Second Lieutenant,
and Walter McChesney, Third Lieutenant.   About ten days after being
organized they joined the Second Regiment under Col. Thomas Woodward, at Clarksville, Tenn, and were with this gallant officer in his subsequent operations in southwestern Kentucky and middle Tennessee.
Having enlisted for a term of one year, they were so tendered to the
Confederate Government by Woodward in December, but being declined,
disbanded, and either returned home or scattered out into other commands.

J. T. Greer of this company, after the disbandment, joined McDonald's Battalion of Tennessee Cavalry, which he subsequently commanded,
and under Gen. Van Dorn operated in north Mississippi, west Tennessee
and Alabama.   Was in the battles of Holly Springs, Corinth and Iuka,
and after the death of Van Dorn was assigned to Chalmers' Brigade of
Forrest's Division.   Under Forrest he took part in the battles of Guntown, Okolona, Memphis, Fort Pillow, etc.   He surrendered with his
command at Jackson, Miss., June 5, 1865.

Company D, Second Regiment of Kentucky Cavalry.—This was the
next company, largely composed of Trigg County boys, to organize for
the Confederate service.   It was composed of about eighty-seven men,
rank and file, and rendezvoused on the Summer farm, on the road be-

tween Cadiz and Hopkinsville. The organization took place in September, 1862, with the following officers: Captain, E. A. Slaughter; First Lieutenant, Ben F. Bacon; Second Lieutenant, William M. Campbell; Third Lieutenant, —— Wallis. A few days after they joined Woodward at Hopkinsville, and with him operated in southwestern Kentucky and middle Tennessee. In December, 1862, Capt. Slaughter and Lieut. Wallis resigned their positions, and Dr. John Cunningham was elected Captain, and R. W. Roach, Third Lieutenant. Shortly after the company was tendered the Confederacy for twelve months, but being declined, also disbanded. About thirteen men remained under Lieut. Campbell, and enlisted for a period of three years; the remainder scattered out into other commands or returned home. The little nucleus remaining with Campbell from time to time received accessions, till in the following February, 1863, they had grown to a full company, and were organized under the following officers: Given Campbell, Captain; J. M. Jones, First Lieutenant; William Campbell, Second Lieutenant, and S. P. Martin, Third Lieutenant. Under Forrest the company took part in the campaign through western Tennessee, and were engaged at Lexington, Jackson, Humboldt and Huntington, Miss. When the Murfreesboro campaign commenced in 1863, they were in front of Rosecrans' army from Nashville to Stone River, disputing every inch of the way, and when the battle came on were on the left of Bragg's army as "flankers." They were subsequently in the battles of Chickamauga, McMinnville, Farmington, Dug Gap, Snake Creek Gap, Resaca, Kenesaw and Peach-Tree Creek, and when Stoneman made his bold but unfortunate raid into Georgia went in pursuit, and had the honor of capturing the redoubtable leader himself, who surrendered to Capt. William M. Campbell in person. After this they were at Triune, Tenn., then at Saltville, W. Va., then back to Georgia again to confront Sherman on his march to the sea. On this memorable campaign through Georgia and South Carolina they were in daily conflict with both infantry and cavalry, performing, with the rest of Wheeler's command, perfect prodigies of endurance and valor.

On the Congaree, under Col. William C. P. Breckinridge, they made one of the last fights of the war, in which the gallant Captain of the company, Campbell, was severely wounded.

At Charlotte, N. C., the command fell in with President Davis and his party, and had the honor of acting as his escort to the final capture.

These were the only regular commands supplied by Trigg County to the Confederate cause, but there were many who went out singly or in squads at various times during the progress of the war, of whom no account has been taken. It is estimated that, first and last, between eight hundred and a thousand men took part in the struggle on the southern side. Notably among those who joined other commands may be mentioned Capt. Ben D. Terry of Company F, First Regiment of Kentucky Cavalry, afterward Morgan's command, Dr. Livingston Lindsay, Surgeon of the Forty-ninth Regiment Tennessee Infantry, and afterward of McDonald's Tennessee Battalion, P. C. Harrell, who went out with a squad of twenty-nine or thirty men in November, 1861, and joined the Fiftieth Tennessee, and afterward promoted to Second Lieutenant of Company F of that regiment, Wiley Futrell, of the same command, Wilson Jackson and Archy W. Clinard.

Federal Side.—Of the Federal side little remains to be said. Besides a portion of Company F, Forty-eighth Regiment of Kentucky Infantry, commanded by Capt. Charles E. Van Pelt, and a " Home Guard " company of forty or fifty men under Capt. H. E. Luton, Trigg County had no regular organization in the Federal army.

Company F was composed of about 100 men, only a part of whom were from Trigg, and was additionally officered as follows : First Lieutenant, Bluford Rogers ; Second Lieutenant, Charles Adams ; Third Lieutenant, not known. The operations of the company were confined to southwestern Kentucky, doing guard and post duty, and, besides a little skirmish at Hopkinsville, were never in a fight.

Capt. Luton's company was raised principally from " between the rivers," and did little other duty than guard the line of telegraph between Fort Donelson and Princeton. They were never engaged in any action of importance.

Of course there were others from Trigg County on the Union side, but they were scattered out into other commands, and no record is to be found of them. It is possible as many as 200 in all represented Trigg on the Federal side.

Besides those mentioned the Adjutant-General's report gives the names of the following additional officers : Robert V. Grinter, Captain Eighth Regiment Kentucky Cavalry ; W. J. McKee, First Lieutenant Seventeenth Regiment Kentucky Cavalry ; W. Randolph, Assistant Surgeon Eighth Regiment ; and William Randolph, Surgeon of the Forty-eighth Regiment Kentucky Infantry.

Though there were a number of individual or personal encounters on Trigg soil there were no organized fights or important skirmishes, and the only occurrence worth recording was in connection with the burning of the court house at Cadiz. In the month of December, 1864, a small company of Confederates, some forty or fifty in number, under Capt. Cole of Lyon's Brigade, learning of the presence of a detachment of negro troops, who were barricaded in the court house at Cadiz, determined to attack and capture them. Under the escort of an intelligent citizen guide they moved rapidly and quietly on the place from the direction of Canton, but on reaching the Dover road near the town learned that the enemy had already passed down that road. Wheeling down the road they followed in pursuit, and about nightfall came up with them near the J. S. McCalister farm, about two and a half miles from Cadiz. The negroes, some 150 in number, scattered out in every direction, a number of them taking protection in a barn on the premises. A few shots were exchanged, but for some reason not known the Confederates drew off, and beyond a few negroes wounded and the capture of Lieut. Schuyler and twelve or fifteen of his men, there were no other results. Cole rode on into Cadiz, where he spent the night. Next morning, ostensibly to prevent the spread of small-pox, which had been introduced into the building by the negroes, and also prevent the enemy from again using it as a place of defense, he gave orders to his men to fire the court house. A number of negroes were gathered in from the town, and the roof and cupola torn away in order to prevent the flames from spreading. On going up into the second story a negro soldier with confluent small-pox, who had been deserted by his comrades and left to die, was found at the head of the stairway where he had dragged himself. Cole caused the invalid to be shot. The excuse given for the act is that the negro was already in a dying condition, and if left on the sidewalk would spread the loathsome disease among the people. The building was then set fire to, and after its destruction Cole and his men withdrew from the town.

It only remains to be said of the people of Trigg who remained at home, both Southern and Union, that they lived in comparative peace with each other. They strove rather to protect than to expose each other to military aggressions and persecutions from either side. The following incident is to the point, and illustrates the spirit of the times in Trigg: Mr. R. D. Baker, of Cadiz, an ardent Union man, was known to have a large sum of money in his possession, and one of his neighbors, Mr. M. A. Smith, an equally ardent Southern man, was approached by a guerilla and desperado, and solicited to assist in its forcible capture. Smith knowing the desperate character of his tempter, and in order to deceive and throw him off his guard, acceded to the proposition. Seeking Baker at once, he notified him of the danger, and urged him to remove the money from the premises forthwith. This Baker did, and much to Smith's surprise and dismay, tendered to him the package with the sententious remark: "There, Smith, keep it for me till I call for it." It is needless to say the confidence so frankly reposed was never abused, and the money, every dollar of it, was promptly returned when all danger had passed. The package is said to have contained $10,000.

A well-known citizen of Cadiz relates that on one occasion he was arrested by the Federal authorities, and carried to prison at Louisville on a false charge. Without solicitation, one of his Union neighbors, Squire T. H. Grinter, by a little diplomacy, secured the necessary papers for his release and at once followed to the city. Presenting his credentials to the General in command, and vouching for the character and innocence of his friend, he soon had him released from prison and safely on his way home. When afterward proffered the amount of his expenses to and from the city, he indignantly declined with the remark : " It's a poor friend who would not do as much for his neighbor." The same worthy citizen, with Mr. R. D. Baker, mentioned above, was, on more than one occasion instrumental in securing the release of Southern sympathizers from Fort Donelson.

These friendly and neighborly acts were generously reciprocated by their Southern friends, whenever the Confederates were in possession, and but few instances of reprisal or retaliation against Union people took place during the war.

Both sides agreed to disagree in mere matters of opinion, and wisely left the fighting to the soldiers in the field. Had other portions of the State been guided by the same wise counsels, they would have been spared on many occasions the bitterness and humiliation of *lex talionis* that fell with a heavy hand upon both person and property. All honor to both Union and Southern men of Trigg, for their moderation and forbearance. Not a dollar of indemnity or blackmail was ever collected from them by the satraps of either side.—*J. M. Tydings.*

CHAPTER VI.

CADIZ PRECINCT is irregular in shape and occupies the central part of the county. It is drained by Little River and its tributaries, the most important of which are Muddy Fork and Bird's Creek. The banks of the river are composed of masses of limestone, which, in places, rise to great heights presenting many romantic and picturesque views. Caney Creek is a small stream fed by springs flowing into Little River near Cadiz. Springs of clear, cold water abound in many parts of the precinct, the most noted of which is the large one at Cadiz and Caney Spring. The country is broken, contains forests of very valuable timber and embraces a goodly area of fine farming lands. Agriculture and stock-raising are the chief occupations of the people, and within the precinct are some of the best improved plantations in the county.

" One of the oldest settlers of Trigg County, whose descendants still retain a residence here, was Thomas Wadlington, the grandfather of Ferdinand, Thomas and William Wadlington. He moved from North Carolina and settled on the east bank of Little River, at a place now known as Kent's Bridge as early as 1792. He had two sons when he set- tled here—Ferdinand and Thomas—the former sixteen and the latter twelve years of age. His nearest neighbors were a few families at Eddy Grove, near Princeton. Benjamin McCulloch who made a small settle- ment not far from the old Dry Fork meeting-house and the Goodwins who lived in the neighborhood of Cerulean Springs." Like the majority of Kentucky pioneers, Mr. Wadlington was skilled in the use of the rifle, and many stories are told of his adventures with wild animals and wild men during the first few years of his residence in the wilderness. We have space for but one incident, which is told as follows : Happening in one of his hunting excursions to pass Caney Spring, near the site of Cadiz, he found sitting around it a number of Indians, who sprang suspiciously to their feet upon perceiving his approach and beckoned him to come near. They were armed only with tomahawks, and seeing that Wadlington carried a long heavy rifle they were desirous of securing it without exciting his suspicion, knowing full well that if they attacked him while he had the gun one of their number at least must die. Wadlington did not fear them, but walked into their midst, and with his finger on the trigger of his trusty weapon asked them what they wanted. One of the red skins stepped to a sapling near by, and blazing a white spot upon it with his tomahawk, replied that he would like to see " white man try skill and shoot at mark." Wadlington knew very well that this was only a ruse to get him to discharge his gun, but he was not to be deceived in any such manner. Stepping back a few paces and bringing his gun to bear he applied several epithets to them, and told them that unless they were gone in five minutes he would send every dirty devil of them to h—l where they belonged. This had the desired effect, and the savages left without further ceremony, leaving Wadlington in peaceable possession of the spring. Mr. Wadlington died on the farm he settled as early perhaps as the year 1803 or 1804. His son Ferdinand fell heir to the old place but did not retain it many years. He sold out in an early day and moved to Caldwell County. Thomas, the younger son, remained in the county all his life. He settled the place where his son William Wadlington now lives in Caledonia Precinct, and was one of the oldest men in the county at the time of his death.

Another early settler was Isaac McCullom, who located in the eastern part of the precinct prior to 1814. "He had a fight at a gathering of some kind on Little River, and met with the misfortune of having one of his eyes put out in the encounter. Having been a considerable fighter in his day and being very boastful of his manhood, this defeat so mortified him that he left the country. He went from here to Illinois and has no descendants in Trigg County. Thomas Young, John Young and Thomas Howard settled on Bird's Creek, near the Old Bethel meeting-house, about the year 1813. They earned the reputation of being reputable citizens, and acquired a handsome property during the period of their sojourn. About this time or perhaps a year later came Benjamin Wallis, and settled near the mouth of Bird's Creek. John Gore settled in the same locality some time during the year 1814. John Stacy settled on the river where Joel McKinney now lives, a short distance below the Street Mill, prior to 1816. John Davenport came about the same year, and made a small improvement on the farm now owned by L. Freeman, near

Bird's Creek. Levi Harland settled about three miles from Cadiz, where Moses Thompson's tanyard now is, but the date of his arrival could not be ascertained. Marmaduke Ingram came as early as 1813 and cleared a small farm between the two bridges over Little River. David Randolph and his father settled near the mouth of Sinking Fork a few years later, where several of their descendants are still living.

Absalom Seavills settled the old Wimberly place in an early day, but prior to his arrival the Husk farm was settled by Sevier Tadlock. This was long before the first cabin was erected within a mile of the town of Cadiz. William Husk afterward bought this tract of land, and can be classed with the early pioneers of Trigg County. Ferman Smith and William Redd were both living within the present boundaries of the precinct as early as 1816, and one year later John Wharton settled near the toll gate on the Canton pike, where his son—George Wharton—lives at the present time. John Langley came as early as 1817 also, and settled near Cadiz on the bottom lands now owned by Robert Wilford. This place was purchased a little later by Thomas Bryant, who in turn disposed of it to Robert Baker about the time the county seat was established.

Prominent among those who secured homes in the vicinity of Cadiz was James Thompson, whose first improvements were made where Robert Wilford lives, within the town limits. He came about the year 1813. An early settlement was made on Caney Creek by Joseph Jones, who opened the farm now owned by Ed Baker; John Williams, a Methodist preacher who settled in the same locality, and Uriah Gordon, who settled near the head of the creek on the place occupied at the present time by William Wallis. The old Carson place was owned by Samuel Orr at the time of the county's formation, and it was at his dwelling that the first courts were held. The place was then known as Warrington, and competed with Cadiz for the seat of justice. An old German by name of French lived at the place now owned by Joel McKinney in 1822. There were a number of other families around him, so many indeed that it was regarded as a kind of Dutch settlement. They and their descendants have all moved away from the county. They were regarded as a thrifty, harmless and industrious class of citizens.

William Roberts came to the county as early as 1804, and settled in the neighborhood of Cerulean Springs, where he lived until 1811, when he removed to what is now Cadiz Precinct and opened up a farm on Little River. Other early comers were: Jesse Adams, Wesley Adams, John P. Wilkinson, James Curran, Z. Thomas, Mr. Cook, Mr. McNichols, William Jones, Mr. Minton, Thomas Bryant, William Young, Ferdinand Young and Mr. McCain. It was on the place where the last named lived that one of the first settlements in the precinct was made, but the

name of the family could not be learned. "George Harland, son of
Levi Harland, owned the old Jackson Mill property in an early day. In
attempting to cross the river to visit some sick member of old man
French's family in a flat-boat, it was drawn over the mill-dam and himself and wife, two daughters and a son were drowned. One of his sons
—Levi Harland—lived for a number of years at the old tan-yard place.
He removed to Illinois, and his family have become prominent among the
brightest and most cultured people of that State." Several other prom-
ident settlers came in an early day and located within the limits of Cadiz,
appropriate mention of whom may be found in the history of the town.

Mills were among the earliest industries of the country, and Cadiz
Precinct has been blessed with quite a number. Little River affords
splendid water power, and as early as 1819 Levi Harland and John P.
Wilkinson erected a small combination saw and grist-mill on the spot
occupied at the present time by the large flouring-mill of Jefferson &
Jones. The first mill, which was composed of logs, stood for several
years and did a good business during the time it was in operation. The
property was purchased by a Mr. Stewart, who afterward erected a good
frame flouring-mill, which was operated until replaced by the present
building belonging to Messrs. Jefferson & Jones. One of the earliest
mills in the precinct was erected by William Jones on his place near Caney
Creek. It was constructed on the most primitive plan and was operated
by horse-power. It ceased operations about the time the first water-mills
were erected. An early mill was built by Presley Slaughter, on Muddy
Fork of Little River, and was in operation until about the year 1858.
It was a combination mill, and did a very good business for a number of
years. William C. Martin was the last proprietor. In about the year
1821–22 Robert Baker built a saw and grist-mill on Little River,
where the Wilford Mill now stands. It stood until the year 1869,
at which time the site was purchased by Messrs. Jones & Gatewood, who
tore down the old structure and commenced the erection of the large one
now standing. They were unable to complete the work begun, and in 1870
Robert Wilford and brother purchased the property, which by a generous
outlay of capital they have made the largest and best mill in the
county. The mill is a frame structure 40x50 feet in size, four stories
high, and has a capacity of eighty barrels of flour per day, and represents a
capital of about $30,000. A small mill was built on Muddy Fork as early as
1842 by Messrs. Alexander & Wimberly, who did a thriving business in
grinding grain and sawing lumber. It was in operation until about the
year 1866. M. A. Smith was the last owner.

Among the early industries of Trigg County were distilleries, several
of which were in operation in Cadiz Precinct shortly after the settlement

of the country. William Jones operated a small still-house on Caney Creek prior to 1820. Z. Thomas had a distillery on his farm two and a half miles from Cadiz about the same time, but all traces of it have long since disappeared. In 1819–20 Spotswood Wilkinson started a tannery in the town of Cadiz which was in operation ten or twelve years. Another tannery was started by Levi Harland on the Thompson place, near the head of Caney Creek, a few years later. Harland operated it for several years and was succeeded by Moses Thompson, who continued the business very successfully until his death in 1884.

Religious.—The highest social progress rests in the church and school. Whatever success the individual lacking these influences may achieve, a community can never prosper without them. The early settlers were considerably scattered and it was for some time a difficult matter to get more than two or three families together for religious services. The pioneer preachers were men of limited education and homely address, but were wonderfully effective in their self-denying earnestness. They visited from cabin to cabin, exhorting, counseling, reproving, as occasion might demand. They became in every home welcome guests. Among the names most familiar here were: Dudley Williams, Fielding Wolfe, Samuel Ross, Reuben Ross, Jesse Cox and Peyton Nance, of the Baptists, and Robert McCullom, Thomas Humphries and John Butcher, of the Methodist Church.

The earliest religious society was the old Mount Pleasant Baptist Church, organized near the site of Jefferson & Jones' Mill in 1810. Later the organization was moved to the southwest part of the precinct, near the Liberty Point Church, where a little log building was erected some time prior to 1820. This building was torn down within a few years and replaced by another log structure built on the ground occupied at the present time by the Liberty Point Church. The second house was known throughout the country as the old "Wolf Pen" Church, so named from the fact that Elder Fielding Wolfe was for many years the pastor of the little flock that met for worship within its diminutive walls. In about the year 1832 a third edifice was erected which is still in use, being occupied at the present time by the Baptist society known as Liberty Point Church. Mount Pleasant was one of the first societies of the Little River Association. It was not materially affected by the rupture of 1833 between the Old School and Progressive wings, but continued in harmony until 1846, when an unfortunate division occurred resulting in a complete dismemberment of the church, the former faction moving to Canton Precinct, where they effected a re-organization which still meets under the original name, while the non-Progressives remained in possession of the building. The Old School society maintained an existence until 1868, when it was abandoned. Among the pastors during that interval were Elders Reuben Ross, Peyton Nance, Joseph Barnes, John Gammon, Samuel Ross and others.

An early Methodist class was organized by Rev. John Butcher in the Young settlement on Bird's Creek several years before the formation of the county. A log house of worship was erected on the bank of Little River, near where the Clarksville road crosses the stream, as early as 1818–19, and stood until some time in the thirties. Among the old families connected with the society were the Youngs and Wallises, and among the earliest preachers are remembered Revs. John Ashley, William Young, Thomas Humphries and —— Corwine. The organization was kept up for a number of years. It was the parent church of the Cadiz society, a history of which will be found further along in this chapter.

Rocky Ridge Baptist Church. This society was established at the village of Wallonia on the 24th day of September, 1840, by a Presbytery composed of Elders Jesse Cox, William Morrison and Joel E. Grace. At the first meeting the following brethren and sisters presented their letters of dismission from Harmony Church (Caldwell County) to wit: Benjamin Faulkner, William Boyd, William A. Faulkner, William Snelling, James T. Snelling, Sallie Blanks, Marium Barton, Sarah Barton and Winfrey Bond; all of whom were given the right hand of fellowship and received into the new organization. William A. Faulkner is the only one of the original members now living. The society was constituted as the Wallonia Baptist Church, and continued to meet as such until April, 1848, when the organization was transferred to a new building erected on the line dividing Cadiz and Wallonia Precincts, and the name changed to Rocky Ridge. This house of worship is a frame building and still used as a meeting place. It has been remodeled at different times, and now has a seating capacity of about 300 persons. John H. Stamps was elected first Church Clerk, and William A. Faulkner, Deacon. The first Pastor was Rev. Joel E. Grace, a man of much more than ordinary natural abilities and an orator of eloquence and power. He preached for the congregation until some time in 1842, when Elder J. F. White became Pastor. With the exception of an interval of three years Elder White has served the church from 1842 to the present time. The interval alluded to was filled by Elder R. W. Moorhead. At the present time there are eighty-six members belonging to the church. The officers are: James H. Blakeley, J. J. Roach and W. Wharton, Deacons: John H. Caldwell, Clerk. Soon after the close of the war letters of dismission were granted to fifty-two colored members, who organized a church of their own in the Wallonia Precinct. They erected a good frame building, which was destroyed by fire in the year 1882, since which time services have been held in a neighboring schoolhouse. They have a strong organization and a very flourishing Sunday-school Elder E. Ladd is their Pastor.

Oakland Methodist Episcopal Church, in southern part of the precinct, was organized in 1859 by Rev. Dr. William Alexander. Among the original members were the following, to wit: David Randolph, Mahlon Belford, Penina Belford, Thomas D. Malone, William Roberts, Nancy Roberts, Thomas Flood, Catherine Flood, J. J. Randolph, J. R. Randolph and T. J. Randolph. The first officers were: Daniel Randolph, Thomas D. Malone and William Roberts, Trustees, they acted as Stewards also; Mahlon Belford, Class-leader. A house was built about the time the organization was effected on land donated by David Randolph, and is still used as a place of worship. The following pastors have ministered to the church since its organization: Dr. Alexander, John Randolph, Gideon Gooch, James Petrie, J. H. Redford, T. C. Peters, L. B. Davidson, J. R. Randolph, Thomas J. Richardson, W. C. Brandon, James Brandon, J. Dowell, Isaac Shelley and John Frayser. Pastor in charge at the present time is Rev. J. L. Reid. Present membership about twenty. The church officers are: J. J. Randolph, Steward and Class-leader, and Drury Sholar, Hawkins Meadow and J. J. Randolph, Trustees.

Dyer's Chapel Methodist Episcopal Church was established in the year 1877 by Rev. Thomas Richardson with a membership of about fifty persons. The organization took place in the Guier Schoolhouse, which was used as a meeting-house until 1881, when a substantial frame house of worship costing $900 was erected on ground donated by J. H. Lawrence. Since its organization the society has been ministered to by the following pastors in the order named:. Thomas Richardson, John D. Frayser, S. G. Shelley, Joseph Love, James Brannon and J. L. Reid, the last-named being preacher in charge at the present time. Present church officers are: J. N. Richardson and James Guier, Stewards; James Battoe, Class-leader; Rufus Dyer, William McAlister, Edwin Guier and James Battoe, Trustees. The organization is in flourishing condition at the present time, and numbers about sixty communicants.

Siloam Methodist Episcopal Church was organized in 1880 by Rev. James W. Bigham, at that time pastor in charge of the Wallonia Circuit. A frame house of worship was erected the same year at a cost of $1,000. Rev. Bigham preached one year and was succeeded by Rev. P. A. Edwards, who remained two years. The next pastor was Rev. J. L. Edrington, after whom came the present Pastor, Rev. E. E. Pate. Church officers are: W. H. H. Alexander and W. A. Shannon, Stewards; —— Banister, Class-leader. At the present time there are the names of eighty-three members on the record. A good Sunday-school is maintained under the superintendency of C. L. Russell.

Liberty Point Baptist Church was organized on the 21st day of August, 1871, by Revs. S. R. McLean and D. S. Hanberry. The names of the original members are as follows : John F. Barnes, W. S. Dismuke, L. B. Edwards, M. N. Mershon, Sarah Edwards, Kittie Hall, Ellen Boyd, Susan Pallard and Isabell Hendrick. The first officers elected were: G. P. Dismuke and Perry Thomas, Jr., Deacons, and James Cunningham, Clerk. The organization was effected in the old Mount Pleasant Meeting-house, which is still used as a place of worship. The following preachers have ministered to the congregation at different times, to wit: D. S. Hanberry seven years; J. W. Oliver two years; C. H. Greystone two years, and J. L. Atwood, present Pastor, who is on his second year's labor. The church has a membership of forty persons, and is reported in good condition. Perry Thomas, Jr., and E. W. Lanieve are Deacons, the former is Clerk also.

Oak Grove Baptist Church was constituted August, 1875, by Revs. George A. Patterson, L. H. Averitt and Daniel Hanberry, with a membership of thirty-nine persons. A house of worship was built the same year on ground deeded by Stanley Thomas and Humphrey Lawrence, and is one of the most comfortable and commodious country church edifices in the precinct. The first pastor of the church was Rev. E. C. Faulkner, who served from 1875 to 1876. Rev. J. H. Spurlin was called the latter year, and has been the regular supply ever since. Under his pastorate the society has increased very largely in numbers and influence, and now has an active membership of 130 persons. The officers at the present time are as follows, to wit: J. J. Thomas, Clerk ; W. B. Thomas, Peter Light and J. J. Thomas, Trustees.

In addition to the churches enumerated the Methodists have a society known as the Bethel congregation, which is one of the oldest religious organizations in the precinct. The early records not being accessible its history was not learned, although it is reported in excellent condition at the present time, and is one of the aggressive churches of the county.

*The Town of Cadiz.**—On the 15th day of May, 1820, Mr. Dion, Mr. Givens, Mr. Thompson, Mr. Sharp and Mr. Vance, five Commissioners appointed by law to locate permanently the seat of justice for Trigg County, made their report, from which the following extract is taken : "After mature and deliberate examination of the many different places proposed as sites for the administration of justice in Trigg County, we are of the opinion that the seat of justice be fixed on the lands of Robert Baker, where he now lives on Main Little River on the top of the eminence above the spring, to include the lot whereon his stable now stands, it being the most central, convenient and eligible site for that purpose."

* The principal facts and material for this sketch of Cadiz were furnished by Maj. McKinney.—ED.

Whereupon the said Robert Baker proceeded to make a deed of transfer of the said stable lot, together with fifty acres of land adjoining, to the newly-organized county.

The first court held in the county was held at Warrington, a place known as the old Carson farm, situated on the Canton & Cadiz turnpike about three miles from Cadiz, and owned at present by Alfred Thomas. By reference to the order books we find at this court the following order, to wit: " It is ordered that the books, papers, etc., of this county be moved to the dwelling of Mr. Robert Baker, and that this court be adjourned until court in course, and then to be held at the dwelling house of the said Baker, afore-said." The next term of the court, on the 19th day of June, 1820, was held as directed at Baker's residence, and the order books show that it was continued at that place up to the October term. At that term on the 17th day of October we find the following order made: " It is ordered that the said fifty-two acres of land shall comprise and constitute a town, and the same is hereby established as such, to be known and called by the name of Cadiz, which shall be contained within the following metes and bounds, to wit: Beginning at a white oak standing south of Baker's stable lot, from thence north 52, west 17 poles 14 feet and 8 inches to a stake marked with two notches, thence north 38, east 17 poles 14 feet and 8 inches to a stake marked with three notches, thence south 52, east 17 poles 14 feet 8 inches to a stake standing in Baker's yard northeast of his dwelling-house, thence south 38, west 17 poles 14 feet 8 inches to the place of beginning, containing the public square of 52 acres and 50 acres besides, which are bounded as follows, to wit: Beginning on the north-west corner of the public square, thence south 38, west 46½ poles to a gum bush and the black stump on Baker's line, thence with said line south 21, east 103 poles to a sugar tree on the south bank of the river, thence north 388, east 117 poles to an ash and two elms, thence north 52, west 70 poles to the east corner of the public square, crossing Little River at 20 poles, thence south 38, west with a line of said public square, thence north 52, west with another of its lines 17 poles 14 feet and 8 inches to the beginning. The whole town of Cadiz aforesaid containing according to the foregoing metes and bounds the quantity of 52 acres and the part besides the said public square that by former order of this court has been laid off into lots of one-fourth of an acre square, being four in a block, and the main and cross streets of the width of sixty feet each, crossing each other at right angles." With the foregoing plat begins the history of the town.

The early inhabitants of the place were the two brothers Robert and Alexander Baker, James Thompson, their stepfather, and his sons, Frederick Holland his son Austin W. Holland, Wayman Crow, Spotswood

Wilkinson, Richard Poston, W. P. M. Scott, M. Mayes and Collins D. Bradley. W. P. M. Scott and Robert Baker were the first merchants. The former occupied a small house not far from the present location of Rash's drug store, and the latter sold goods from the corner house on Main Street just opposite the grocery house of G. W. Lindsay. These stores were stocked with miscellaneous assortments of merchandise, and seem to have been extensively patronized by the early inhabitants of the village and surrounding country. James Thompson kept the first hotel in a two-story log-house situated on the lot where John L. Street's large brick storehouse now stands, and if he failed to accumulate a fortune by plying the occupation of "mine host" we may find a partial elucidation of the mystery in mentioning the fact that law only allowed him to charge 12½ cents for a pint of whisky, 25 cents for a quart of porter, lodging per night 12½ cents, and furnishing a stable for a horse twenty-four hours with three feeds, including corn, oats or fodder, 50 cents. We may mention too as a singular fact that Sevier Tadlock, William Redd, Charles Jones, Absalom Seavills, David Cooper, Levi Harland and James Harland comprised the first Board of Trustees, and none of them living at the time resided within less than four miles of the town. The second board was composed of the following gentlemen: James Thompson, John A. Caudle, B. Alexander and Richard Guynn, all residing within the corporate limits of the town. This board continued in office until May, 1823, when the third board was elected, composed of Richard Guynn, James Thompson, Robert Baker, William McWaters and George Venable, who continued in office until 1830. The members comprising the fourth board were the following gentlemen, to wit: Philip Frayser, Robert Baker, Henry W. Crow and William Cannon. We have been thus particular in mentioning these early boards, not because their official actions connect them with any great public enterprise, but merely to recall and aid in perpetuating the names of respectable bodies of old citizens that few of the present population will remember at all.

No positive material improvement of the town was attempted until about 1850, and the entire duty of the Boards of Trustees seemed to be confined to a few town ordinances, such for example as imposing a fine of $3 on all shows or exhibitions of any kind that should charge an admission fee within corporate limits of the village; $3 for showing a horse within 100 yards of the court house; $5 for delivering a load of tobacco on Sunday, or if it be a negro, twenty stripes in lieu of money, and $1 for all violations of the ordinance that forbade the washing of clothes within sixty feet of the spring lot.

In 1833 the Town Assessor was instructed to make out a full list of all taxable property within the corporate limits of the town and report the same to the Board of Trustees. This he did, the whole amounting to $375.90. No tax, however, was imposed on this amount, and the only object in taking the list was doubtless an ambition to make some official record of the immense wealth of the growing city. A town tax, however, was levied the same year, at the rate of $1 on each white tithe.

In October, 1820, on application and motion of Robert Baker, a part of his land adjoining the town, containing eighteen acres, was added to the original plat. In January, 1821, John G. Reynolds platted an addition to the town, containing twenty-six acres.

The first blacksmithing in the town was carried on by Mr. James Wallis, whose shop was situated where the dwelling house of Mr. M. S. Thompson now stands, and the first cabinet shop was that of Pursley & Cofer, situated on the lot on which the residence of John C. Dabney has been recently erected.

Early Business Men.—As already stated, the first merchants who offered goods for sale in Cadiz were W. P. M. Scott and Robert Baker, the latter of whom was identified with the business interests of the town for a period of about five or six years. The third merchant was one John Hill, who opened a store in a little house where the Cadiz House now stands, and sold goods for about five years, when he disposed of his stock to Hiram Thompson, who continued merchandising some years later. James E. Thompson was another early merchant, as was also Wayman Crow, who conducted a successful business in a house which stood on Main Street. Mr. Crow was one of the most successful business men ever identified with Cadiz, and acquired during the period of his residence here a handsome fortune, and is now one of the leading wholesale merchants of St. Louis. Another prominent merchant was Josiah Miller, who also became wealthy during the early days of the town. Among the tradesmen of the town deserving special notice may be mentioned, John Roach, now in Evansville; Josiah Gardner, F. H. Ragon, Q. Miller, Robert D. Baker, Jr., and E. G. Ragon, all of whom were successful business men and added character to the village. The oldest merchants at the present time are John L. Street and J. W. Chappell.

The second hotel was kept by Robert Baker. Alexander Baker opened a public house for the entertainment of the traveling public in an early day also, and followed the occupation of " mine host" for a period of about twenty-five years. His house was a frame structure and stood on the corner where the new Cadiz Hotel now stands. James O. Cooper succeeded Baker, and was in turn succeeded by L. Barnes. The present hotel was built in the year 1880 by Thomas H. Grinter, and is one of the largest and most commodious structures of the kind in southern Kentucky. The present proprietor is Abe Quick, Jr., who has achieved an enviable reputation as a successful hotel man.

Physicians and Lawyers.—The first doctors, and they were all gentlemen of a considerable degree of eminence. were W. B. Dozier, Abram Venable, Thomas B. Jefferson, Isaac Burnett and W. C. Russell. The first resident members of the bar were Major M. Mays, Judge C. D. Bradley and Esq. T. W. Hammond.

Tobacco Interest.—A very heavy tobacco trade was always done here and at an early day the great bulk of the crop of the county was shipped from this place. Mr. Robert Baker had a rudely constructed warehouse which he kept for storing tobacco, and himself and brother and Silas Alexander usually shipped the entire lot in flat-boats up to about 1837 to 1841, their principal market being New Orleans. About this time the tobacco business attracted the attention of gentlemen possessed of means, better credit and a more comprehensive business capacity, and the old shipping system was compelled to give way to the buyers and professional tobacconists.

The first legitimate operators in this branch of business were the firms of Messrs. Joseph McAlister & Sons, Messrs. Kinson & Street and Mr. Barrett of Henderson, whose business was conducted through his agent Mr. George Robertson, and at his death continued by his son Edmund. Various other firms followed who did for a time a very heavy and successful business. The Dupuys, Wesley Gunn, J. S. and J. P. Thompson were of Louisville and Cincinnati. But the gentlemen of the longest continuation in the business and by far the most successful are the Messrs. White, the present operators. Few men have ever been so successful in any branch of hazardous operation as these gentlemen. They have paid the highest prices, outlived every formidable opposition, gone contrary to the advice of all other well-informed men in the business, and have never met with a reverse.

The first pretentious business houses that were ever erected in the place were: the old house built for the dry goods business that is still standing on the old Poston corner, the one room of which is now used for a shoe store, and the other for a butcher shop; and the others the dry goods and grocery houses built by Messrs. Terry & Wilkinson, and which have been so completely surpassed by those of more recent construction, and which for the last three or four years they have not been able to find an occupant for either.

During the last ten years most of the old business houses of the town have been torn away, and in their stead have been erected fine brick blocks which will compare favorably with the buildings of any other town in southern Kentucky.

Business Register.—The present business of Cadiz is represented by the following men and firms: John L. Street & Son, dry goods; J. W.

Chappell & Son, dry goods and general merchandise; J. J. Garton, dry goods; M. S. Thompson, dry goods; Wilford and Jagoe, dry goods; G. Willis Lindsay, groceries; G. T. McClain, groceries; P. S. Jefferson, groceries; Hancock & Bro., groceries; H. M. Garton & Son, hardware; W. F. Hamilton, hardware and saddlery; —— Wallace, confectionery; —— Newton, confectionery; Mrs. Rawlins, millinery; W. L. Hillman, boots and shoes; Theobald & Son, boot and shoe manufacturers; J. S. Malone & Son, carriage makers and blacksmiths; T. K. Torian, livery stable; Walter Gray, livery stable; Abe Quick, proprietor of the Cadiz House.

Methodist Episcopal Church South of Cadiz*.—In making up the history of this church we meet with difficulties hard to surmount, yet by patient inquiry and diligent research we have reached something near the requisite information, as to details not what we desired, but as to general facts sufficient for all ordinary purposes.

The territory including the present site of Cadiz was originally embraced in Christian Circuit. As early as 1811 we note the appointment of Peter Cartwright, Presiding Elder of the above circuit, which at that time was included in the Nashville District of the Western Conference. But there is no indication of the formation of a class at Cadiz as early as that date. Indeed, Cadiz was not then in existence, nor have we any authentic account of the organization of a society at or near the present site of the town for several years afterward.

In 1812, the notable Peter Cartwright was returned as Presiding Elder, with Jacob Turner as Preacher in charge.

Peter Cartwright served until 1816, the Preachers during that time being S. H. Thompson, John Johnson and Claiborne Duval. In 1816 James Axley was Presiding Elder, and Peter Cartwright Preacher in charge. Axley served the following year, with Benjamin Malone and John Davar, Preachers.

Marcus Lindsey was Presiding Elder from 1818 to 1820 inclusive, the preachers being John Cragg for the former year, Peter Cartwright and Martin Flint for 1819, and Cartwright and William McReynolds for 1820.

This was about the time of the organization of Trigg County, and the location of its seat of justice at Cadiz. The place was visited soon afterward by circuit riders who held public worship in the little log court house. Tracing the succession of preachers we find from the records the district was regularly supplied as follows: 1821, Charles Holliday was appointed Presiding Elder, and served until the year 1825; T. A. Morris and Philip Kenesly were the Preachers for 1821. In 1822, Morris and

---

* By Rev. E. E. Pate.

Major Stanfield were Preachers in charge; the following year George McNelly and A. Long had charge of the circuit. Revs. McNelly and N. G. Berryman were the Preachers during 1824. In 1825, T. A. Morris was Presiding Elder, William Peter and B. Ogden Preachers in charge ; T. A. Morris served as Presiding Elder in 1826 also, with William Peter and D. Tunnell, Preachers. G. McNelly was appointed Presiding Elder in 1827, B. C. Wood and Samuel Kenyon serving as Preachers during that year; 1828, G. McNelly, Presiding Elder, John Sinclair and T. Warren, Preachers ; 1829, McNelly, Presiding Elder,.G. W. Robbins and William Philips, Preachers in charge; 1830, McNelly, Presiding Elder, I. Denham and C. L. Clifton, Preachers; 1831, John Johnson, Presiding Elder, John Redman and W. S. Evans, Preachers ; 1832, Johnson, Presiding Elder, N. G. Berryman and John Redman, Preachers; 1833, Isaac Callard, Presiding Elder, W. S. McMurray and B. Faris, Preachers ; 1834, I. Callard, Presiding Elder, L. Campbell and A. Kelly, Preachers; 1835, I. Callard, Presiding Elder, L. Campbell and R. W. Landrum, Preachers ; 1836, at this time Cadiz was embraced in the Lafayette Circuit, Isaac Callard being the Presiding Elder, and E. Sutton, Preacher in charge ; R. Corwin was Presiding Elder in 1837, and R. F. Turner, Preacher. About this time the class at Cadiz took permanent form, and a house of worship was built on the ground occupied by the present brick edifice, the title to the property not being secured until some two years later. The Rev. R. F. Turner is still living, and is a local Elder residing near Cerulean Springs in Christian County. Coming on down we have the following line of succession : 1838 and 1839, R. Carmine, Presiding Elder, and A. Long, Preacher; 1840, R. Carmine, Presiding Elder, and J. J. Ferree, Preacher; 1841, E. Stevenson, Presiding Elder, A. Long and J. J. Ferree, Preachers ; 1842, E. Stevenson, Presiding Elder, and J. E. Nix, Preacher ; Stevenson served as Presiding Elder in 1843, with Z. M. Taylor, Preacher. In 1844 the name of the circuit was changed to Cadiz, E. Stevenson still serving as Presiding Elder, with J. H. Bristow, Preacher in charge; N. B. Lewis was appointed Presiding Elder in 1845, and served until 1847, the Preachers in the meantime being R. Fisk and J. W. Rhodes. In 1847 T. Bottomly was appointed Presiding Elder ; he served until 1850, with the following preachers, to wit: J. W. Rhodes, J. H. Bristow and W. H. Morris; 1851, N. H. Lee was appointed Presiding Elder this year, and served until 1854, the Preacher in charge during that time being A. Quick, who is still living in Trigg County within two miles of Cadiz on the Hopkinsville turnpike. In 1853 the circuit was known as Lafayette and Cadiz Circuit, the preachers during that year being William Neikirk and J. C. Petree ; 1854, Z. M. Taylor, Presiding Elder, William Neikirk and C. G. Boggess, Preachers; 1855, William Randolph, Preacher; 1856, John Randolph; 1857, William Randolph; 1858, A. Aikin, Presiding Elder, A. Quick, Preacher; R. C. Alexander was Preacher from 1859 to 1861; J. C. Petree served from 1861–62 till 1864; W. H. Morrison succeeded Aiken as Presiding Elder in 1862, and served until 1867; J. F. Redford and H. C. Settle were Preachers in charge from 1864 to 1867; T. C. Frogge was appointed Presiding Elder the latter year, and L. B. Davison, Preacher in 1867–68; F. C. Peters preached for the circuit. The following list comprises the Presiding Elders from the years 1869–70 to 1883–84, the names being in the order they served: L. B. Davison, H. M. Ford, J. A. Lewis, T. G. Bosley, R. C. Alexander and E. M. Crowe. The preachers during that time were T. C. Peters, P. T. Hardison, T. J. Randolph, J. A. Lewis, J. W. Shelton, J. M. Crowe and E. Pate, the last named being Pastor in charge at the present time.

As before stated, the first house of worship was built where the present one stands, on Washington between Montgomery and Franklin Streets, the ground being deeded to Robert Baker, W. C. Russell, A. H. Poston, Thomas B. Jefferson and J. E. Thompson, Trustees. The church continued to worship in this house until the year 1870, when the present edifice was erected at a cost of $4,500. It is a neat brick structure, 40x 60 feet in size, and will comfortably seat 350 or 400 persons. A parsonage was built in 1855 and used five years, at the end of which time it was sold, and other property lying on Little River purchased. The latter house was used until 1872, when it was exchanged for the present parsonage by the payment of $800 difference.

The number of members belonging to the church at the present time is 130, among whom are many of the leading citizens of the town and surrounding country. From 1813 to 1821, inclusive, this section was embraced in the Tennessee Conference and Green River District. In 1822 it was changed to the Kentucky Conference in which it has remained ever since.

Cadiz Christian Church.*—The Church of Christ in Cadiz was organized between the years 1838 and 1840, and was composed of a few scattered members in the town and vicinity. Spotswood Wilkinson, a resident merchant and tobacconist of the town, being an earnest, devout and cultivated Christian, gathered these scattered members in the court house, and taught and exhorted them from Lord's day to Lord's day. Elders George P. Street and other transient preachers occasionally visited and preached to this congregation in the court house from its organization until 1842, when Elder Henry T. Anderson was employed as pastor for some years. He being a man of decided ability and culture, and more

---

*By Judge J. C. Dabney.

recently the author of "Anderson's New Testament" (a translation from the original Greek) with the aid of Elder G. P. Street, largely built up and increased the membership of the church. The membership during this period and more recent years was composed in part of the following persons :

Spotswood Wilkinson and wife, Margaret N. Moore, Mary E. Moore, Maj. M. Mayes and wife and family, James Q. Miller and wife, Dr. Isaac Burnett and wife, Albert S. Dabney, John L. Street, Thomas C. Dabney, Dr. R. A. Amastead and wife, Sydney Hopson and wife, Alexander Baker and wife, Dr. Lunsford Lindsay and wife and family, John S. Fisher and wife, Judge J. J. Harrison, John Cameron and wife, S. W. Van Culin (now of Philadelphia), William Redd and wife and family, Peterfield Jefferson, Albert Jefferson, John Mabry (the old surveyor), Henry C. Burnett, Robert A. Burnett, Capt. R. L. Nance and wife, John H. Boyd, Mrs. Linn Boyd, George L. Torian and wife, and many others. Of these original members many have died, and many have moved away.

The first church edifice was erected in the fall of 1844, on a lot now owned by Moses Thompson, and donated to the church by M. Mayes, in which this congregation continued to meet and worship until the completion of their present brick edifice in the rear of the court house in the fall of 1854.

The Pastors of this congregation have been Henry T. Anderson, G. P. Street, W. E. Mobley, W. C. Rogers, R. M. Giddons, Bela Metcalf, R. B. Tremble, J. W. Higbee, Prof. B. C. Deweese, H. C. Waddell, and from time to time they have enjoyed the visits and protracted meetings held by many distinguished preachers, such as John T. Johnson, the Fergusons, George W. Elley, Jacob Croath, Brown, Howard, John J. Rogers, G. E. Flower, Prof. R. C. Cave, Prof. T. A. Crenshaw, J. T. Hawkins, W. L. Butler, Lipscomb, etc. The Local Elders of the congregation at this time are T. C. Dabney, J. L. Street and J. W. Crenshaw. The Deacons are Robert Crenshaw, Henry C. Wilkinson and J. J. Garton.

From the organization of the church to the present time, with exceptions of short intervals before and during the war, the church has kept up in addition to its regular Lord's day meeting for worship, a Bible Class or Sunday-school, and prayer-meeting. Dr. J. W. Crenshaw is the present Superintendent of the Sunday-school, numbering some forty pupils and six teachers. Various members of the congregation have given much of their time and means in promoting domestic and foreign missions, and the spread of the Gospel of Christ.

*Baptist Church.**—April 15, 1842, the members of the Baptist denomination living in the town and vicinity of Cadiz, according to previous

*By H. B. Wayland.

appointment, met at the house of brother C. A. Jackson, when, in accordance with their request, they were examined by a presbytery composed of Elders William Morrison, John Hubbard, R. W. Nixon and T. G. Keen, who believed them to be orthodox, and were upon their adopting a declaration of faith and church covenant constituted into a church under the name of the Cadiz United Baptist Church. Elder Morrison acted as Moderator.

Church Covenant.—Having been, as we trust, brought by Divine Grace to embrace the Lord Jesus Christ, and to give up ourselves wholly to Him, we do now solemnly and joyfully covenant with each other *to walk together in Him with brotherly love* to His glory as our common Lord. We do, therefore, in His strength engage,

That we will exercise a mutual care, as members one of another, to promote the growth of the whole body in Christian knowledge, holiness and comfort; to the end that we may stand perfect and complete in all the will of God.

To promote and secure this object we will uphold the public worship of God and the ordinances of His house, and hold constant communion with each other therein; that we will cheerfully contribute of our property to the support of the poor, and for the maintenance of a faithful ministry of the Gospel among us.

That we will not omit closet and family religion at home, nor allow ourselves in the too-common neglect of the great duty of religiously training up our children and those under our care, with a view to the service of Christ and the enjoyment of heaven.

That we will endeavor to walk circumspectly in the world, that we may win their souls, remembering that God hath not given us the spirit of fear, but of power and of love, and of a sound mind; that we are the light of the world and the salt of the earth, and that a city set on a hill cannot be hid.

That we will frequently exhort, and if occasion shall require, admonish one another according to Matt., 18th, in the spirit of meekness; considering ourselves lest we be also tempted, and that as in baptism we have been buried with Christ and raised again, so there is on us a special obligation thenceforth to walk in newness of life.

And may the God of peace, who brought again from the dead our Lord Jesus, that great Shepherd of the sheep, through the blood of the everlasting covenant, make us perfect in every good work, to do His will; working in us that which is well pleasing in His sight through Jesus Christ, to whom be glory forever and ever. Amen.

The following brethren having adopted the articles of faith and covenant were enrolled as members of this church, viz.: John Jackson, John

W. Jackson, Charles A. Jackson, Daniel M. Ragon, George L. Torian, Mrs. Elmira Gilfoy, Catharine Baker, Mary Jackson, Susan E. Jackson, Misses Eliza Jane Kelly, Ann Eliza Thompson, Martha J. Jackson and Nancy Perry. C. A. Jackson was chosen Clerk and John W. Jackson was recognized as Deacon, having previously held that office. In June, the church resolved to apply for admission into Little River Association. D. M. Ragon was appointed Treasurer. At present the total membership of the church is thirty-one communicants.

Cadiz Methodist Episcopal Church (colored) was organized in the year 1873 by Rev. Christopher Humphries, assisted by Rev. D. Bagby. At the first meeting seventy names were enrolled as members and the following officers elected : Handy Wilford, Class Leader ; Jones Mayze, Eli Early and Harvey Young, Stewards ; and Jacob Young, Handy Wilford, Jones Mayze, Henry Carloss and Nelson Morgan, Trustees. Christopher Humphries was the first Pastor. He was succeeded by D. A. Bagby, after whom came in regular order the following ministers, viz.: Green Bibb, B. C. Tolbert, Mr. Spurlin, A. Samples, G. W. Landers and D. A. Radliff, the present incumbent. A neat, frame house of worship was built in 1874 at a cost of $900. At the present time there are 126 members belonging to the society, which is reputed in flourishing condition. The present officers of the church are the following, to wit : Jones Mayze, Handy Wilford, Joseph Poston, Nathan Martin and Jacob Young, Trustees ; Henry Redd, Andrew Stubble, William Wilford and R. Ragon, Stewards ; Handy Wilford, Henry Redd and Joseph Poston, Class-leaders. A fine Sunday-school is maintained under the efficient superintendency of R. Ragon.

Second Baptist Church (colored).—This church was organized in the year 1871 by Rev. Mr. Morehead, with a constitutional membership of about twenty persons, a number which has since increased to 230, being one of the strongest religious societies in the county at the present time. A frame house of worship was built shortly after the organization and used jointly by the Methodists and Baptists for a couple of years, at the end of which time the latter denomination disposed of their interest in the building and erected their present edifice, a good frame structure costing the sum of $400. The pastors of the church have been Elders Morehead, Waddell, Skinner and Ridley, the last named being the present incumbent. The officers of the church are Robert Slaughter, R. Crump and A. Alexander, Deacons ; D. M. Brown, Clerk.

Second Methodist Episcopal Church (colored) was established by Revs. Christopher Humphries and D. Bogy in the year 1873. At the first meeting the names of seventy persons were enrolled as members and the following officers elected : Handy Wilford, Jacob Young, Jones Mayze,

Henry Carloss and Nelson Morgan, Trustees; Harvey Young, Jones Mayze and Eli Early, Stewards; Handy Wilford, Class Leader. The following pastors have had charge of the church since its organization, to wit: Christopher Humphries, D. A. Bogy, Green Bibb, B. C. Tolbert, —— Spurlin, A. Samples and G. W. Landers. Present Pastor is Rev. D. A. Radliff. The house of worship in which the society meets was built in 1874, and cost the sum of $900.

The church officials at the present time are as follows: Jones Mayze, Nathan Martin, Handy Wilford, Jacob Young and Joseph Poston, Trustees; Henry Redd, Andrew Stubbles, William Wilford and R. Ragon, Stewards; Handy Wilford, Henry Redd and Joseph Poston, Class Leaders. Present membership 126.

*Schools.**—About the year 1840 a Mr. Curlin by will left an estate consisting of land and negroes *"for the benefit of a Seminary."* Five Trustees were elected every four years by the legal voters of the county. Property was purchased and the school located in Cadiz, consisting of a male and female department, but in separate buildings. The land was leased for ninety-nine years. The negroes were freed by President Lincoln's proclamation. From 1860 to 1865 the annual income from this source—$300—was divided *pro rata* amongst the pupils who came to the school, by which the subscription was reduced to that extent. The tuition in full of two female pupils was paid two years after 1860 from the Curlin fund. The last of this fund went in part payment for the present High School building. Some of the earlier teachers were Messrs. Anderson and Rumsey, also Miss Norris, and then her sister.

J. Q. A. Tyler taught eleven years in the Male Seminary, ending with the spring term, 1860. H. B. Wayland and his wife, J. S. Wayland, took charge of the Female Seminary in September, 1860, Mrs. Wayland teaching music. In the spring of 1862 they resigned in consequence of disturbances resulting from the war. Rev. Petre taught one session. In September they took charge of the Seminary and taught until 1869, when they resigned. During 1863 and 1864 the music class numbered twenty-seven; number in school about eighty, and at one time there were about forty boarders in the town. Miss Leonora Prescott and Mrs. L. E. Cook were Assistants.

During the war board having been raised to $5 a week, and difficult to obtain, H. B. Wayland and wife purchased land at the cost of nearly $3,000, and put on it improvements at a cost of $8,000. H. B. Wayland took charge of the Male Seminary one year in 1871. He then opened a private school on his premises, and taught until June, 1873. Mrs. Wayland was teacher of music. Her health failed and October 30,

* By H. B. Wayland.

1873, she departed this life, and the Cadiz Institute closed. The assistants in the Cadiz Institute were Misses Willia Faulkner, Laura Gary, Nannie Duncan and Mary E. Guthrie. Miss Willie Elliot taught in the Female Seminary nine years, beginning with September, 1869. She was succeeded by John C. Dabney, B. C. Dewees and —— Wyatt. Other teachers since 1860: Gentlemen—Randolph, Harwood, Jefferson, Boggs, Jones, Pomroy, Harvey, Hancock, Woodson, Watson. Ladies—Mrs. Dabney, Mrs. Pettis, Misses Poston, Faxon, Pursley, Terry, Pursley, Wilkinson. The present public school building, standing on the principal street of the town, is one of the most commodious and convenient school buildings in southwestern Kentucky. It is a substantial brick edifice and well adapted to school purposes. Excellent schools are taught in it each year and for the usual period by competent teachers.

Freemasonry.—The history of Masonry is more or less familiar to all the civilized world, and, as the order claims, to many of the semi-civilized, and even good Masons are to be found among barbarous peoples. Among its claimed chief merits and glories are its great age—the oldest organization in the world—antedating all sects, religions, and even all organized social life since the coming of Adam and Eve. Again, it is sometimes given as the history of its foundation that, as its name indicates, it was founded and organized among the workmen for mutual protection, at the building of that historical structure—Solomon's temple. But like everything else it has adapted itself to the inevitable that follows the workings and growth of the human mind, and now they have attached to the order well regulated benefit associations, and distribute much real and beneficial charity and aid to fellow members and the widows and orphans of deceased brethren. The cardinal ideas of Masonry have perhaps always been a high morality founded on the Bible, and a law of mutual protection of a brother toward a brother.

A lodge was chartered in Cadiz on the first day of September, 1841, under the name of Cadiz Lodge, No. 121. The first officers were William C. Grafton, W. M., Matthew Mays, S. W., and Joel Wilson, J. W. The society held meetings at different houses until 1850, at which time a large and commodious hall was built in connection with the Christian Church, the Masons occupying the upper story. The society at one time was the strongest in the county, but of recent years, owing to the establishment of other lodges in the neighboring villages, its membership has considerably diminished, until now there are only about thirty-eight names on the roll. The present officers are: A. F. Rash, W. M.; P. H. Allen, S. W.; John C. Curling, J. W.; R. W. Major, Treas.; J. F. Gentry, Sec.; J. D. Shaw, S. D.; Armstead Moody, J. D.; John W. Russell, Steward and Tyler.

Cadiz Lodge, No. 1,635, K. of H., was organized on the 19th of August, 1880, with the following charter members, to wit: John G. Jefferson, J. E. Edwards, John W. Pursley, W. T. Smoot, Thomas L. Bacon, Thomas T. Watson, C. H. Hawkins, John D. Shaw, H. B. Wilkinson, G. Willis Lindsay, F. G. Terry, W. C. White, M. S. Thompson and R. A. Burnett. The present membership is fifty-six. The present officers (1884) are: G. W. Lindsay, P. D.; John G. Jefferson, D.; W. L. Hillman, V. D.; W. T. Smoot, Assist. D.; M. S. Thompson, Sec.; F. G. Terry, Financial Reporter; H. B. Wilkinson, Treas.; T. T. Watson, Chaplain; Perry Thomas, Jr. Guide; John D. Shaw, Sr. Guide, and J. W. Russell, Guardians.

Ophelia Council, No. 11, Chosen Friends, was established on the 11th day of October, 1882, with thirty-eight charter members, a number in excess of the present membership, which is only thirty-five. The officers of the society at the present time are J. C. Dabney, P. C. C.; T. F. McBride, Chief Counselor; John Theobald, Vice-Counselor; John G. Jefferson, Secretary; H. B. Wilkinson, Treasurer; J. W. Crenshaw, Medical Examiner; E. S. Sumner, Prelate; Robert Crenshaw, Marshal; W. H. Timmons, Warden; L. Freeman, Guard.

Good Templars was an older society than the Knights or Chosen Friends, and so far as we can learn deserves the first place in history, but in seeking after the facts of its organization we ascertained that it ceased to exist a few years since. It was organized on the 23d of July, 1876, with twenty-eight charter members, and terminated its existence in 1879.

The Hamiltonians.—We go to school from the cradle to the grave, and this is one of the inexorable laws of our being. These schools or fountains of education are nearly infinite in variety, and have little in common save the imperfections that pervade all. A careful investigation of the influences of the mind go far to demonstrate the fact that real education comes with our joys, our pleasures and the social intercourse of congenial spirits, that is the highest mark of our civilization. The mind must be developed as in the perfect physical nature. It is not hard dull work that molds the child into beauty and strength, perfection and grace, but on the contrary, too much of this dwarfs and stunts the young into ungainliness of person and feature. But it is the happy heart, the rippling laugh, joined with agreeable mental culture, by which strong, active, graceful and well poised intellects are created. We mean that intense mental activity that comes of keen jest, of mental play work, of that social and intellectual life that is made up of the associations of congenial companions where "youth and pleasure meet" at the weekly assemblings of the *Hamillomans*, a society of the intelligent and literary young men of Cadiz, organized on the 8th of March, 1884. As best stated by one of its members, the objects of the association are literary and social enjoyment, the promotion of a spirit of good fellowship among the members, the acquirement of the art of public debate, the attainment of a higher mental culture and a steady growth toward enlarged usefulness. The officers of the society are as follows: Webb Watkins, President; Joseph P. Gill, Vice-President; Paul A. Curling, Secretary. The following gentlemen comprise the membership, viz.: Paul A. Curling, Muscoe Burnett, Joseph P. Gill, Edwin F. Dabney, C. D. McKinney, Webb Watkins, J. W. Sawyer, James E. Burnett, J. E. Kelly, A. S. Dabney and Henry Malone.

In conclusion of our brief sketch of Cadiz, we will add that it fulfills the scriptural text; it is a "city set on a hill, and cannot be hid." It does stand on a hill, and is one of the handsomest and neatest little cities we have ever become acquainted with. And its people are as courteous as the city is handsome. Among them we have some friends we are proud to reckon as such, and when they read this it will remind them that we shall not soon forget them.

CHAPTER VII.

CANTON AND LINTON PRECINCTS—TOPOGRAPHY OF CANTON—ITS AGRICUL-
TURAL RESOURCES—EARLY SETTLEMENT—ABRAHAM BOYD—SETTLE-
MENT ON DONALDSON CREEK—THE WILSON FAMILY—OTHER PIONEERS
—MILLS AND DISTILLERIES—BIRTHS, DEATHS AND MARRIAGES—RE-
LIGIOUS, ETC.—TOWN OF CANTON—ITS BIRTH AS A TOWN—GROWTH
AND DEVELOPMENT—THE METHODISTS AND BAPTISTS—SECRET SOCIE-
TIES—PHYSICAL FEATURES OF LINTON PRECINCT—ITS EARLY OCCUPA-
TION BY WHITE PEOPLE—SKETCH OF ITS SETTLERS—MASONIC—CHURCH
HISTORY, ETC., ETC.

CANTON PRECINCT lies a little southwest of the geographical center of the county, and is bounded on the north by Little River, on the east by Cadiz Precinct, the south by Linton Precinct, the west by Cumberland River. The face of the country is very uneven and broken, especially along the rivers, where are high hills and rocky, precipitous bluffs. Back from the river the country is not so abrupt, although the entire precinct possesses but a small area of level land. Among the hills and contiguous to the smaller water-courses are tracts of comparatively even land, possessing a deep alluvial soil, the fertility of which has been but slightly diminished by seventy years' almost constant tillage. The broken portions of the precinct are not so well adapted to agriculture, many of the hills being characterized by a thin gravelly soil, which a few years' cultivation renders sterile. Consequently much of the rolling land has never been cleared, and large areas are covered with a forest growth and present the same appearance they did when seen by the first settlers at the beginning of the present century. The timber embraces the varieties usually found growing in this part of the State, maple, oak, beech, hickory and ash predominating. Limestone abounds in all parts of the precinct, and an abundance of excellent sandstone is found in various localities. The water-courses are Donaldson Creek, Craig's Branch, Beech Fork and Muddy Creek, all of which are running streams throughout the greater part of the year. They traverse the country in almost all directions, and empty into Cumberland and Little Rivers.

The chief products of the precinct are tobacco, corn, wheat, oats and the usual varieties of vegetables found in this range of climate. Wheat is not found so well adapted to the soil as to form a staple crop in recent years, and while it is still sown to a considerable extent, it is not the crop upon which the farmers place the most dependence. Corn and tobacco are the principal crops upon which they rely for revenue, and much of this is sold for exportation. But few attempts have been made as yet to enrich the soil with commercial fertilizers, although some of the farmers are growing clover successfully and turning it under with good effect upon the soil.

Settlement by White Men.—The settlement of Canton Precinct dates back prior to the dawning of the present century, though at what year the first pioneers made their appearance is a matter of mere conjecture. Traces of rude log-cabins were found in many places along the Cumberland River when the first permanent settlers came, and the belief is current that families of trappers and adventurers made this a rendezvous many years before any effort was made to open up and improve the country. "As early as 1799, a party of emigrants called a halt on the river at a point where now is situated the town of Canton, who were destined to leave a record in the public archives of this Commonwealth that has been and will continue to be read from the beginning to the ending of the present century. We allude to the family of Abraham Boyd. He was a native of North Carolina, but had been a resident of Tennessee in the neighborhood of Nashville, a number of years, and removed thence to the point above stated. The trip must have been made in flat-boats, for there were no roads, and an old settler remarked that he assisted them in cutting a road through the cane from the river bank to the top of the hill for their wagons, and it took several days to complete it. He erected his first dwelling on the ground where the present church stands. His father-in-law, Adam Linn, accompanied him, and made a settlement three miles out from the river on the Luster place. He was a native of Scotland, and a blood relation of the poet Burns. Abraham Boyd was a man of remarkably fine intellect, and for that day a man of considerable culture. He represented the people a number of times in the Legislature when this was a portion of Christian County and afterward when Trigg was formed into a distinct division. He has been represented as the superior of his afterward distinguished son, Hon. Linn Boyd, upon the stump, was a man of very thorough business training, and the presiding Justice of the County Court in the organization and formation of the county."

About the same time of Boyd's arrival, or perhaps a little earlier, a small settlement was made on Donaldson Creek. Among the first to settle in this locality were John and Shadrach Futrell, Josiah Lindsay and his brothers James L., Caleb and Carleton. Basil Holland settled near the Perry Thomas farm as early as 1800, and died forty-five years ago. James Dixon and his sons Hiram and James, Jr., made improvements in the Holland neighborhood about the year 1802 or 1803.

The Wilson family, consisting of the father, John Wilson, and his sons

John, Ben, James, natives of South Carolina, secured homes on Craig's Branch, an affluent of Donaldson Creek, as early as 1803, and John Craig, after whom the stream was named, came a little earlier and settled on the place now used as a poor-farm. In 1804 and 1805 came Joel Cohoun and settled where William Turner lives; Josiah Outland and Enos Outland, who improved a part of the Lindsay land; Charles Boren, Sr., and Charles Boren, Jr., who settled where Blunt Turner lives. About the same time came William Ross and settled on the Whitmill Holland farm. Drury Bridges came as early as 1804 and located near Beech Fork on the place now owned by his grandson, C. T. Bridges. One daughter of this stanch old pioneer, Mrs. Perry Thomas, is still living in the precinct. Mr. Bridges died in 1840. Lawrence Killabrew settled on land adjoining the Bridges farm about the year 1804. He was one of the earliest preachers in the county, and a man of character and influence in the community where he resided.

Prominent among the settlers on Donaldson Creek was James Thomas, who moved to the State from North Carolina in 1806, and located where his grandson Peyton Thomas now lives. The following sketch of this noted pioneer is from McKinney's historical articles: " He was born in North Carolina in 1761, when that country was a province of Great Britain, and long before the inhabitants had conceived the thought of throwing off the yoke of the British Empire. Living through the storm of the Revolution, he inherited that patriotic devotion to his country so peculiar in those days, and gave as a reason for not moving West earlier than he did, that he recognized the same obligations to the State of North Carolina until he was forty-five years of age that he did to his parents until he was twenty-one. Taking leave of the country, then, soon after his second maturity, he turned his face to the great West, and after a long and tedious journey arrived on Donaldson Creek, in what was then Christian County, the latter part of November, 1806. Not possessed of the restless disposition of most men, when they have once torn away from the place of their birth, he felt perfectly satisfied in his new home, and resolved at once to spend the residue of his life there. He never broke the resolution, but died in 1832 where he first settled. Old Uncle James Thomas was a man of more than ordinary ability. He was a man of good morals, and a consistent member of the Baptist Church." In company with Mr. Thomas came his sons, Cullen, Perry and Starkie, all of whom were prominently identified with the early growth and development of the county. Cullen Thomas lived and died on the place settled by his father. Perry Thomas, the second son, is still living, having reached the rare old age of eighty-eight years, in full possession of all his mental and physical powers. He has been a very active business man, and has been called at various times to fill offices of public trust.   He was the Assessor of the county for twenty-one consecutive years, and the date of his induction into official life extends away back to the time when two-thirds of the present old men in the county were merely in their swaddling clothes.   He is a man of more than ordinary culture, even for the present day, and takes an active part in all measures calculated to benefit the public. Starkie Thomas, the third son, became a very successful business man, and his descendants are among the well-to-do and respectable citizens of the county.   James and Stanley Thomas were born after the family came to the State, and were equally prominent with the three described.

Other early settlers of the precinct were Alexander George, Edwin Noel, Richard Bell, Joshua Underwood, James Kinchen and Jordan Lasseter.   Later came Allan Showler, Joshua Showler, William Barnes, James Barnes, Allen Barnes, Robert Hardin, Luke Thomas and Ezekiel Thomas, all of whom had homes in the precinct prior to 1812.   Since that period the influx of population has been steady and constant, and many of the old landmarks have forever disappeared.

Early Industries.— The first mill in the precinct was erected about the year 1803 or 1804, and stood on Donaldson Creek, about two miles above its mouth.   It was a small log building, contained one buhr operated by a "tub" wheel, and made a coarse article of meal.   It was in operation about thirty years, and seems to have been well patronized during the greater part of that period.   The last owner was Henry Hansbarger.   Another early mill was built by Cullen Thomas, and operated by horse-power.   It was what is termed a "tramp-mill," and did a fair business during the time it was in operation.

Abraham Boyd erected a horse-mill at the landing shortly after his arrival, and operated it about twenty years.   He constructed a cotton gin about the same time also, with which he did a thriving business during the early days of the county.   The second water-mill in the precinct was put in operation by Cullen Thomas about the year 1840.   This was a combination mill, manufactured both lumber and meal, but did a limited business, owing to the scarcity of water in the creek.

In the year 1811 James Thomas and Shadrach Futrell erected a distillery on the land of Allen Showler, which they operated with fair success for a period of six or seven years.   This was one of the first distilleries in the county, and early achieved the reputation of turning out the very finest quality of whisky.   Cullen Thomas constructed a small distillery on his place in 1815, and ran it until 1835.   Later, Hiram Dixon engaged in the distillery business on Craig's Branch, but owing to a want of patronage was obliged to close out in a short time.   The distillery of **Mize & Cliner** was erected near Canton about the year 1864.   They did a fair business until 1867, at which time the enterprise was abandoned.

A tannery was started on the Sumner place near Donaldson Creek in 1851 by —— McReynolds, of Christian County, who ran it until 1854, when George C. Graham became possessor. He operated it until 1868 or 1870, when it passed into other hands, and finally went down.

A steam-mill was erected by William Williams near Canton about the year 1859. It was afterward purchased by Peyton Thomas, and moved to his place on Donaldson Creek, where it was in operation about three years. It was afterward purchased by a Mr. Gordon, and moved to the west side of the Cumberland. Mr. Thomas operated a small tannery also, and was well patronized until the yard was overflowed and destroyed by the creek. The first blacksmith in the precinct was Basil Holland. Shadrach Futrell was an early mechanic also.

Among the first summoned away by death in the precinct were Dicey Showler, sister of James Thomas in 1806, and Mrs. James Dixon, in the winter of the same year. Other early deaths were Temperance Thomas, Shadrach Futrell and wife, Sarah Futrell, and members of the different families previously referred to.

Early Marriages.—Among the early marriages in the precinct are remembered the following: Winborne Futrell and Charity Colston, 1809; Stephen Boren and —— Colston, the same year; John Allen and Sallie, daughter of John Craig, as early as 1808; William Barnes and Sarah Lawrence, in 1809; Denson Deese and Rachel Holland, 1808 or 1809; Ezekiel Thomas and Temperance Thomas, in 1812. Other early marriages were a Mr. Ford to Nellie Craig; David Cohoun and Rebecca Futrell; Cullen Thomas and Elizabeth Futrell. Among the earliest births were Stanley Thomas, son of James and Mary Thomas, in 1807, and Mary Thomas, in 1809.

The pioneers of Trigg County were a church-going people, and the gospel was introduced in a very early day. The first preachers in this precinct belonged to the Baptist Church, and for several years religious services were held from house to house. Among these pioneer missionaries are remembered Elders Dudley Williams, Lawrence Killabrew, Thomas Ross, James Dixon and Reuben Ross.

The Donaldson Creek Baptist Church was constituted in 1814 by Revs. Thomas Ross, Dudley Williams and Thomas McLean. At the time of its organization it was an arm of the Dry Creek Church in Canton Precinct, and numbered twenty-four members. The first house of worship was a little log building erected on one acre of land donated by Basil Holland, and was used as a meeting-place for about twenty years. At the end of that period another log structure, more commodious than the first, was built.   It stood until 1854, at which time the present frame edifice was erected.

The first regular pastor was Rev. Thomas McLean ; John Mallory and Alfred Lindsay preached for the congregation in an early day.   Later came Revs. A. P. Hodges, William Skinner, —— Trimble, L. McLean and R. Allen.   The present incumbent is Rev. Mr. Tidwell.   At one time the organization was very strong, but owing to the division between the progressive and conservative wings in an early day the members were greatly diminished.   The present membership is about seventy.

Early educational facilities were meager, and the children of the pioneers had few advantages in that direction.   A few months in the log-cabin schoolhouse, with its puncheon or dirt floor, and big fire place, was the extent of learning they received, and the advantages the precinct afforded.   For forty years or more after the first settlement education was at a low ebb.   Like stagnant water in the creek bottom swamps, it was difficult to tell whether the current flowed backward or forward.   The schoolhouses, school books, teachers and the manner of instruction were of the most primitive character.

A man by name of James Gray was one of the first teachers, not only in this precinct but in the county.   Wilson Wallis, Christopher Pritchard and David Barton were early teachers also.   The first public school was taught in the Donaldson Creek Church building by a Mr. Gray, not the one mentioned above.

An early schoolhouse stood near Peyton Thomas' residence, and another not far from the town of Canton.   The precinct is fairly supplied with schools at the present time, and the advantages of an education are within the easy reach of all.

Town of Canton.—The first settlement on the present site of Canton was made, as before stated, by Abraham Boyd, about the close of the last century.   For several years the place was known as Boyd's Landing, and early acquired considerable prominence as a shipping point.   Up to the completion of the railroad to Hopkinsville more freight was received and more tobacco shipped here than at any other point on the Cumberland River, with the exception of Clarksville, from Burksville to the mouth.   The first road that was opened from the place was before the village was laid out, and is still known as Old Boyd's Landing road, leading to Hopkinsville by Thompson's tan-yard, Kent's Bridge and Cherry Hill.   The second road was between the rivers to the old Pentecost Ferry. They were both opened by order of the County Court of Christian County, and the order establishing the ferry across the Cumberland at the landing, and the old Pentecost Ferry across the Tennessee required the consent of the Indians who inhabited the western bank of the latter stream before the privilege was granted or the ferry established. The favorable location early attracted settlers to the vicinity, and as early as the year 1809 or 1810, a small store was started by one James Warren. How long he remained and with how much success he met in his business venture are facts not now known, as all traces of him and his store have long since been forgotten.

In the year 1823 the village was regularly laid out and the plat placed upon record. The order for the town reads as follows: "On motion of Abraham Boyd for the establishment of a town at Boyd's Landing, on Cumberland River, he having produced satisfactory proof to the county of his holding a good and undisputed title to the said land, as also of his having given such notice of this application as required by law. It is therefore ordered that said town be, and the same is hereby established, to be known and called by the name of Canton, which shall be contained within the following metes and bounds, to wit: Beginning at a sycamore on the bank of Cumberland River, and thence running south 75 degrees, east 120 poles to an elm; thence south $23\frac{1}{2}$ degrees west, 150 poles to a stake in the field; thence north 75 degrees west, 121 poles to a black walnut on the bank of said river at the mouth of Lick Creek; thence down aforesaid river north 35 degrees, east 82 poles to the landing; thence north 12 degrees, east 70 poles to the beginning, containing 105 acres. It is further ordered that Ferdinand Wadlington, James Daniel, Lipscomb Norvell, Jesse Wells, Charles Caldwell, Reuben Lynn and William Deason be appointed trustees of said town."

Several business men came to the town shortly after it was laid out, and its importance as a trading point continued to grow until the completion of the Louisville & Nashville Railroad to Hopkinsville. This road seriously interfered with the river trade, and since its construction the town has been gradually losing its original vitality, although it is still the distributing point for Cadiz and a number of other places. Among the early merchants were Jesse Wells, William Wells and James Cox. William Durette came later and acquired a competent fortune. James T. Gore & Co. engaged in merchandising in an early day, and conducted a very successful business until the breaking out of the war. Another merchant deserving of special mention was William Soery, who went to the town a poor boy, and by diligent attention to business acquired a handsome fortune. The firm of Richardson & Ford were successful merchants, as were also E. C. Spiceland and John D. Tyler. Philip Anderson sold goods for several years, and afterward moved to Cerulean Springs. The Fuqua Brothers were prominent business men of the place, and W. J. Fuqua, the present merchant, has perhaps amassed a greater fortune than any we have spoken of. A number of warehouses have been built at different times, the most important of which were those belonging to J. F. Dyer, Cobb & Boyd, Ford & Tyler, and a large one owned by a stock company and operated several years by W. D. Grace and later by Col. J. F. Gentry. A steam-mill was erected by W. D. Grace in an early day, and operated several years. His successors were Whitlock, McNichols & Co.; the last owners were Linson & Clinard.

Canton Methodist Episcopal Church South.—This society dates its origin from the year 1845, at which time meetings were held in an old schoolhouse which stood in the northeast part of the town. Among the early members were W. R. Lee, A. J. Lee, M. Adkins and wife, Sandy Wail and wife, and S. Light. Among the pastors prior to 1878 are re-membered Revs. Davidson, King, Redford, Randolph, Hardison, Rhodes and Petrie. Since 1878 the following pastors have had charge of the church, to wit: James Frayser, Thomas Richardson, Joseph Love, James C. Brandon, and J. L. Reid, present incumbent. In 1874 the society united with the Baptists in the erection of their present house of worship. The officers of the church at this time (1884) are as follows: G. W. Cobb, W. M. Brandon, Stewards; J. H. Lackey, Class Leader.

The Methodist Episcopal Sunday-school was organized in 1880, and with the exception of one season has been held every Lord's day since. The first Superintendent was Mr. Chitwood. The present officers are W. M. Brandon, Superintendent; Dr. J. H. Lackey, Assistant Superintendent; S. E. Lacy, Secretary; and William Malone, Treasurer.

Baptist Church of Canton.—This church was constituted May, 1855, by Elders Meacham and Trimble, with the following members, viz.: S. Finley and wife, E. C. Spiceland and wife, C. H. Major and wife, Wesley Adair and wife, Catherine Durette, William Bell and Ellen Holland. The village schoolhouse was used as a meeting-place until 1874, at which time the Union Church was erected. This house is a handsome structure, representing a capital of about $2,500, and is used by the Baptists and Methodists. The pastors of the church since its organization have been the following: Revs. Trimble, J. H. Spurlin, — Moorhead, C. H. Greg-ston and A. W. Meacham; A. G. Cobb, T. H. Atwood and C. H. Major are Deacons; T. H. Atwood, Clerk. The membership is forty. A flour-ishing Sunday-school is sustained, the officers of which are the following: C. H. Major, Superintendent; W. J. Holland, Assistant Superintendent; and James Holland, Secretary and Treasurer.

Masonic.—Canton Lodge, No. 242, A. F. & A. M., was organized in the fall of 1852, through the instrumentality of J. E. Thompson, of Cadiz, and Mr. Weller, of Princeton. On the charter are the names of the following persons, to wit: Lemuel Sills, Kinchen Battoe, Robert Shaw, A. R. Wallace, N. R. Wallace and W. L. Fuqua. The first officers were Lemuel Sills, W. M.; K. Battoe, S. W.; W. L. Fuqua, J. W.; and Robert Shaw, Sec.   An upper room of the village schoolhouse was fitted up for a hall at a cost of $200, and served as a lodge-room until 1879, when it was destroyed by fire.   The society then purchased a vacant building, and fitted up a very neat room which is still in use.   The present membership is twenty-two, a number much smaller than in former years, owing to the organization of other lodges in the neighboring towns. The following are the officers at the present time: J. H. Lackey, W. M.; C. T. Bridges, S. W.; J. N. Haydon, J. W.; L. R. Wallace, Treas.; T. N. Ingram, Sec.; W. D. Lancaster, S. D.; N. R. Wallace, J. D.; Isaac B. Yates, Steward and Tyler.   Among the many charitable acts of the lodge may be mentioned the liberal contribution of $300 to the widows' and orphans' fund of Louisville.

Cruson Council Chosen Friends, No. 5, was established in 1880 by James Cruson, with twenty charter members, among whom were G. W. Cobb, F. P. Cobb, J. W. Logan, J. D. Logan, Mrs. Myra Hopson, W. J. Hopson, J. W. Chitwood and wife, Mr. and Mrs. John R. Blake, and Dr. J. H. Lackey.   The society has a membership of twenty-five at the present time, and holds its meetings at the residence of Dr. J. H. Lackey. The following officers were the last ones elected; G. W. Cobb, C. C.; Dr. J. H. Lackey, P. C. C. and Medical Examiner; W. M. Brandon, Secretary; and W. J. Hopson, Treasurer.

Linton Precinct.—Linton is voting precinct No. 11, and with Canton forms a magisterial district.   It lies south of Canton, east of the Cumberland River, west of Roaring Springs, and borders upon Tennessee on the south.   The greater part of the precinct is very broken and contains but a small area of good land, which is confined principally to the Cumberland bottoms and Dry Creek.   The latter stream is the most important water-course, and it was along its banks that one of the oldest and most important settlements in the county was made.   " It is a singular fact that the first settlements of this county as in most other counties of Kentucky, were made on the most sterile and unproductive lands, leaving all the rich barrens as comparatively worthless and of no earthly value to the agriculturist."   " The time has never been that the lands upon which the first settlements of Trigg County were made could have been sold for 50 per cent above the original cost of the survey, while other lands lying contiguous to them, that could have been obtained for even a less price, have since been sold as high as $75 per acre."   " The settlement on Dry Creek is an illustration very much in point; except in narrow bottoms immediately on the stream the lands for miles around are of the very poorest quality."   It is a well authenticated fact that there were a few white people in the county before this division was settled, but the

majority of them were transient hunters and had no settled abodes.
" Those from whom sprang the present population were a much better
and more thrifty class of people." " Restless, daring and uneducated,
they had few wants that were higher than an abundant stock of wild meat,
a suit of dressed buckskin, or a moderate portion of ' John Barleycorn '
could supply."

A large family of the Westers came from North Carolina and settled
on the creek as early as 1798. They were a hardy, energetic and upright people, and loved the excitements of pioneer life. As the population began to increase they disposed of their little farms, and moved into Jackson's purchase, for the purpose they said of securing more " elbow
room." The names of the older heads of these families were Fulgrum
Wester and Eli Wester. Abel Olive, a brother-in-law of the Westers,
came about the same time and settled near the river. He was a man of
considerable energy, and opened the first road in the southern part of the
county, and established a landing at Linton, which was long known by
river men as Olive's Landing.

A little later, probably in the year 1802 or 1803, a large family of
the Joiners and Pittses settled in the same neighborhood. " Israel Joiner
and Thomas Joiner settled farther up the creek toward the neighborhood
of Flat Lick, while their mother, who was a widow lady, settled on the
place now known as the Pitts farm."

The Skinner family, consisting of Samuel, William, Joseph, Theophilus and Wiley, all brothers, came about the year 1803 or 1804, and secured tracts of land lying along the creek. They were among the substantial citizens of the county, and have a number of descendants living
at the present time. " Two of the very oldest families, whose descendants still remain in the county, were the Carrs and Sheltons. William
Carr was a native of Pennsylvania, but moved to Virginia in a very early
day. He came to Kentucky and settled in Fayette County, and from
thence came to Trigg in 1804, and located on the farm known as the Old
Greenwade place." " He is remembered as a very humorous old man,
and like all the rest of the early settlers was especially fond of his glass
of ' grog.' " " Whenever he took a drink, it seemed to arouse all the mu-
sical inspiration of his soul, and he could be heard singing for miles
around. On one occasion he was coming home from a still-house on Saline Creek with a barrel of whisky, and meeting his old neighbor, Shelton, he remarked that there were a thousand good songs headed up in
that one cask. Unfortunately, however, before journeying far, it was
accidentally thrown from the wagon, the cask burst, and the whole of
the precious contents thrown upon the ground. The old man contemplated in sullen silence for a while this shipwreck of his Christmas joys,

and turning to his old friend remarked that he was a little mistaken in his estimate of the number of songs the barrel contained, for indeed there seemed but one and a d——d doleful one at that.'' His son John came the same time and was a resident of the precinct until 1820, at which time he moved to Mississippi, where he remained until 1824, when he again came back to Trigg County. David Rogers, father of Richard Rogers, was one of the earliest settlers, and his descendants are among the prominent and well-to-do citizens of the precinct. William Scott settled near the site of Linton as early perhaps as 1805 or 1806. He was a native of Virginia and came to this county accompanied by his sons-in-law, John Tinsley, William Bibb and Benjamin Bibb, all of whom secured lands in the neighborhood of the village. A man by name of Ryan came about the same time. He was probably the first mechanic in the precinct, having opened a blacksmith shop soon after his arrival.

Village of Linton.—The spot occupied by the village of Linton was formerly known as Olive's Landing, and was a stopping-place for steamboats as early as 1820. In 1830 the name was changed to Shipsport, and about that time the place acquired some prominence as a shipping and distributing point for a large area of territory lying on the east side of the river. The first store was started in 1830 by a man by name of Good, who kept a small stock of general merchandise in a small log building which stood near where the Stacker furnace was afterward erected. He did a small business and removed from the place in about the year 1832. In 1845 the Stacker iron furnace was built, and soon after quite a number of families settled in the neighborhood, forming the nucleus of a flourishing little village. The furnace was abandoned in 1856, after which nothing of importance transpired in the locality until 1858, when S. A. Lindsay purchased the iron company's survey, consisting of some 11,000 acres. Soon after Dr. Whitlock, of Christian County, and his brother Thomas Whitlock effected a partnership with Lindsay and together they laid out seven acres in town lots which were offered for sale. At the same time Joseph Dyer started a small store in a log building that had formerly been used as an office by the furnace company. Following this, in the same year, Lindsay & Whitlock commenced building a large warehouse, but before it was completed, Whitlock purchased Lindsay's interest and continued business until 1859, when Washington Jarrett was taken in as partner. In 1882 the house was purchased by Frank McRae, who still operates it. In 1859 Whitlock & McNichols put up a dry goods store. They did business as partners until 1882, when Frank McRae purchased Whitlock's interest. In 1863 R. L. Crow opened a store building which he used for a short time, when he sold out to Whitlock & Co. They afterward disposed of it to C. C. Flore, who sold goods until 1865. J. M. Champion engaged in merchandising about the year 1870, and continued until some time in 1880.

In 1873 A. L. Carr started in business and sold goods until 1876. Other merchants of the town were Carr, Rogers & Co., who engaged in business shortly after the town was laid out. They continued until the fall of 1865, at which time E. C. Spiceland & Sons became proprietors. They are still in the village and have one of the best country stores in the county. Penner & Northington put up a store in 1864, and continued in business one year, when they were succeeded by Messrs. Carr & Lock, who in turn sold to J. M. Champer in 1871. Mr. Champer is doing business at the present time.

Linton Lodge, No. 575, A. F. & A. M., was organized November 15, 1874, by C. L. Bacon, of Roaring Springs Lodge. The following are the names of original members: Perry Thomas, A. L. Carr, E. A. Nunn, J. S. McNichols, William Rogers, F. S. Carr, A. S. Ford, J. M. Carr, William Futrell and Dr. Henry Blane. The organization worked two years under dispensation, the charter not being granted until 1876. The present membership is seventeen. The officers at the present time are Jonathan Herndon, W. M.; A. S. Ford, S. W.; E. A. Nunn, J. W.; J. S. McNichols, Treasurer; F. S. Carr, Secretary; A. J. Boyd, S. D.; A. Scott, J. D.; W. R. Futrell, Steward and Tyler.

Churches.—The oldest religious organization in Linton Precinct is the Dry Creek Baptist Church, organized as early as 1805. The first preachers were Elders Dudley Williams, Reuben Ross, Jesse Cox and others. The first house of worship was a log building which stood on land donated by Samuel Skinner. It stood a number of years, and was afterward replaced by another log structure, which was used until about the year 1850, at which time the present frame edifice was erected. The organization is not strong in membership, numbering only about thirty communicants at the present time; present pastor is Elder William Dyer.

Linton Methodist Episcopal Church South was organized in 1867, by Rev. Thomas Randolph. The first members were Mrs. J. F. Gentry, Mr. and Mrs. McNichols, Riley Vinson, E. Shepherd and wife and James Herndon. Meetings were held in a tobacco warehouse until 1869, when a house of worship was erected in the village. Since its organization the society has been ministered to by the following pastors in the order named, to wit: Thomas Randolph, G. T. Cundiff, Thomas Richardson, Carter Brandon, Richard Randolph, John Frayser, James Brandon and Joseph Love. The present pastor is Rev. J. L. Reid. The organization is not very strong, numbering only about twenty-five members at the present time.

There have been but two mills in the precinct. The first was built in 1858, by Whitlock & Lindsay, who operated it a couple of years, when they sold out to Thomas Sowell, who ran it until 1866. E. A. Nunn purchased it in 1881 and moved it to Tennessee. Booth, Delaney & Co. erected a mill on Cumberland River in 1877. They moved it to Canton Precinct in 1880, where it is still in operation.

CHAPTER VIII.

CERULEAN SPRINGS is voting precinct No. 7, and occupies the northeast corner of Trigg County, with the following boundaries, to wit : Christian County on the north and east, Montgomery Precinct on the south, and Caldwell County on the west. The general character of the land is what might be termed undulating, and as an agricultural district it stands second to but few divisions of the county. The soil is principally a red loam resting upon an impervious clay subsoil, and well adapted to all the fruits and cereals indigenous to this part of the State. Limestone of a fine quality is found in many parts of the precinct, and along the banks of the streams are large sandstone bluffs which afford an inexhaustible supply of building material. Much of the stone has been utilized by the farmers in the construction of chimneys and in building foundations for houses and barns. The precinct was originally well timbered, the leading varieties being walnut and the several species of oak, with cedar on the rocky knolls and along the bluffs of the water-courses. Much valuable timber was ruthlessly destroyed in an early day by the settlers in clearing their farms, and a large area of that which is standing at the present time is of comparatively recent growth.

The principal water-course is the Muddy Fork of Little River which enters the precinct from the northeast, and flowing in a southwesterly course crosses the southern boundary not far from the Caldwell County line. It is a stream of considerable importance, and receives in its course several small affluents, none of which are designated by any particular name.

Farming is the chief occupation of the people, the principal crops being corn, wheat and tobacco. Considerable attention is paid to stock-growing, which promises to become the leading industry at no distant day.

Settlement.—The neighborhood of the Springs is one of the oldest settled portions of what is now Trigg County, and must have had a beginning at a very early day after the visit of the North Carolina and Virginia Commissioners in 1790 and 1800. The first settlers were attracted thither no doubt by the heavy growth of timber rather than by the productive properties of the soil, the thick undergrowth of cane, grapevines, haw bushes, etc., affording a fine covert for such game as deer, elk, bear, which afforded the early comers their principal means of subsistence. Early in the year 1789 a small company of emigrants might have been seen making their toilsome journey slowly across the hills and through the unbroken forests of South Carolina and Tennessee toward the then insignificant settlement of Nashville. This little band was well organized and armed in order to repel the attack of savages who at that time were very hostile toward the whites, and gave them every possible annoyance. It might be interesting to state that the leader of this party was a man who afterward became the popular hero of New Orleans and the iron-willed President of the United States—Andrew Jackson.

In the same company was one Robert Goodwin, who had been a companion of Jackson's in his younger days, and who now under his leadership was with his family going to seek a home in the rich and newly-settled Tennessee country. After a long and perilous journey the hardy emigrants reached their destination and were obliged to take refuge in the block-house at Nashville until the Indian hostilities ceased, which was not until about a year and a half later. In 1792 or 1793 Samuel Goodwin and his family, together with a few spirits as hardy and daring as himself, left the Nashville settlement and came to Kentucky. Goodwin found his way into what is now Trigg County, and settled a short distance from Cerulean Springs on what is known as the Gardner farm, where he erected a diminutive log-cabin and cleared a small farm.

This in all probability was the first permanent white settlement in the county east of the Cumberland River, although it is claimed by some that a few cabins had been built previous to this time near Boyd's Landing or Canton. With Goodwin came his sons Samuel and Jesse, both of whom were men grown. The former settled about one mile above the Springs, where his son Robert Goodwin now lives, while the latter improved the land now known as the Wake place, near the village, on which he resided until the year 1825. Robert Goodwin, Sr., died prior to 1812. Samuel was an honored citizen until the time of his death in the year 1843. His son Robert Goodwin, Jr., was born in the year 1811, and has lived on the old homestead continuously from that time to the present. He is one of the oldest residents of the county, and justly esteemed one of its most intelligent and honored citizens. A man by name of Spencer came to the county a few months after Goodwin's arrival and settled on land adjoining the latter's place. Spencer was the father of two sons, James and George, both of whom achieved some reputation in an early day as mechanics, and much of the furniture used by the first settlers was made by them.   Another very early settler whose arrival antedates 1795 was James Daniel, who located about one and a half miles east of the farm now owned by J. Stewart.   His sons Elijah, John and George came the same time and figured as prominent citizens at a later day.   George became Sheriff of the county in 1830.   John Blakely settled two miles southeast of the Springs as early as 1792, and was joined soon after by William Johnson and John Roberts, both of whom came from South Carolina.   Joel Thompson was among the first pioneers, and made a home on land adjoining the old Goodwin farm.   John Goode settled on Dry Fork one and a half miles from the Springs prior to 1800, and was one of the earliest magistrates in the county.   Jacob Stinebaugh came in an early day and settled where his son Daniel lives, a short distance from the Springs.   The latter was born on the place where he now resides, and has been a citizen of the precinct for seventy-five years.

Among other very early comers were Benjamin Ladd, Elisha Harber, John Jones, Richard Stowe, Robert Rogers, H. Hayden, John McAtee and James Brownfield, all of whom located within a radius of three miles of the village.   Later came David Haggard, John Guthrie and his sons Vincent, Patrick, Jesse and Erby, William, James and John Blanks, Samuel Campbell, Wiley Wilson, Joel Wilson, William Wilson, Seth Pool, Adam Thompson and J. Pool.

Early Events.—The first death in this precinct as far as known was a man by name of Upton, who died prior to the year 1804.   He was the first person buried in the Guthrie Graveyard.   Robert Goodwin, Sr., and Jesse Goodwin died in a very early day, and were among the first laid to rest in what is known as the Military Cemetery.   Balaam Izell was the first person interred in the Thomas graveyard, his death having occurred prior to 1820.   Among the very early marriages were the following : John Goodwin and Elizabeth Griffith, Joseph Goodwin and a Miss Edwards, Gustin Cook and Mary Goodwin, David Martin and Martha Goodwin, Josiah Blakely and Elizabeth Goodwin, Richard McAtee and Anna Goodwin.   In the year 1806 Jackson Daniel, son of James Daniel, was born, and a year later Samuel, son of Robert Goodwin, Sr., was ushered into the world.   These as far as known were the first births that occurred in what is now Cerulean Precinct.   Other early births were, Green Daniel born in 1808, Leah Goodwin in 1809, Lewis Daniel in 1810, Benjamin Woodson, John and Harry Goode, sons of John Goode, prior to 1812, and Robert Goodwin, Jr., in 1811.

Mills and Other Industries.—The first settlers were obliged to undergo many hardships during the early days of the country, and for a number of years wild game and a coarse bread made from pounded corn was the daily bill of fare. The nearest mill where meal could be obtained was on Red River, fifty miles away, and it was a very rude and imperfect affair. Small horse-mills were erected as the population increased, and were kept running constantly in order to supply the growing demand for meal. The first mill of this kind was erected by James Brownfield, and stood on the farm now owned by the Richardson heirs. It was in operation for a number of years, and did a thriving business for a mill of its capacity.

The first water-mill in the precinct was built by Jesse Goodwin about one mile above Cerulean Springs, on Muddy Fork. It was erected about the year 1797, and stood until the year 1800, at which time it was washed away by an overflow of the creek. The next water-mill was erected a number of years later by a Mr. Butler, and stood a short distance above the first named. It ground both wheat and corn, and seems to have been extensively patronized in an early day by the settlers in this and adjacent territory. It passed through several hands and underwent many improvements, and was abandoned about sixteen years ago on account of the dam having been destroyed by a freshet. In the year 1870 G. G. Goodwin built a combination saw and grist-mill on Muddy Fork, at a point between the two mentioned. Two years later it was washed out, since which time no mills have been operated in the precinct.

Among the early industries of this part of the county was a distillery operated by Jacob Stinebaugh about the year 1800. The first blacksmith in the precinct was one Uriah Cato, who ran a shop on the Goodwin farm a few years after the arrival of the first settlers. A second distillery was started by John Rogers, who did a good local business as early as 1812. One of the first orchards in the county was set out by Samuel Goodwin soon after he came to the country.

Schools.—The early schools of Kentucky were supported by subscription, and were few and far between. Many of the first settlers were men of limited culture, and did not seem to appreciate the advantages of education, and as a consequence many years elapsed before schools became general throughout the country. A man by name of Maxwell is thought to have been the first pedagogue in what is now Cerulean Precinct, as it is known that he taught a little school in the winter of 1803–4. Another early teacher was William Bradley, who wielded the birch in the old log church the same year of its erection, 1806. Other schools were taught in private dwellings from time to time, and it was not until a comparatively recent period that houses were erected especially for school purposes. Among the earliest teachers are remembered J. Pool, R. Jones, and a man by name of Knight ; the last-named came from Massachusetts, and seems to have been a man of splendid acquirements and an excellent instructor.

Religious.—The pioneer church of Trigg County was the Baptist, and among the earliest Preachers were Elders Dorris and S. Brown, who preached from house to house as early as the years 1795 and 1800.   The first society was the Muddy Fork Baptist Church, which dates its organization from the year 1806, at which time it was constituted as an arm of an older organization known as the Eddy Grove Church, in Caldwell County.   Among the earliest members were Samuel Goodwin, Jesse Goodwin, Benjamin Ladd, John Goode and wife, Samuel Goodwin, Jr., Robert Rogers and wife, B. Sizemore and wife, Anderson Sizemore, Benjamin Vincent and William Snelling.   The first house of worship was a small log structure erected in 1806.   It stood until 1836, at which time it was torn away and replaced by a substantial frame house, which is still in use.   The pastors and regular supplies of the church since its organization have been the following : Elders Fielding Wolfe, Reuben Rowland, Peyton Nance (who was pastor for over twenty years), John Gammon, and Hezekiah Smith, the present incumbent.   It is a point in the Little River Association, and numbers about sixty-five or seventy members at the present time.

Cerulean Missionary Baptist Church was organized about the year 1858, with a membership of forty persons, a number which has since increased to 160.   A beautiful temple of worship was erected soon after the organization on land donated by Col. Philip Anderson, one of the most influential and active members of the society.   This house was a frame structure, 40x60 feet, and cost the sum of $3,400.   It was burned in the year 1867, and soon thereafter the present edifice was built at a cost of $1,000.

The following pastors have ministered to the church in the order named : William Gregston, W. Meacham and James Spurlin, the last named being Preacher in charge at the present time.

Village of Cerulean Springs.—This neat little hamlet is situated in the western part of the precinct on Muddy Fork and occupies one of the most romantic and beautiful spots in Trigg County.   Indeed, it would be difficult to find within the bounds of the entire state a location embracing as many pleasing features and enjoying such a healthful climate.   The chief attraction is a spring of never-failing water of a milky white appearance and strongly impregnated with mineral properties.   The following sketch was written by Maj. McKinney in his reminiscences of the county : "The waters of these springs have attracted the attention of the humble and the scientific from their earliest discovery.   The first settlers of the county had a high appreciation of them, because, when almost overcome by thirst and heat they could drink to satiety without oppression. Well-beaten tracks, coming from all directions, led to these springs long before there were any distinguishable pathways to any other point in the county, and invalids for their curative properties sought relief from these waters before the beginning of the present century.

"A careful analysis of the water has been made by a number of distinguished chemists. It is highly spoken of by all as a most delightful water, not only as a beverage, but also for its fine medicinal properties. The temperature is fifty-six degrees Fahrenheit, while that of the air is eighty degrees. It issues at the rate of one gallon or one and a half gallons per minute. The spring is strongly impregnated with both sulphate and chloride of magnesia with soda, bicarbonate of lime and free sulphuretted hydrogen. Up to 1812 the water was much more strongly impregnated with iron than it is to-day, and the magnesia that gives it the white milky appearance was never observed until after the 'shakes' of February, 1812."

"Among the first owners of the old spring tract was Richard Stow, who transferred it to Kinchan Killabrew, and he to Joseph Caldwell. Killabrew erected some rude log-cabins on the premises for the comfort of invalid visitors about 1819, which were added to as necessity required afterward, until the property, finally falling into the hands of Henry Crow, began about the years 1834–1835 to attain some little celebrity under the more euphonious and pretentious appellation of a watering place. In 1835 Mr. Crow disposed of the property to Col. Philip H. Anderson, who commenced at once a more tasteful and elaborate system of improvement, only, however, to be checked again in a very short time by discovering a vital defect in his title. This having been at last perfected, the ownership of the property in 1880 passed into the possession of the present owners, Messrs. White and Harper. These gentlemen are both possessed of ample means. They are liberal and enterprising, and are determined to spare no expense in making it one of the most pleasant and attractive places of summer resort in the West." A large, commodious hotel capable of receiving several hundred guests has been erected, with a number of outer buildings for servants, washing, cooking, etc., which add very much to the comfort and appearance of the place.

The village numbers about 100 inhabitants, and its future outlook is encouraging from the fact that a railroad will soon be completed through the county, thus affording easy communication with the principal cities of the State. The business of the village is represented at the present time by three general stores and one blacksmith shop. Drs. A. B. Cullom and B. F. Felix practice the healing art in the town and adjacent country.

Wallonia Precinct.—Wallonia is voting precinct No. 6, and was named in honor of Maj. Braxton Wall, one of the early settlers and prominent citizens of Trigg County. The topographical features of this division of the county are agreeably varied. The surface is undulating or gently rolling and affords ample facilities for drainage without any waste lands, while from the tops of any of the slight knolls or ridges, the eye is delighted with miles of corn, wheat and tobacco fields diversified with rich pastures and beautiful woodland. The soil is mostly a yellowish and reddish.clay, the decomposition of carboniferous lime rock imparted by rivers anciently flowing at this level. It is rich in tree food and was originally clothed in dense forests of oak, hickory, maple and other varieties. Immense quantities of blue limestone are found in various parts of the precinct, and clear, cold springs are numerous. Beautiful cedar groves have of late years sprung up on the rocky knolls, and their brilliant green against the somber trunks of deciduous groves lends a pleasing variety to the scene. Muddy Fork and Dry Creek are the principal water-courses. Bingham's Branch and several small rivulets traverse the country in various directions, but the majority of them contain running water only a part of the year.

The Pioneers.—It would be difficult to determine who was the first white man to settle in this part of the country as there is but little definite information accessible of that early period. It is known that William Barton, Hezekiah Watkins and his father-in-law, Robert Wade, Daniel Cameron, William Hagerty, Maj. Braxton Wall, S. Dunning and Hardiman Dunning were living within the present boundaries of the precinct as early as 1820. Barton settled on Muddy Fork about one mile below Wallonia Village. Watkins settled where his son now lives, and Cameron located east of the Wade and Watkins settlements.

Maj. Wall was perhaps the most prominent man in the neighborhood. He was a native of Virginia, but in an early day emigrated to Tennessee, from which State he moved to this county. He started the first store in Wallonia, and was also the pioneer mill builder in the precinct. He died prior to 1844. A man by name of Hansbarger was one of the earliest comers, and settled near the village. Benjamin Faulkner settled where D. D. Wall now lives; David Jennings and William McDaniel, on portions of what now comprises the present plantation of Thomas Boyd. Levi Dunning, a relative of Hardiman Dunning, settled west of the creek in an early day on the farm still in possession of members of his family. Among others who came when the country was young and who participated in the trials and hardships of pioneer life were Custis Gray, a man by name of Kennedy and his son Josiah, Irwin and John Brandon and John Wall, brother of Braxton Wall; Thomas and D. D. Wall, sons of

John Wall, came with their father to the new country, and for fifty-six years have been leading citizens of the precinct.   Other names could be added to those enumerated, but the space of this chapter forbids a further mention.

Mills and Distilleries.—The first mill in the precinct was built by Maj. Wall in the year 1825 or 1826, and stood on Muddy Fork .a short distance below Wallonia Village.   This was a combination mill—made lumber and ground grain—and did a thriving business during the time it was in operation.   A few years after its erection the mill was moved further down the stream under the following circumstances :   " Before erecting his mill Mr. Wall made an effort to buy the privilege of building a dam across the mouth of the Lee Dunning Spring, as Bingham & Kevil did before building their mill, but Mr. Kennedy, who owned the property, persistently refused.   The result was that upon the completion of the dam at the Wall Mill the whole body of water except at flood time found an outlet through Kennedy's Creek, affording a much better mill seat on the creek than the one Maj. Wall had selected. So old man Kennedy immediately went to work and built him a handsome little water-mill on the creek.   Old man Wall kept dark until Kennedy got his mill completed and started off in fine style, when all of a sudden he tore away his dam and moved his mill a mile lower down the river.   This left Kennedy's Mill high and dry, and the only alternative left was for him to convert it into a horse-mill."   The present mill was erected by Messrs. Bingham & Kevil in 1873, and stands on the site of the old Wall Mill.   The building is a large two-story frame, and the proprietors are doing an extensive custom and merchant business.

The first distillery in the precinct was put in operation by Maj. Wall about the year 1824 or 1825, and stood on what is known as Bingham's Spring Branch.   Mr. Wall did a fine local business, and had the reputation of making a fine article of the " O be joyful ! "'   The Dunnings operated a small distillery as early as 1823, but seem to have done but a very limited business.

Wallonia Village.—The history of this little city dates from about the year 1837, at which time Maj. Wall erected a commodious storehouse on the lot where the Wallace building now stands, and himself and William Gray, of Princeton, formed a copartnership under the title of Wall & Gray, and in the spring opened up a heavy stock of miscellaneous merchandise.   They continued in business until the fall of 1838, when not meeting with the success they anticipated, they disposed of the remnant of the stock to Abner R. Terry and Samuel McKinney.   The latter firm, with means to prosecute an extensive business for that day, opened up a large stock, and ere long their business swelled in proportion far beyond their original expectations or hopes. Their sales during the years 1841 and 1842 aggregated $27,000 per year. A postoffice was established and Mr. McKinney appointed Postmaster. The mail route was from Princeton by way of Wallonia through Cadiz and on to Clarksville. William Wallace was the contractor and mail carrier. McKinney & Terry sold out to Josiah S. Gardner and Lewis McCain, who did a successful business for a number of years. About this time John A. McCain commenced a small grocery business, and in a few years with O. T. Gardner and J. R. Hays bought out the firm of Gardner & McCain. Mr. McCain remained in active business for a number of years. Among the different merchants of the place were S. W. Gray, Jones & Harper, G. W. Dunning, W. J. Wilson, Mr. Wolfe, D. W. Kennedy and William S. Coy. The present business men of the village are Dyer & Hayden, the Brandon Brothers, Hopson and W. H. Pomeroy. The medical profession has been represented by the following disciples of Esculapius : Drs. Wall, Allison, Foster, Pool, Standrod and Lindsay.

Wallonia Christian Church.—The first meetings by the church known as Christians or Disciples were held in the village schoolhouse in 1849 by Elder John Ferguson, who preached at intervals thereafter for several years. In 1852 a permanent organization was effected with the following members, to wit : J. B. Wall, Harriet C. Wall, A. C. Mart, Evaline H. Mart, Elizabeth J. Swatswell, William S. Coy, Virginia S. Coy, Elizabeth Wall, D. D. Wall, Mary E. Wall, E. N. Amoss and Ann Amoss. The first officers of the church were J. B. Wall and E. N. Amoss, Bishops ; A. C. Mart and D. D. Wall, Deacons ; William S. Coy, Clerk. The organization was brought about by the labors of Elder Enoch Brown, of Christian County, who preached for the congregation two years. There was no regular preaching there until 1865, the church in the meantime meeting for social service each Lord's day, and depending upon such transient ministers as happened to be passing by. In 1865 steps were taken to build a house of worship. Prior to that time public worship was held in the schoolhouse and private dwellings. In connection with the Masonic Lodge a house was erected at a cost of $1,741. During the year 1865 Elder R. Dulin preached for the congregation once a month. The next pastor was Elder Giddens, who remained but a few months. He was succeeded by Elder B. Metcalf, who preached till 1875. J. W. Higbee came next and remained one year. Other preachers who visited the church at different times were Elders Street, Ferguson, Hancock, Mobley, Howard, Marshall, Anderson, Keith, Albert Mills, James Mills, Long, Hatchett, Gass, Walthall, Lindsay, Lucas, Dimmit, Hardin, Trimble, Johnson and Marshall. Present officers : E.

N. Amoss, Elder; Samuel Hopson and Thomas Amoss, Deacons. The society is in good condition, and numbers about seventy members.

Mount Zion Methodist Episcopal Church.—The history of this organization dates back to the year 1832, at which time a small class was established at the residence of Robert Hawkins, about two miles from the village of Wallonia. Among the original members of the society were Robert Hawkins and family, Peter Wade and family, Jesse Adams and family, Erwin Brandon and family, Isaac Husk and wife, Lewis Husk and family and Jackson Huston. Meetings were held for four years at the dwellings of Robert Hawkins and Jesse Adams, and at the end of that time a house of worship was erected on a lot donated to the church by Erwin Brandon. This building was a log structure, and stood where the present edifice stands. It was in use until 1848, at which time a new frame building was erected, the same that is still standing. The building is 40x36 feet in size, and with improvements added since its erection represents a capital of about $1,000.

The society was first attached to the Little River Circuit, and later became a prominent point on the Circuit of Wallonia. It belongs to the Cadiz Circuit at present.

The following preachers have ministered to the church, to wit: Lewell Campbell, Elijah Sutton, Robert Turner, James Bristow, Abraham Long, Abraham Quick, Dr. William Randolph, Thomas Randolph, P. T. Harderson, Richard Love, T. Peters, James Bigum, P. E. Edwards and J. C. McDaniel, the last named being pastor in charge at the present time.

Present officers are: James Richardson, Robert Wade, David Hancock, T. C. Brandon and J. R. Watkins, Trustees; James Richardson, Robert Wade, Jabez Bingham and C. R. Watkins, Stewards; Jesse Cameron and J. R. Watkins, Class Leaders. The organization is in flourishing condition at the present time, and numbers about 110 communicants. A good Sunday-school is maintained under the efficient superintendency of H. T. Watkins, assisted by W. H. Rector.

There is a Masonic lodge in the village, also a society of the Chosen Friends, both of which are in a healthy condition. We, however, failed to obtain particulars of them.

A MODERN COUNTRY SCHOOLHOUSE.

CHAPTER IX.

CALEDONIA AND MONTGOMERY PRECINCTS—PHYSICAL FEATURES—BOUND-
ARIES, ETC.—EARLY SETTLERS—MILLS—EDUCATIONAL AND RELIGIOUS
—CALEDONIA VILLAGE—DESCRIPTION AND TOPOGRAPHY OF MONTGOM-
ERY PRECINCT—ITS AGRICULTURAL RESOURCES—THE FIRST PIONEERS
—EARLY INDUSTRIES AND IMPROVEMENTS—MONTGOMERY VILLAGE—
CHURCHES, SOCIETIES, ETC.

CALEDONIA PRECINCT lies in the eastern part of the county, and is bounded as follows: Montgomery and Cadiz Precincts on the north and west, Cadiz and Roaring Springs on the south, and Christian County on the east. The principal water-course is Little River, which flows along the southern boundary. It receives a number of small tributaries which traverse the precinct in various directions, chief of which is Sinking Fork. Along the river the land is broken, but beyond the bluffs north and northeast is a fine undulating region unsurpassed in the county for its agricultural excellence, and is occupied by a class of thrifty and enterprising farmers. Corn, wheat and tobacco are chiefly produced, although the soil is well adapted to all the cereals and fruits indigenous to the climate of southern Kentucky. Many farmers, too, devote some attention to stock-raising, a business that is becoming of more importance every year. The original timber was chiefly black and white oak, hickory, poplar, gum, dogwood, sassafras, with elm and sycamore along the water-courses. Limestone abounds in immense quantities, and clear, cold springs are to be seen in many places throughout the precinct.

The settlement of Caledonia dates back almost to the beginning of the present century, and from the most reliable information accessible, Thomas Wadlington, Jr., appears to have been the first permanent settler. Mr. Wadlington came to Trigg County in company with his father, Thomas Wadlington, Sr., as early as 1792, and lived with the latter on his farm at what is known as Kent's Bridge in Cadiz Precinct, until 1803, at which time he fell heir to a tract of land in this precinct, where his son William Wadlington now lives. He moved to this land the same year, and at once began to improve it, and as early as 1804 he had a goodly number of acres cleared and in cultivation. He was an energetic man, thrifty and impulsive, and loved the wild free exercises of pioneer life as he loved his own being. He killed the last bear and prized the first hogshead of tobacco in Trigg County, and at the time of his death had probably lived here longer than any other man since the country was first settled. His death occurred in the year 1868. He had five sons, three of whom survived him; Ferdinand, William and Thomas are still living, the first being a resident of Cadiz Precinct while the other two are citizens of Caledonia.

Jesse Wall settled where William Humphries lives about the year 1804 or 1805. Absalom Humphries came about the same time and was followed shortly afterward by his brother, Capt. Thomas Humphries, both of whom were prominently identified with the early history of the county. They were members of a very prominent Virginia family, and achieved some distinction in the war of the Revolution, Thomas having risen to the position of Captain in the army of Washington. Absalom settled on Sinking Fork, and died on the place first owned by his father-in-law, Jesse Wall, the same farm now owned by William Humphries. Thomas settled on Little River in 1810, on what is known as the Carloss place. He was a Methodist preacher of some note and preached in various places throughout the county during the early years of its history. Another early pioneer deserving of special mention was William Armstrong, also a Revolutionary soldier, whose arrival in the precinct is fixed at the year 1808. He located on Sinking Fork and made his first improvements on the place now in possession of Burnett Wilford. David Macky settled where Thomas Wadlington lives, about the year 1810; he sold the place to John Roberts in an early day, and emigrated further West.

Other settlers came in from time to time, among whom are remembered Thomas Armstrong, son of William Armstrong, Joel and Alexander Wilson and James Coleman. "The neighborhood of Caledonia Village was not settled at so early a date as some other sections of the precinct, and consequently the traces of the more prominent families residing there do not lead us so far back into the twilight of the present century. "Judge Jouett, the name more frequently of late years erroneously written Jewett, settled the place and built the residence now owned by John A. Tuggle. Our information relating to this very worthy old citizen is not so satisfactory as we could have otherwise wished, but if it can be at all relied upon, he was at one time a prominent officer in the United States Army with the rank of Major, and was commander of the post of Chicago, Ill., when that magnificent city of the West could not boast of a population superior to Caledonia. He was a native of Virginia, a gentleman of learning and varied accomplishments, a Chesterfield in manners and a paragon of integrity and kindness; he died about the year 1830." Maj. Dabney, father of Judge J. C. Dabney, and A. S. Dabney were for a number of years residents of this neighborhood. Other prominent early families in the same locality were the Wilfords, Campbells, Ogles, Cravens, Joneses, Hardys, Sallies, Waterfields, Woodses, Faulkners, Bennetts and Carlosses, several of whom lived across the river in the edge of Roaring Springs Precinct.

The first industry of any note in the precinct was a distillery put in operation by William Armstrong about the year 1825. He did a good business until his death, at which time the building was allowed to fall into decay. About the year 1826, Jesse Ogle built a small water-mill near the mouth of Potts Creek on Little River. It was in operation until about the year 1836, at which time the greater part of the building was washed away by a freshet. About the year 1855 or 1856 S. P. Sharp built a flouring-mill on Sinking Fork not far from Caledonia Village. It passed through various hands and underwent many improvements and is at present known as the Peal Mill. A very extensive distillery was started in the same neighborhood some time prior to 1860, by Messrs. Wilford and Lindon, who did a flourishing business for a period of three or four years. At the end of that time they discontinued the business and moved to Cadiz.

The first school in the precinct was taught by W. A. Wadlington in a little cabin on the farm where William Wadlington lives.

The earliest preachers who visited this section of the county were Dudley Williams, of the Baptist Church ; John Barnett, a Presbyterian ; Jesse Cox and a man by name of Spraggins, both Baptists.

The first house erected for public worship stood on the farm of Thomas Wadlington. Mr. Wadlington built the house himself and opened the door to all denominations. The building was a log structure and has been torn away forty-five years.

The Cherry Hill Methodist Episcopal Church was organized near the village of Caledonia, some time during the fifties.

A neat house of worship was erected and services were regularly held until about the year 1859, at which time the society disbanded. The building was sold to the Baptists, who organized the Locust Grove Church about one year later. This society is an offshoot of the old Antioch Baptist Church in Roaring Springs Precinct, and its organization was brought about chiefly through the efforts of Rev. Mr. Morehead. The original membership numbered something like twenty or thirty persons. The present membership is about sixty. Rev. Morehead was the first pastor. After him came Rev. Mr. Meacham, who preached for several years and was succeeded by Rev. C. H. Gregston. After Gregston's pastorate expired Meacham was again called, and is pastor in charge at the present time. The present officers are Lewis Averitt, Clerk ; Mark Jones and John A. Tuggle, Deacons.

The Mount Tabor Church building was erected under the auspices of the Christian Church in the year 1868, and stands on ground donated by Thomas Averitt. The size of the house is 30x40 feet and the original cost was $1,500. The Christians, contrary to their expectations, failed to effect an organization, and the house was generously placed at the disposal of such denominations as saw fit to use it. The various sects have in turn used the building, and the neighbors have had ample opportunities of hearing the Gospel "each in his own tongue." An organization known as the "Christian Union" sprang into existence in 1882, and is now using the house. They have a fair congregation and are accomplishing much good in the community.

Cherryville.—This little hamlet, known also as Caledonia, is situated in the eastern part of the precinct and is the youngest village in the county. The first store was started by James B. Carloss and J. H. Hammond. They commenced business under the firm name of Carloss & Hammond, and soon acquired a large and lucrative trade. Mr. Carloss remained only a few years as active partner, closing out to Mr. Hammond about 1878, who continued the business up to the close of 1881.

In the meantime a second store was started by Joe Wooten, who sold his building soon after to Carloss & Hammond. The present merchants are Messrs. Wall and Hammond.

Montgomery Precinct.—Montgomery Precinct, named in honor of Thomas Montgomery, one of the earliest prominent settlers, lies in the northeast part of Trigg and embraces one of the finest and most productive agricultural regions in southern Kentucky. Indeed it would be difficult to find within the limits of the entire State an area of similar proportions, possessing as rich a soil and combining as many advantages for the agriculturist as does this banner division of Trigg. The surface of the country is sufficiently undulating to make an easy natural drainage and every acre is susceptible of almost unlimited cultivation. The only broken part of the precinct is along the southern border, the rest being comparatively level and known as "barrens" land. Cultivation has wrought marked changes in the topography of Montgomery during the sixty-five or seventy years which the white man has possessed the land. What appeared to the early settlers an expanse of worthless boggy land is now a pleasant rolling area of thrifty farms. This transformation has been brought about not by physical changes but by the natural effects of the farmer's occupation. The open land was originally covered with a rank growth of tall grass; on the high lands the grass did not reach its normal height, while on the lower lands its growth was of astonishing proportions, frequently reaching a height which would almost hide a man on horseback, and this would tend to create the illusion of a nearly level plain. Groves of scraggy oaks were to be seen at intervals, but the greater part of the timber now growing in the precinct has made its appearance within the memory of old settlers now living. In the woodlands the change has been very marked also. The dense forests of young growth, underbrush and saplings did not exist fifty years ago. Then the timber, save along the streams, was characterized only by scattered oaks and hickories, which favoring localities preserved from the annual fires that swept over the country. Unlike the experience in a timbered country, here the wooded area has increased. The young growth and saplings which the fires of those times kept in check have developed into large trees, and the timber has encroached upon the open lands so that the area of woods is now much larger than fifty years ago.

The barren lands were not understood by the early settlers who passed by rich black soil and secured homes among the hills and along the streams of those parts of the county which to-day are of less value then when first opened for cultivation.

The agricultural resources of Montgomery are unsurpassed; the principal crops being wheat, corn, oats and the usual varieties of fruits and vegetables found in this range of climate. All classes of stock are found also, but horses and cattle predominate, as the wide ranges of grazing are best adapted to raise them with profit. As a stock country this division is without an equal in the county and cannot be easily surpassed. Grass grows in rich abundance, and truly, cattle are made to "lie down in green pastures." Some of the finest stock that goes from grass to market goes from this precinct. Among those who have made stock-raising a profitable business is Henry Bryant, on whose beautiful and well-cultivated farm can be seen some of the finest and most valuable improved herds ever brought to this part of the State. The other leading farmers and stock-raisers of the precinct are the following gentlemen, to wit: Robert Roach, James H. Gaines, Robert Hill, J. J. Gaines, Clarence Blakemore, James Beasley, James Rasco, John Rasco, Tandy Wadlington, Jefferson Moore, Wilson Stewart and W. J. Stewart.

Early Settlers.—Montgomery was not settled as early as many other portions of the county, owing to the fact that the pioneers did not understand the nature of the land, and looked upon it as wholly unfit for agricultural purposes.

From the most reliable information obtainable, Thomas Montgomery appears to have been one among the first if not the first permanent settler, as he was living within the limits of the present precinct as long ago as the year 1816. He located near the village which bears his name, and secured a large area of grass lands at very moderate figures, and was one of the first stock-raisers in Trigg County. But little is known of this

stanch old pioneer, save that he was considered a very estimable citizen
and did much towards shaping the character of the community in which
he lived.   The farm on which he settled was always considered and is perhaps the best place of its size in the county, and a simple mention of the
fact will be sufficient to show how much even in as small a territory as a
precinct the estimated value of a tract of land is governed by its location.
In 1839 or 1840 the place was offered for $3.25.   At that time land in
the neighborhood of Wallonia was valued at double the estimate that was
placed on similar lands in Montgomery.

Joshua Cates settled near Montgomery Village in a very early day, as
did also J. J. Morrison and Dr. Wooldridge.   Henry Sheton was an early
comer and located not far from the Rocky Ridge Baptist Church.
John Stephens and " Ki " Edwards secured homes in the same locality.

Another early resident was John Roberson, who made a farm not far
from the village.   Adam Stinebaugh originally settled in the Cerulean
Springs Precinct, but came to this part of the county as soon as the value
of the land was ascertained.

Jonathan, James and Harrison Stewart were among the pioneers of
this section.   They purchased land in the vicinity of Montgomery Village
and made good farms.   Other settlers came in from time to time, and by
the year 1845 the precinct was populated by an industrious and thrifty
class of citizens.

Village of Montgomery.—This most beautiful little village of Trigg
County is situated in the eastern part of the precinct and dates its history proper from the year 1866, at which time Gen. John W. Gaines, of
Virginia, purchased the land on which the town is situated, and erected a
store building and engaged in merchandising.

Prior to that date, however, a man by name of Ashford had kept a
small stock of general goods in a little house which stood near the central part of the present village plat, but all traces of his building had
disappeared before the place achieved any prominence as a trading point.

Mr. Gaines laid the village off into lots on which he erected a number of residences, shops and other buildings for the purpose of attracting
people to the place.   He conducted a very successful business for about
eighteen years, accumulating in the meantime a handsome fortune.   He
is remembered as one of the most active and enterprising citizens of
Trigg County, and died a few years ago, respected and honored by all
who knew him.

His son J. J. Gaines began business in the village in 1872, and is one
of the leading merchants of the county at the present time.   In 1880
the McGehee brothers brought a miscellaneous stock of merchandise to the
place, and are still in business with a large and constantly increasing
trade.

The first mechanics of the town were John Stewart and J. A. Powell. The present mechanic is J. W. Wooten, who runs a wood-working establishment and blacksmith shop.

The medical profession has been represented in the village by the following gentlemen, to wit: Drs. Withers, Smoot, Allen and Cullom. The present physician is Dr. Henry Blaine, who has a large and lucrative practice.

J. C. Whitlock Lodge, No. 487, A. F. & A. M., was organized at the village of Cherry Hill or Caledonia, and moved to Montgomery several years ago. It has a good membership at the present time, and is reported in a fair condition. The officers last elected are the following, viz.: Andrew J. Pilkinton, W. M.; Taylor Tompkins, S. W.; Jasper J. Roach, J. W.; R. H. Wilson, Sec.; A. J. Humphries, Treas.

Montgomery Methodist Church South was organized by Rev. J. W. Shelton in the fall of 1879 with a membership of about twelve persons. A beautiful frame house of worship was built in the year 1883 at a cost of $1,100. The second pastor was Rev. T. C. Peters, after whom came Rev. J. M. Crow. Pastor in charge at the present time is Rev. E. E. Pate. The society is not in a very flourishing condition, there being the names of only seven active members on the church record at the present time.

ROARING SPRINGS PRECINCT.

CHAPTER X.

ROARING SPRINGS PRECINCT—TOPOGRAPHICAL AND PHYSICAL FEATURES—
CAVES AND CAVERNS—COMING OF THE PIONEERS—THEIR SETTLE-
MENTS—EARLY INDUSTRIES AND IMPROVEMENTS—EDUCATIONAL FA-
CILITIES—CHURCHES—SKETCHES OF THE DIFFERENT ORGANIZATIONS—
VILLAGE OF ROARING SPRINGS—GROWTH, DEVELOPMENT, ETC., ETC.

ROARING SPRINGS is voting precinct No. 10, and embraces a larger geographical area than any other division of the county. It is bounded on the north by Cadiz and Montgomery Precincts, on the east by Christian County, on the south by the State of Tennessee, and on the west by the Precinct of Linton. The surface of the country is agreeably varied, and contains many natural scenes to delight the eye. Casey's Creek rises near the Tennessee line, flows through the central part of the precinct in a northerly direction, and empties into Little River. This is one of the most beautiful and romantic streams in the country, being fed along its entire course by springs of the purest water issuing from rocky bluffs and caves, with which the country abounds. One of these caves, called McGovern's Cavern, is a place of some note, and is visited yearly by a great many sight-seers. It is about fifteen feet from the roof to the bottom ; from sixteen to twenty feet wide, and has been explored for a distance of 300 yards, beyond which it is impossible to go on account of the depth and coldness of the water which issues from the cave.

Little River forms part of the northern boundary of the precinct, and receives in its course a number of small tributaries which traverse the country in various directions. A place of considerable note near the river is a cave on the Garland Jones farm which was used as a place of concealment by runaway negroes during the days of slavery. This cavern is twenty feet in height, fifteen feet in width, and extends into the earth for a distance of about two miles. Hardy's Cave, another spot of interest on the river, differs from the ones named on account of the interior being perfectly dry. It has been explored for over a mile, and the supposition is that it extends much further.

The southern part of the precinct is drained chiefly by Saline Creek, which rises near the State line, and flowing a northwesterly course empties into the Cumberland River. There are several other small streams in different parts of the precinct, none of which is deserving of special mention. Near the State line is the highest part of Trigg County. This region is known as the "flat lick" or "flat woods" and contains a large area of very level land, much of which is too wet for tillage without being artificially drained. Owing to this fact it was not settled in a very early day, and its resources have been developed within a comparatively recent period. Agriculture is carried on very extensively, the best farming lands being in the northern and central parts of the precinct, and especially along Casey Creek and its tributaries, where can be seen some of the largest and best improved plantations in the county. Perhaps the most interesting spot in the county, and certainly its greatest natural wonder, is the roaring spring which gave name to the village and precinct. This spring, or torrent rather, issues with great rapidity and a loud roaring noise from a limestone cavern about one hundred feet below the line of the surrounding country, and after running for a distance of perhaps sixty feet enters an opening in a large rocky cliff opposite the mouth of the cave and is lost sight of. The cavern, which is very broad and high, was explored a few years ago by a party of gentlemen who penetrated it for a distance of three miles without finding the terminus. The atmosphere of the interior is said to be very invigorating and retains a temperature of sixty degrees Fahrenheit throughout the entire year. At one time in the early history of the county the waters of this stream were utilized to operate a small mill built at the mouth of the cave, to reach which it was necessary to descend a flight of steps 100 feet cut in the stone bank.

Settlement.—Roaring Springs is one of the original voting precincts of the county, and was settled shortly after the beginning of the present century. Among the first white men who sought homes here were Robin and Josiah Boyd. They settled on the farm owned at the present time by Mrs. Robinson, and came perhaps as early as the year 1805. The Joiner family came about the same time and settled in the southern part of the precinct on Dry Creek, where several descendants are still living. Jesse Cox, a Baptist preacher, came from South Carolina about the year 1803 or 1804 and secured a tract of land lying in the southwest corner of the precinct, on which he lived until the time of his death in 1849. His son, George Cox, was born near the original homestead in 1817, and is still an honored citizen of the precinct. John Potts came in a very early day and located near the creek which bears his name. The place on which he made his first improvements is owned at the present time by Lewis Garnett.

Ebenezer Boyd settled in the southwest corner of the precinct as early as 1810. Paul Patrick came the same year and settled the Rasco farm, about three miles from the Springs on Casey Creek. Joseph Ledford settled in the central part of the precinct about the year 1815. J. Mills and a man by name of Wood came a few years later and located near Casey Creek, the former on a part of what is now the Crenshaw farm and the latter on the Greenwade place. John Cower settled on the Crenshaw farm about 1817 and remained two years, when he sold out to Cornelius Crenshaw. Thomas Mathers settled in the southeastern part of the precinct in a very early day. The Dawson family became residents as early as 1817, settling near the head waters of Casey Creek, where several descendants are still living. John Mathers and William Gillum settled on Gillum Creek in the southwest corner of the precinct prior to 1818. A man by name of Greer came about the same time and located on the Widow Dunn's place. Among other families who resided in the precinct anterior to 1820 were those of Elias Burbridge, Lewis Izell, Hugh Gray, William Reed, James Daniel, John Ford, Cornelius Burnett (father of Dr. Isaac Burnett), John Greenwade, the Northingtons, McCulloms, Lindsays, Blantons, Millers, Torians, Colemans, Cornelius Crenshaw and John H. Scott, Thomas Nance, and in 1820 Thomas Crenshaw. Later came Lewis and James Garnett, Elder Peyton Nance, Lesenberry Nance, John T. Hays, Alexander Harrell, all of whom were residents prior to the year 1830, many of whom are mentioned in a preceding chapter.

Mills, etc.—The honor of erecting the first mill in Roaring Springs Precinct belongs to Saxe Lindsay, who in the year 1819 or 1820 built a small structure on Little River. Lindsay operated the mill with tolerable success for several years and finally sold out to Jesse Carter, who put up a frame building which he supplied with good machinery, and valued the property at $3,000. At his death Elbridge A. Coleman purchased the mill, which he has continued to improve until it is now one of the best mills in the county, and represents a value of $5,000. The second mill in the precinct was built by Thomas Nance in 1825, and stood at the mouth of Roaring Springs Cave. This has already been alluded to. Mr. Nance built a distillery which he operated in connection with his mill, and with the two did a good business until the time of his death in 1835. For ten years the mill stood idle, but at the end of that time the property was leased by a Mr. Foster, who operated it until about 1849 when it was abandoned and allowed to fall into decay. At the present time no vestige of either mill or distillery is to be seen.

Schools.—" The early education of that day was obtained under many disadvantages, and there was very little of it. The spelling book, the English Reader, Pike's Arithmetic and Murray's Grammar were the text books in most of the schools. A session was from ten to twelve weeks with five days in the week and a few hours each day. The houses were made of logs about twenty feet long, with one window between two logs, under which a plank was placed on pins for a writing desk. The seats were made of logs, ten to fifteen inches in diameter, split in two, out of which a pair of benches were made and put on legs about two feet high, so the boys' legs could dangle down and be convenient for the teacher's switch. When the hickory failed to secure the proper discipline the ferule was applied to the palm of the left hand, so that the bruises occasioned by a too vigorous application would not interfere with the writing lesson. The only retaliation a pupil was allowed for this cruelty was the privilege of ' turning out ' the teacher in order to force him to give a recess during the holidays. In this all the children were allowed to take part, forcing him by threats or the actual administration of a good, sound ducking, which had the effect not only to secure the recess but also a ' treat ' of whisky and egg-nog to boot. Among the early teachers of the precinct was Mrs. Mays, who taught in a little building which stood on the Canton and Lindsay Mill road one mile northeast of the spring. This building was used for school and church purposes until 1849. A schoolhouse was built the latter year near the spring, and stood on ground now occupied by the Methodist Church. The first pedagogue in the building was Alfred Lindsay. Wesley Warrell and Miss Carland (wife of Thomas Crenshaw) taught here also. Other teachers at the same place were William Glover and Cornelia Auburn."

Churches.—There are several religious organizations in the precinct, the oldest of which is the Long Water Old School Baptist Church, about three miles south of Roaring Springs. This society was organized in a very early day, and at one time had a good membership, which has greatly diminished of late years. The house of worship is a log structure, which like the organization bears many marks of decay.

The Antioch Baptist Church near Little River was perhaps the first religious society organized in the precinct. It was established when there were but few sparse settlements in the county, and during the early days of s history supported a membership scattered over many miles of country. A log building was erected and used until about the year 1859, at which time the existence of the society terminated. Among the pastors of the church were Elders Jesse Cox, L. H. Averitt, Reuben Ross and Dudley Williams. The last regular preacher was Elder George Patterson.

Roaring Springs Christian Church, as an organization, dates its history as far back as 1833, at which time a meeting was held in what was known as the Buford's Springs Schoolhouse, by Elder George P. Street, of Christian County, and a society established which took upon itself the name of the Lebanon Christian Church. The original members were William Northington, John Dawson, E. G. Lewis, L. T. Calloway, Andrew Lewis, Penina Dawson, Mary Calloway, Phebe Garnett and Martha Ledford. The schoolhouse was used as a meeting-place until 1835, when a log building was erected which served the congregation for a number of years. A frame building was afterward built and used until 1878, at which time the present commodious temple of worship was erected at Roaring Springs, at a cost of $1,500. A re-organization was effected in 1878, under the name of the Roaring Springs Christian Church, and the following officers elected: Albert Crenshaw, J. W. Hays and William Lewis, Elders; Thomas Crenshaw, Matthew Jones and John Rasco, Deacons; Thomas Crenshaw, Clerk; T. P. Campbell, J. W. Hays, Albert Crenshaw and M. Jones, Trustees. The ministers of the church have been Elders George P. Street, Samuel Calloway, M. Metcalf, John Ferguson, Jesse Ferguson and W. E. Mobley, the last named being preacher in charge at the present time. A Sunday-school was organized shortly after the church was established at the Springs, which has continued to increase in interest and numbers until it is now one of the most flourishing schools in the county. The first Superintendent was Henry Richards; present Superintendent is Robert Crenshaw. The present membership of the church is 115, among whom are many of the leading citizens of the community.

Shady Grove Baptist Church was organized in 1850 by Rev. George Patterson with the following members, to wit: Lee S. Harrell and wife and N. Harrell and wife, formerly members of the old Dry Creek Church on Saline Creek, which ceased to exist in 1849. Of the original organization nothing could be learned owing to the fact that the early records were not accessible. The four members mentioned formed the nucleus around which a flourishing society soon gathered, and among those who came in shortly after the organization were James Mathers and wife, Mrs. James Hester and daughter, Mrs. William Hester and William Cox and wife. A log-house was built in 1851 and stood until 1873, at which time the present substantial frame edifice was built at a cost of $950. The following preachers have ministered to the church at different times: Revs. James Preer, John B. Smith, David Bronson, Samuel McClain, L. McClain and Samuel Sumner. The present incumbent is Rev. W. L. Tidwell. Officers are: L. S. Harrell, N. Harrell, J. Harrell and John McCowen, Deacons; J. Harrell, Clerk. At present it has 110 members.

Methodist Episcopal Church South* at Roaring Springs was organized in July, 1852, by Rev. James R. Dempsey. The following names are those of the original members, viz.: Ephraim Blane, Miss Mary Blane, Miss Bettie Blane, George Blane, James T. Jones and wife, James H. Hamil-

---

* By Dr. Thomas L. Bacon.

ton and wife, Thomas M. Ogburn, Charles Ranson, Thomas L. Bacon, Mathew L. Bacon, Charles P. Bacon and William Smith. The first pastor was James R. Dempsey in 1851–52; in 1852–53, Thomas M. Penick; in 1853–54, —— Neikirk and J. C. Petree; in 1854–55, —— Neikirk and C. Y. Boggess; in 1855–56, D. D. Moore; in 1856–57, J. C. Petree; in 1857–58, W. W. Lambreth; in 1858–59 and 1859–60, William Alexander; in 1860–61, Gideon Gooch; in 1861–62, H. M. Ford was appointed but failed to come and his place was supplied by James Gray. In 1862–63 and 1863–64, Gideon Gooch; in 1864–65 and 1865–66, J. C. Petree; in 1866–67 and 1867–68, Wilbur L. King; in 1868–69 and 1869–70, Thomas J. Randolph; in 1870–71 and 1871–72, Bryant A. Cundiff; in 1872–73, R. B. McCown; in 1873–74 and 1874–75, Robert C. Alexander, in 1875–76 and 1876–77, John W. Price; in 1877–78, 1878–79 and 1879–80, Joseph F. Redford; in 1880–81 and 1881–82 and 1882–83, James W. Bigham, and at present Ben F. Biggs.

The membership never increased any till the second pastorate of Gideon Gooch, when there were about fifteen added to it, and again, during the third pastoral term of J. C. Petree there were several more added as also was the case during the terms of Bryant A. Cundiff, J. F. Redford and James W. Bigham. When first organized the organization took place in the dwelling house of Ephraim Blane, but a schoolhouse was used as a place of worship until 1865; the present church house was erected at a cost of $2,500, James T. Jones and Thomas L. Bacon constituting the building committee. There is no Sunday-school at present, nor has there been save one or two years a denominational school there; for several years there was a school on the union basis in successful operation.

In the southern part of the precinct is a Presbyterian Church which was organized about thirty years ago. The society meets for worship in a neat frame building, and has a good membership.

Joiner's Chapel Christian Church was organized about 1869 by Elder James Hester. Present preacher is Elder —— Smith; present membership about thirty communicants.

Village of Roaring Springs.—In 1846 Mr. C. A. Bacon purchased a tract of land from Ed Dawson, and removed to the neighborhood. He erected the first business house in the fall of 1847 and from a "local habitation and a name" sprang suddenly into existence an enterprising business point and one of the most thrifty villages of the county. Captain Bacon continued in the mercantile business until 1852, at which time he sold to Dycus & McNichols. The latter firm remained about two years, when the building was purchased by William Richards, who later took in Thomas Crenshaw, Joseph Ledford and Carter Ledford as partners. This firm continued in business for several years, and finally failed, owing to some mismanagement on the part of the senior partner.

In 1848 William Landrum built a log storehouse and sold goods for a few months. H. Robbins engaged in the grocery business in 1852, but closed out soon after and moved from the place. James Moss started a small store about the same time and ran it until the breaking out of the war. Among the other merchants of the place were A. McKinney, who is now one of the leading business men of St. Joseph, Mo., E. A. Stephens, Ephraim Weeks, H. C. Richards and J. J. Roach. In 1883 William Rasco came to the place, and is running a good family store at the present time. Milton Brandon has a general store also, and Mr. McGraw keeps the village hotel.

Roaring Springs Lodge, No. 221, A. F. & A. M., was organized in 1848. The first officers were C. M. Bacon, W. M.; Anthony Garnett, S. W.; Thomas Garnett, J. W. Present officers: C. M. Bacon, W. M.; James Hamilton, S. W.; John Donald, J. W.; John A. Bacon, S. D.; W. W. Lewis, J. D.; William Bradshaw, Sec., and Samuel Joiner, Tyler. First meetings were held in Capt. Bacon's office, which was used until 1852, at which time a room was fitted up in a vacant store building at a cost of $200. The present hall was built with the Methodist Church and represents a capital of $2,700.

CHAPTER XI.

ROCK CASTLE AND BETHESDA PRECINCTS—GENERAL DESCRIPTION, BOUND-
ARIES AND TOPOGRAPHY—SETTLEMENT—A PROLIFIC FAMILY—OTHER
PIONEERS—FRONTIER HARDSHIPS—ROCK CASTLE VILLAGE—HURRICANE
BAPTIST CHURCH—BETHESDA METHODIST CHURCH, ETC., ETC.

ROCK CASTLE AND BETHESDA PRECINCTS, forming of themselves a magisterial district, lie in the northern part of the county between Wallonia Precinct on the east, and Cumberland River on the west. Little River flows along the southern border, and Lyon County forms the northern boundary. Contiguous to the Cumberland River the land is undulating, with stretches of bottoms the soil of which is of great depth and fertility. In some places along the stream are large embankments of limestone rising to a height of many feet, one of which—Castle Rock—which gave name to the precinct and village, is considered one of the most interesting natural features in the northern part of the county. Back from the river the country is more uneven, stretching away into hills which were originally clothed with a dense forest growth of oak, hickory, maple, poplar, ash and many other varieties of timber found growing in this portion of the State. The soil on the uplands is clay mixed and comparatively fertile, although for general farming purposes it ranks far below the alluvium of the bottoms and creek lands. When first cleared these hill lands are said to have been unexcelled for their productiveness, but as years passed by the soil became thin by continuous tillage, while a great portion of it was washed into the ravines and bottoms, until now the district is considered about a second-class farming region.

The district is principally drained by the Cumberland and Little Rivers, which receive a number of small creeks traversing the country in various directions. The most important of these minor water-courses are Hurricane Creek and Hawkin's Branch, both of which flow a westerly course, and empty into the Cumberland near Rock Castle Village. They are fed principally by springs, many of which are found throughout the precincts. Another small stream known as Dyer's Creek rises near Trigg Furnace and flows through an irregular channel and empties into Cumberland River a few miles from the village of Rock Castle.

Pioneer Settlement.—In tracing the history of the early settlement of this district we have drawn largely from Mr. McKinney's published reminiscences, the credibility of which is generally conceded.   The settlements on Dyer's Creek were among the first in the county and date back as early as the year 1796.   At that time or perhaps a little earlier there was living near the head of the stream where the old Trigg Furnace stands, one John Mayberry, who is remembered as one among the very first permanent settlers of the county.   He settled on the farm owned at the present time by Bob Cunningham, and appears to have been a man of considerable intelligence and an honorable and upright citizen.   He was a man of some attainments, and filled the office of surveyor in an early day.   His descendants are all dead.   Near the head of the same creek, on the place now owned by James Burnham, lived an old man by name of Thedford, who came to the country as early as the year 1798.   He was the pioneer mill builder of this part of the county, having erected a rudely constructed horse-mill near the site of Trigg Furnace before the beginning of the present century.   His brother, James Thedford, who came about the same time, settled where the widow Wallace lives.   Their descendants have all died or left the country.   Another very early comer was a Mr. Gillahan, grandfather of William Gillahan, who lives between the rivers.   Mr. Gillahan settled opposite the old Empire Iron Works at a place known as Ferry Corner, and is supposed to have immigrated to the locality in the year 1798.   John Grasty moved from South Carolina and settled not far from the location of Trigg Furnace early in the present century.   "He was a man of great industry and manifested a disposition, so far as their meager facilities would allow, to improve the morals and the intelligence of the little community."   "He taught near the old Cunningham place perhaps the first school that was ever taught in Trigg County, giving it up to an Englishman by name of Price, who continued to teach it for several years."   Mr. Grasty was the father of several sons, one of whom—John M.—is still a resident of the precinct, living at the present time near the old Hurricane meeting-house.

Jesse Birdsong, a brother-in-law of Grasty, came about the same time and made his first improvements on the Baker place, settling on a hill not far from the old graveyard.   He sold this farm several years later to Blake Baker.   Isaac Burnham came from North Carolina and located near Ferry Corner about the year 1805.   Isham Osborne, a Virginian, came in a very early day and settled in the same locality.   His descendants moved West a number of years ago.   "What is known as the old Dyer place was first settled by a very indolent old man by name of Curtis, who was the original Izaak Walton of the country.   He had no occupation but that of a fisherman, and would do nothing but fish and talk of nothing else.

"In relating the most enjoyable and remarkable episodes of his life they were all connected with the capture of some vast monster in the shape of a seventy-five pound cat-fish, and was never so happy as when snugly settled down with half a dozen fishing poles at some favorite 'hole' on Little River. He would make a lusty snatch with his ' grabs ' or fight mosquitoes alternately from the rising to the setting of the sun. He sold the place to Gen. John J. Dyer, and moved off in search of a location where fish were more abundant and a gourd of worms could be obtained without digging for them.

"Among the most noted families of the early settlers of this neighborhood was the old family of Standrods. They were natives of New Jersey, their father moving to North Carolina, and from there here in the year 1805. He settled on the Rock Castle and Princeton road in 1807. He had two sons, Samuel and Basil." The former settled about one mile southeast of Rock Castle, and the latter secured a home a short distance east of the Hurricane Baptist Church. Basil Standrod was a man who did as much if not more toward shaping the character of the early settlement of Rock Castle than any other person who ever resided in the district. Elected to the office of magistrate in an early day he discharged the duties of the position in a manner creditable to himself and satisfactory to the people, who looked to him as a kind of leader and legal adviser from whose opinion there were few appeals. A son, D. W. Standrod, one of the prominent business men of Trigg County, is living in Rock Castle Village at the present time. " A short distance from the old Hurricane Church and about three hundred yards from the residence of John Grasty, old man James Bourland settled in an early day." His son Andrew K. lived in the same vicinity for a number of years, and was the first shoemaker in this part of the country. Shadrach Jenkins and Henry Martin were both very early comers. They settled near the present residence of James Holland, but no facts concerning them could be learned.

Among those who came in a little later were William Shannon and a Mr. Hawkins, both of whom located in the neighborhood of Hurricane Church, where the former died more than forty-seven years ago. Richard Holland, a Virginian, settled in the northern part of the district, not far from the Caldwell County line in an early day, and became one of the wealthiest men and largest land-owners in the district. His son James M. Holland is a respected resident of the precinct at the present time. Freeman Baker came from North Carolina and settled near Rock Castle Village some time prior to 1820. He lived in the precinct until about the year 1829, at which time he was drowned in the Cumberland River. Blake Baker, a brother of Freeman, came the same time and settled northeast of Rock Castle on land which he purchased from Jesse Birdsong.

Thomas L. Baker settled in an early day on a place which was afterward bought by the Standrods.

"One of the most respected and certainly one of the most fruitful families that ever claimed a residence in the county was that of William Cunningham, a native of Scotland, who settled where Trigg Furnace now stands as early as the year 1817. The mere mention of the fact that within the present century and within the recollection of men still living a pair of old people should have settled in this county whose posterity at this day would number perhaps over 800 living souls, and all of the highest respectability, has a tendency to recall, and without aid of revelation, render both possible and probable the promise that God made to Abraham. It is like some indubitable fact clothed in the habiliments of romance, and almost startles at once our reason and our credulity. Still it is but a simple truth without exaggeration or adornment." Mr. Cunningham during his life-time accumulated a handsome competency. The names of his children were as follows: John, Gideon, Buck, Malinda, Andrew, Dabney, James, Mickens, Alexander and Robert, all of whom were heads of large families.

Prominent among the early pioneers was Gen. John Dyer, a man whose general character was respected throughout the county as much perhaps as any other citizen who ever claimed a residence in Trigg. He was elected General of Militia in an early day, and was looked upon as a kind of leader by his neighbors, all of whom had unbounded confidence in his abilities. George Creekmer, Malachi Creekmer, Thomas Sevills, Hardy Smith, Thomas Evans and John Curlin were all early settlers in the northern part of the district. Reuben Harris settled at Rock Castle, and Thomas Mitchell secured land about a half mile northeast of the village early in the twenties. William Campbell came from Christian County and settled close to the town of Rock Castle prior to 1826. He married a daughter of Freeman Baker, and was considered one of the leading citizens of the district. Thomas Wadlington, another early settler, located on land which he afterward sold to the Standrods. He is remembered as a very singular character, but withal a reputable citizen.

Among those who settled back from the river in what is now Bethesda Precinct, were James Caraway, who improved the place where Benjamin Shryer lives, on the Rock Castle and Princeton road, and Stephen Pearl, who settled in the same locality. Abner Crump came in an early day also. Mordecai Fowler settled near the Caldwell County line, in the northern part of the precinct, as did also John Hanberry, both of whom were very early residents. Jarrett Mitchell improved the place where Mollie Mitchell lives, in the southern part of the precinct, and can be classed among the pioneers of the county. The above list, we think, comprises the earliest and most prominent settlers in the two precincts. Other names could be added, but the limits of this chapter forbid a more extended mention.

Village of Rock Castle.—" Up to 1842, Old Ferry Corner, opposite Empire Iron Works, was the shipping point for all the northern part of Trigg and the southwestern portion of Caldwell Counties. As a business point it was discontinued after the erection of the furnace on the opposite bank, the property having been purchased by Messrs. Watson & Hillman, the owners of the iron works." The furnace store was kept in the old storehouse that is yet standing on the east bank of the river, up to 1848 or 1849, but the point from this date was used only as a boat landing for the individual interest of the furnace. The first store in Rock Castle was kept by Messrs. Marshall & Bradley, who engaged in business as early as 1835 or 1836; they kept a general stock of goods, and were well patronized by the citizens of the northern part of Trigg and the southern portion of Caldwell Counties. No great amount of business was done, however, until D. W. Standrod and George Creekmer obtained possession of the property. They continued as partners about four years, at the end of which time King Baker purchased Creekmer's interest, and under the firm name of Baker & Standrod, a successful mercantile and commission business was carried on until 1862. Standrod carried on a commission business until within the last two years, and is still a resident of the village.

J. H. Whitney started a store in 1869, and keeps a fine stock of goods at the present time. Several warehouses have been built in the town, the largest of which were those belonging to D. W. Standrod, Joseph T. Harris and John Grasty. The first physician of the place was Dr. A. Calloway, who located in the village soon after its settlement; since then the following medical gentlemen have practiced their profession here, to wit: Doctors Inge, Samuel Standrod, K. S. Campbell and Samuel E. Standrod.

Hurricane Baptist Church, the only religious organization in Rock Castle Precinct, was established in the year 1845, by Rev. J. F. White. Among the constitutional members were the following: Thomas Wadlington and wife, Miles Osborne, and Alexander Cunningham and wife. The first meetings were held in an old log schoolhouse, on Hurricane Creek, which was also used for a preaching place by the Methodists at the same time. A house of worship was afterward erected on John Grasty's land, and cost the sum of $600. Since its organization the church has been ministered to by the following pastors, viz.: J. F. White, George Patterson, C. Meacham, Elder Rowland, J. H. Spurlin, James Oliver and John Spurlin. The present officers are: Robert Allen and Blake Baker, Deacons; Robert Wallace, Clerk. The society is one of the aggressive organizations of the county, and numbers at the present time about 132 communicants.

Bethesda Methodist Episcopal Church.—The society was organized in 1845, with thirty members, among whom were: William Larkins, Penelope Larkins, Samuel Larkins, Henry Larkins, Mrs. Sallie Mitchell, David Etheridge, Mrs. Ann Sanders, Mrs. Elizabeth Savills, D. C. Savills, Miles Savills, Rebecca Hanberry, D. S. Hanberry and J. W. Hanberry. The first Class Leader was Robert Hawkins; the first Steward was Samuel Larkins. The organization took place in Duvall's Schoolhouse, which was used as a meeting place for about four years, when a frame church was built one mile southwest of the present edifice. It was built on land donated by Colmore Duvall, and stood until 1877. The present temple of worship was erected on ground donated by John Larkins, and cost about $600. The first pastor of the church was Rev. Zachariah M. Taylor. The present pastor is Rev. J. R. McDaniell. There are the names of about 100 members on the church book.

Under the labors of Rev. Samuel Feltener in 1877, the church enjoyed a most successful revival and perhaps one of the best ever held in this part of the county; some sixty persons professed conversion, and more than forty were added to the church.

CHAPTER XII.

BETWEEN THE RIVERS — A DISTRICT THAT COMPRISES LAURA FURNACE, GOLDEN POND AND FERGUSON SPRINGS PRECINCTS—DESCRIPTION OF THE LAND—ITS OCCUPATION BY WHITE PEOPLE—SOME OF THE PECULIARITIES OF THE PIONEERS—WHERE THEY LOCATED—A BAND OF FREE-BOOTERS—RELIGIOUS HISTORY—SKETCHES OF THE NUMEROUS CHURCHES —VILLAGE OF GOLDEN POND, ETC., ETC.

THE section of country lying between the Tennessee and Cumberland Rivers comprises the precincts of Laura Furnace, Golden Pond and Ferguson's Springs, which together form the first magisterial district. The physical features of this region are considerably varied, the country along the Tennessee being high and broken, and in some places rising in precipitous bluffs of sand rock and limestone; back from the river the land is not so abrupt, but stretches away in undulations covered with a forest growth of deciduous timber of the varieties usually found growing in this latitude. The land lying contiguous to the Cumberland is more "checkered," with sloughs and swamps intervening among the hills, while skirting the water-courses that empty into the rivers are level lands of average fertility and productiveness. Taken all in all it is not what might be termed a good agricultural region, although there are a number of well improved farms in various parts of the district. "Seventy-five years ago 1,000 acres of land between the rivers would not have been exchanged for the same quantity of the richest 'barrens' in the neighborhood of Montgomery, Wallonia or Roaring Springs. Timber and water regulated the value of real estate in this country then, and in this section of the county the settlers were blessed with an abundance of both. The finest springs, the coolest water gurgled up in the sandy bottoms, or came pouring out from the hillsides, and the whole country was covered in a growth of timber as luxuriant as could be found in any other portion of the State, whilst in the other rich 'barren' sections of the county there were few springs, and scarcely a sufficiency of timber to afford roosts for the wild turkeys at night.

"Notwithstanding the gibes and ridicule heaped upon the early settlers for selecting the locations they did, we think it most likely the present population, if thrown into a new country, would do precisely as they did. The cultivation of the soil was not at that time profitable. The settlers had no markets for the products of their farms; the country afforded an abundant supply of meats in the shape of wild game ; and a spring of cool water, a few acres of Indian corn, filled the measure of both their ambition and comfort." This region is rich in mineral wealth, the finest quality of iron ore being found from the Tennessee line to the northern boundary of the county. It is easily accessible, and was worked very extensively in an early day, several large furnaces having been erected at different points, some of which are still standing. An account of the iron industry will be found on another page.

Pioneers.—The first white men who came to this part of the county were the hardy adventurers from North Carolina already alluded to, who floated down the Tennessee and Cumberland Rivers on rafts. They seem to have been actuated by a spirit of adventure, and beyond erecting a few rude huts contiguous to the streams, made no further improvements. Following these came a few families of a more thrifty class of people, but these too have disappeared, leaving but faint traces behind them. As early as 1793 there was a small settlement near the present location of Redd's tan-yard, where a block-house was built as a means of defense against the Indians, hostile bands of whom kept the frontier settlers in a constant state of alarm. This was the second permanent settlement in this county, the first having been made in the neighborhood of Cerulean Springs a year or two previous. Unfortunately, the names of the persons who constructed the block-house have been forgotten, nor could any facts concerning them be learned.

Among the first permanent settlers was Allen Grace, the grandfather of W. D. Grace, who located near the site of Redd's tan-yard some time prior to 1800. He was a man of considerable prominence in the early history of the county, and his descendants are among its most intelligent and substantial citizens at the present time. Moses McWaters settled in the northern part of the district about the year 1802 or 1803, and improved a small farm in what is now Ferguson Springs Precinct. He had a family of grown up sons who secured tracts of land in the same vicinity. Levi Davis settled a place on Turkey Creek, known as the Vinson farm, about the same time. He earned the reputation of being a good citizen, and was thought well of by his neighbors. He died in a very early day, and most of his descendants moved off to other parts of the country. Robert Fergeson settled in the northern part of the district shortly after the year 1800. Robert Ferguson, after whom the northern precinct was named, came a little later and secured a tract of land lying a short distance from Cumberland River. Another early comer in the northern part was Abraham Lash, who settled near the Tennessee River. Eli Kilgore, Eli Ingram, John Blue, James Blue, Wiley Rhodes, James Barham and a man by name of Gregory were all living in the northern part of the district as early as 1812. Following close upon these were other settlements extending from the Tennessee line all the way down to the old Fulton Furnace section. Nathan Futrell settled where Laura Furnace has since been located in the southern part of the district. He owned the place for a number of years and planted a large apple orchard, the first in the county, a few trunks of trees of which may be still seen standing above the old furnace property. He was a relative of John Futrell, one of the earliest settlers on Donaldson Creek.

Frederick Jones settled the old John Futrell place. He disposed of it a great many years ago and moved to Canton. Few of the old settlers are more kindly remembered. Beman Fowler settled the Andy Gordon farm. He was a resident of the place at the time and long before the formation of the county. He was a man greatly respected, and was for a number of years one of the early Justices of the Peace. He moved away at an early day, his destination being unknown. —— Bradbury settled in an early day on the Cumberland River, in Golden Pond Precinct. An old gentleman by name of Young settled on the place now owned by William Gray. He was regarded as a thrifty, energetic and industrious old man. His death occurred a few years after the formation of the county. Joe Gilbert was an early settler, and lived for a number of years on Elbow Creek. He subsequently moved across the river and settled on Donaldson Creek, where his death occurred many years ago. David Grace, the third son of old man Allen Grace, and uncle of W. D. Grace, settled a short distance up the hollow from the present village of Golden Pond.

Charles Anderson, a worthy old gentleman, settled a place on Crooked Creek, not a great distance from Ferguson's Springs. Two or three miles in a northerly direction, at what is now known as the old Foley place, lived in an early day James Cummins and Van Anderson, the grandfather of Hon. Lush Anderson of Graves. " About the same time and in almost the same neighborhood, were a batch of settlers who were not spoken of so kindly. Jake McFadden, Herbert Wood, James Phillips and a few kindred satellites, whose names are not remembered, were very bad men. They came to the country as early as the year 1804, and their huts were scattered from the Oakley place to the Tennessee River. They belonged evidently to an organized band of plunderers, and were shrewdly suspected of being partizans of a lot of adventurers who made their appearance in the neighborhood several years before, and abandoned the country because there was nothing in it to make the avocation of the robber profitable." The presence of these characters gave the country an unsavory reputation, and while their depredations were not committed so much upon the people here they made this region a resort to evade the pursuit from other quarters.   For a time their depredations were carried on with impunity, and while they scrupled at the commission of no form of crime, they were especially annoying in their principal business of horse-stealing.   Their plan of operations was to run in large numbers of horses and keep them concealed among the hills and ravines until fears of pursuit were ended, when they would take the animals to Nashville and other points, where they were disposed of at good prices.   The early settlers did not submit to this state of affairs without some efforts to bring those persons to justice, but singly the pioneers proved poor trappers of this game.   The robbers were known to be desperate characters, adepts in the use of weapons, and it often happened that when a party got close upon the thieves "discretion seemed the better part of valor," and the chase was given up.   Civil authority seemed hopelessly incapable of remedying the evil, and accordingly the citizens took the matter into their own hands and organized a band of regulators, the effect of whose work was prompt and salutary.   The honest residents cordially aided the company, which in a few months rid the country of the gang which infested it.   McFadden and his accomplices succeeded in successfully evading the vigilants, and the reputation of the Jailor of Christian County at that time suffered by reason of a suspicion that he facilitated their escape.

The settlement of the country increased but slowly for a number of years, and those who came in belonged chiefly to the poorer classes. Improvements were few and of the most primitive kind.   Small horse-mills or corn-crackers were put up in various settlements, but these did but little better work than the mortars with which almost every house was supplied.   They did the work quicker, and such a mill was often kept running night and day, while the patrons coming from distances of several miles would wait patiently a day or two to get their grists.   One of the two earliest of these primitive mills was erected by Nathan Futrell, and stood near Laura Furnace.   It was used by the neighborhood for several years and did a good business for a mill of its capacity.

Churches.—There are several religious organizations in the district, the oldest of which is Pleasant Hill Baptist Church in Laura Furnace Precinct, which dates its history from the year 1842.   It was organized by Revs. T. L. Baker, Jesse Cox and —— Barnes, with helps from the Mount Pleasant and Crooked Creek Churches in Tennessee.   The first meeting was held at the dwelling of David Calhoun, and after the society acquired a permanency, religious services were conducted at different residences in the neighborhood.

In 1844 a log house of worship was erected on land donated by David Calhoun.   It has been remodeled since and a second story built for the use of the Patrons of Husbandry, a lodge of which met in the hall for a couple of years. Since its organization the church has been min-istered to by the following pastors, to wit: T. L. Baker, William Skinner R. R. Allen, S. R. McLane, W. E. McCaulley, D. S. Hanberry and A. J. Bird. The present incumbent is Rev. J. M. Ross, who reports an active membership of seventy-eight persons.

Cumberland River Baptist Church in Ferguson Springs Precinct was organized, in 1843, by T. L. Baker and Rev. Mr. Daniel, assisted by others whose names could not be learned. Meetings were held at the dwellings of different members until 1847, in which year a log house of worship was built on the land of Harrison McGregor. This building was used until 1868, when a new and more comfortable frame edifice was erected at a place known as Willow Springs. The following pastors have had charge of the congregation at different times: Revs. T. L. Baker, Jesse Cox, —— Hanberry, G. A. Patterson, Thomas Montgomery, E. L. McLane, William McCaulley and J. M. Ross. There are sixty communicants at the present time and the church is reported in good condition.

Pleasant Valley Baptist Church in Golden Pond Precinct was estab-lished in the year 1854, by Revs. T. L. Baker and George Patterson. The constitutional membership consisted of about thirty persons, and services were held for two years at a schoolhouse on Crooked Creek near the residences of Joel Coulsen and E. Grace. A temple of worship was erected in 1856 or 1857 on B. F. Luten's land, and cost the sum of $800. Among the pastors of the church are remembered the following: T. L. Baker, George Patterson, Thomas Montgomery, S. Y. Trimble, S. R. McLane, D. S. Hanberry, F. M. Holland and J. M. Ross, the last named being in charge at the present time. The records show an active mem-bership of seventy persons.

Long Creek Old School Baptist Church is in Voting Precinct No. 2, and dates its origin back to an early period of the country's settlement. At one time it was a very active organization, but its strength has dimin-ished considerably of recent years owing to deaths and removals.

The Walnut Grove Union Church in the southeastern part of Laura Furnace Precinct was built several years ago, and is used at the present time by the Methodists and Baptists, both of which denominations have small organizations. The house was erected under the auspices of the Christian Union Church, a society of which was kept up for some time, by Rev. J. M. Cress.

A society of the Methodist Church was organized at Redd's tan-yard, near the Tennessee River in Laura Furnace Precinct several years ago. Meetings were held in a hall, and for some time the society bid fair to become an aggressive organization, but owing to some cause unknown, services are rarely held at the present time.

Another Methodist society known as the Indian Springs Church, in Golden Pond Precinct, was established a number of years ago, but like the one mentioned above its strength is gradually decreasing.

Turkey Creek Baptist Church, five miles from Laura Furnace, was established by Revs. E. L. McLane, G. A. Patterson and J. Outland. A building was erected one year later at a cost of $1,000. The society is making substantial progress, and the records show an active membership of fifty persons at the present time. The preachers have been Revs. McLane, Knight, Tidwell and Allen. At the present time the church is without a pastor.

Pleasant Hope Baptist Church in the northwestern part of Ferguson Springs Precinct was organized in the year 1880, with a membership of eight, which has since increased to sixteen. F. M. Holland is pastor at the present time and W. N. Ingram, Clerk.

Ferguson Springs Church, which is also a Baptist organization, was established about the year 1879, by Revs. W. L. Rowland and F. M. Holland, with an original membership of about eight persons. The society has increased but slowly since its organization, and numbers only thirteen communicants at the present time.

Near Laura Furnace is a Catholic Church organized by a few German families under the supervision of Rev. Father Hasley in 1882. A loghouse was built the same year, and the society is now maintained by about eight families, all of whom emigrated from Germany between the years 1880 and 1883.

Village of Golden Pond, which gave name to the second voting precinct, is situated a few miles west of the Cumberland, and is the only village between the rivers. It is a small hamlet of a couple dozen houses and serves as a trading point for a large scope of country. The first store in the place was kept by Frank Ingram, who handled a general assortment of merchandise, and for several years did a fair business. There are two stores at the present time kept by Bogard and Haydon respectively.

MEMORANDA

—OF—

HISTORICAL EVENTS

OCCURRING SUBSEQUENT TO THE PUBLICATION
OF THIS WORK.

BIOGRAPHICAL SKETCHES.

CADIZ TOWN AND PRECINCT.

DR. THOMAS L. BACON was born January 19, 1832, in Halifax County, Va.; he is the eldest child of Charles A. and Susan (Rowlette) Bacon; the former was born February 15, 1807, in Charlotte County, Va., now a resident of Roaring Springs; the latter was born in Halifax County, Va.; she died in 1841. In 1832 the parents removed to Montgomery County, Tenn., remained there one year, then came to Christian County, where they remained till 1846; they then removed to Trigg County where his father now resides. At about the age of twenty-two he commenced the study of medicine with Dr. John C. Metcalf, of Christian County, and later attended the medical department of the Louisville University; there he graduated in 1855; he then commenced the practice of medicine in North Christian; remained there but a short time, and removed to Princeton, where he practiced about one year. In the fall of 1856 he removed to Henderson County; there practiced his profession till 1860; he then went to Philadelphia and received a course of lectures at the University of Pennsylvania, from which he graduated in March, 1861; he then returned to Roaring Springs; there continued in the practice of his profession till 1874, when he removed to Cadiz, where he has since resided. Dr. Bacon was married in 1857 to Miss Martha E. Bacon, who was born in Muhlenburg County, Va.; she died in January, 1860, aged thirty; his second marriage was November 1, 1865, to Miss Elizabeth E. Edwards; she was born in Christian County. This union has been blessed with five children, two of whom are now living—one son and one daughter.

JAMES BATTOE was born January 30, 1826, in St. Clair County, Ill. He is the fourth of a family of seven children, born to John and Annis (Hodges) Battoe. The father was a native of Kentucky; he died in 1832, aged forty. The mother was born in Trigg County; she died in 1846, aged forty. Our subject remained with his mother till about the age of ten years, he then worked out by the month and year till 1848, when he came to Trigg County; here he worked on rented farms. In 1869 he bought his present farm of 214 acres, where he has since lived and has cleared about fifty acres; his buildings which he has placed on this farm cost about $500. Mr. Battoe was married in 1869 to Eliza Lawrence, a native of Trigg County; two daughters have blessed this union. Mr. and Mrs. Battoe are life-long and devoted members of the Methodist Episcopal Church South.

THOMAS BOYD was born January 28, 1826, in Halifax County, Va. He is the youngest of a family of four children born to Thomas and Elizabeth (Stamps) Boyd, also natives of Virginia. His father died when the subject was quite young, and in 1838 the mother emigrated with the family to Trigg County where she died in 1877, at the hale old age of eighty-six. The subject of this sketch was raised on his mother's farm, where he remained until the age of twenty-six, and then purchased a farm of 127 acres and commenced life for himself. Through his own exertions he has since increased his farm to 500 acres, where he now resides, and also owns 250 acres elsewhere in the county and 180 in Caldwell County. The home place is considered to be one of the best in the county, and he now devotes his main attention to the raising of live stock. He now has from fifty to seventy-five head of short-horn cattle, forty to fifty hogs and about 150 head of sheep on his place. At present his son Charles manages the farm, which lies eight miles northeast of Cadiz. On January 10, 1881, he was appointed to fill the vacancy of Sheriff, and in the following August was elected to fill the office. He had prior to this time collected the taxes of 1879. In August, 1882, he was re-elected, and has since filled the office. Mr. Boyd was married on October 1, 1850, to Miss Martha, daughter of Maj. George Daniel. Mrs. Boyd is a native of Trigg County, and is the mother of ten children, six of whom—five sons and a daughter—are living.

JOHN H. CALDWELL was born August 22, 1842, in Trigg County, and is a son of John H. and Martha W. (Barksdale) Caldwell; the former was born June 6, 1817, in Halifax County, Va.; he died December 27, 1848; they were married May 16, 1838, and emigrated to Trigg County in 1841; the latter was born June 11, 1821, also in Halifax County, Va. She died July 18, 1846. The subject of this sketch is the eldest of a family of three. After the death of their parents, they were reared by their guardian, Capt. C. W. Roach. John's early education was received at Cadiz, Q. M. Tyler and James Rumsey being his teachers, after which he attended the Bethel College three years. After five months' study at the Cumberland University, Lebanon, Tenn., he returned to the Bethel College, Russellville, there graduated in the class of 1861; he then entered the Confederate Army, Company A, Ninth Kentucky Infantry, commanded by Col. Thomas H. Hunt, of Louisville, and served to the end of the war; he participated in the battle of Shiloh, was under fire at Vicksburg, battles of Baton Rouge, Murfreesboro, Jackson and all the battles from Dalton to Atlanta, and Jonesboro; after the battle near Statesboro, S. C., on capitulated terms of surrender, they were paroled at Washington, Ga., May 6, 1865, and were the last troops that fired a gun east of the Chattahoochee, where they surrendered; he then returned to Trigg County, where he has since been engaged in agricultural pursuits, except two years as teacher of the Wallonia Institute. He was married December 16, 1868, to Cornelia F. Boyd. She was born June 21, 1848, in Trigg County; she died September 6, 1881, leaving a family of four children—two sons and two daughters. His brother Thomas B. was killed at the battle of Pittsburg Landing, April 6, 1862; his brother Dr. J. W. Caldwell served during the late war in Company A, Woodward's Cavalry, after which he attended the University of Virginia, and graduated at the Baltimore Medical College in 1866. He then engaged in the practice of his profession in Belleview, Christian County; after practicing several years he went to Louisville for the purpose of having an operation performed, from which he died November 4, 1873.

JOHN W. CHAPPELL, merchant, Cadiz, was born March 19, 1824, in Christian County, Ky.; he is a son of Dickie and Susan (McCarty) Chappell, who were natives of Halifax County, Va.; they came to Christian County at an early day; he first engaged in teaching school, and later followed agricultural pursuits. They lived on one farm forty-three years. October 1, 1853, they removed to Washington County, Texas. There his mother died August 10, 1855. His father died in July, 1870. The subject of this sketch was reared on his father's farm, where he remained till January 1, 1844. He then came to Cadiz and was clerk for Hiram Thompson in the dry goods business. November, 1848, he opened a general store; with the exception of being interrupted three years during the war, has continued this business since, and with the exception of Mr. Street is now the oldest merchant in Trigg County. He first opened a store in the old Baker Hotel, with a stock of about $4,000, and since this time has done a business of upwards of $35,000 a year; he continued business at the Baker Hotel eighteen years; he then removed to Mrs. Terry's storehouse, where he remained five years. In 1873 he removed to his present store, situated on the west side of the court house. Mr. Chappell was Postmaster from 1858 to 1861; he is a member of the Methodist Episcopal Church South, and Chosen Friends. He was married May 21, 1845, to Sarah, daughter of the late Dr. Thomas B. Jefferson. She was born in Sumner County, Tenn. This union has been blessed with seven children, three sons and four daughters. His son, John J., is a partner in this business.

JOHN J. CHAPPELL is one of the most promising of the rising young men of the county; he was born in Cadiz December 16, 1855, and is a son of John W. and Sarah (Jefferson) Chappell; his education was received in the schools of his native town; his first instructor was Prof. F. F. Jones; among his other teachers were J. J. Nall, Prof. Hancock, Prof. Pomeroy and Prof. H. B. Wayland. In 1873 he was a student at the College of Arts and Sciences at Lexington, Ky., and graduated from this institution of learning in the class of 1875; he then returned to Cadiz and entered his father's store as a clerk in 1876. He served in that capacity until January, 1884, when he became a partner in the firm under the title of J. W. Chappell & Son. This firm is at present one of the leading houses of the place. Mr. Chappell was married in Hopkinsville, Christian County, March 6, 1884, to Miss Ida, daughter of James O. Cooper, proprietor of the Phœnix Hotel at that point.

JUDGE ROBERT CRENSHAW was born in Trigg County, Roaring Springs Precinct, June 4, 1847; he is the fourth of a family of six sons born to Robertson and Mary (Walden) Crenshaw. The father was born in Halifax County, Va., in September, 1816, and was a son of Cornelius and Nancy (Kent) Crenshaw; he came here in 1819 with his parents (see sketch of Thomas Crenshaw), grew to manhood, and married here in 1839; he resided here until his death, which occurred February 12, 1853; he was a member of the Christian Church and of the Masonic fraternity; the mother was born in Halifax County, Va., in 1819, and died in this county December 31, 1851. Our subject was reared by his uncle, Thomas Crenshaw; he was educated by Prof. Wyatt and Prof. G. P. Street; at the age of twenty he took up the study of law under the preceptorship of Judge Thomas C. Dabney; he was licensed to practice in 1868; soon afterward he was elected County Attorney for four years, and during this time also held the office of School Commissioner; while serving in the latter office he made the tour of the country, delivering addresses in the interest of education; he was a candidate in 1878 and also in 1882 for County Judge, but was defeated both times by Judge Dyer by a small majority. At these elections Judge Crenshaw received more votes than had ever been polled for any other defeated candidate prior to that time. In the summer of 1883 he was a candidate for the third time, and at the primary election he defeated Judge Kelley, Squire W. G. Blaine and Prof. H. B. Wayland. At the following general election in August he was elected over S. I. Spiceland, who was the nominee on the Republican ticket. This position he is still satisfactorily and creditably filling. Judge Crenshaw was married, in 1877, to Miss Minnie, daughter of Judge Thomas C. Dabney. Three children—two sons and a daughter—have blessed this union. He is a member of the Christian Church, and of the Odd Fellows and Chosen Friends.

JUDGE THOMAS C. DABNEY was born in Louisa County, Va., on September 20, 1823. He is the second son of Albert G. Dabney and Ann Eliza Catlett, his wife, formerly of Louisa County, Va., who came to Christian County in the fall of 1830, with a family of four sons. Albert S. Dabney (now deceased), was the third son and held the offices of County and Circuit Clerk of Trigg County for a number of years, and afterward was cashier of a bank in Hickman, Ky., where he contracted a disease from which he died in Cadiz, leaving three sons and one daughter. The brothers, E. W. and C. J., removed to Austin County, Tex., in 1853, where E. W. Dabney now resides, and C. J. Dabney died in June, 1882, both having large families. The subject of this sketch was educated by Elder George P. Street. After receiving a good education, at the age of eighteen he took up the study of the law and came to Cadiz, and lived with the family of the late J. E. Thompson, who was at that time County and Circuit Clerk. Our subject became the Deputy in both offices, and

while discharging these duties continued the study of law, under the
direction of Hon. C. D. Bradley, now deceased. He procured license to
practice in the fall of 1844, and located in Cadiz, where he has since followed the profession. Though at all times decided in his political convictions
he has never sought any political offices ; he was several times elected and
served as County Attorney of Trigg County.   Upon the adoption of the
new Constitution in 1852, he was elected the first County Judge in Trigg
County, under the new Constitution.   In July, 1857, he was elected Circuit Judge in the Second Circuit Court, Judicial District in Kentucky,
which at that time, extended across the State, and included the counties of
Trigg, Christian, Todd, Muhlenburg, Hopkins, Henderson and Caldwell.
Judge Dabney's term expired in August, 1862, and he declined to be a
candidate for re-election and retired to the practice of his profession, to
which he has since devoted his entire attention.   On March 7, 1848,
Judge Dabney was married, in the city of Hopkinsville, to Miss Susannah,
only child of the late James D. Rumsey.   Mrs. Dabney was born and
reared in Hopkinsville, Ky.   Her father was a lawyer by profession, a
teacher by occupation, a man of much learning and marked ability and
descended from a family noted for their rare talent.   He was near kins-
man and named after his uncle James Rumsey, who is the first
to have discovered and applied steam power to navigation, and experi-
mented in propelling a small steamboat on the Potomac in 1784 ; he died
in London, England, of apoplexy, while lecturing on the application of
steam-power to navigation before the Royal Society.   This union has been
blessed with nine children, one of whom (Thomas C., Jr.), died at the
Kentucky University (at Lexington), on April 13 ,1873. Eight children—
four sons and four daughters—are now living.   Judge James R., the
eldest son, is a lawyer by profession and is now County Judge of Henderson County, Ky.   Lieut. Albert J., the second son, is now a Lieutenant
in the United States Navy, where he has been for the past seventeen
years.   E. F., the third son, is a graduate of the Louisville Law School,
and is now a partner with his father in the practice of law.   Dr. Archie
S., the fourth, has lately graduated at the Baltimore College of Dental
Surgery, and has since opened dental rooms at Cadiz.   Of the daughters,
Minnie is now the wife of Judge Robert Crenshaw, now County Judge of
Trigg County ; Cornelia, the eldest daughter, was recently made a widow

by the death of her husband, John R. Averitt, who was a young lawyer of promising attainments, and was filling the office of County Attorney at the time of his death ; Misses Annie and Carrie, the two youngest daughters, are still living at home with their parents.

JOHN C. DABNEY was born January 14, 1852, in Cadiz. He is the second of five children born to Albert S. and Pamelia (Middelton) Dabney. His father was born in Louisa County, Va., and emigrated to Trigg County when about fourteen years of age ; he was a highly cultivated Christian gentleman, a member of the Christian Church and one of the purest and best men that ever lived ; he was exceedingly popular, and filled with marked ability and credit, for about sixteen years, the office of County Clerk ; he died in Cadiz in 1860, in his thirty-sixth year. His mother was the eldest daughter of the late John Middelton of Shelby County, Ky. She was a lady of superior intelligence and culture, and also possessed rare business qualifications. She is said, by those best acquainted with her, to have been the brightest scholar of her classes. She obtained a profound knowledge of the classics, and as a Latin scholar had but few equals and no superior. She was a faithful and devoted mother, an earnest and conscientious Christian, a member of the church of her husband and brought up her children—three sons and a daughter— " in the nurture and admonition of the Lord." She had the consolation of knowing and seeing her children profess Christ before she was called to her sweet reward ; this estimable lady died in December, 1875. Our subject received his primary education while working on the farm and helping to support his widowed mother and family, and studied night and day at home under the instruction and tutelage of his mother, and later attended the schools in Cadiz, where he won prizes for his studious habits, scholarship and gentlemanly deportment. In 1869 he left Cadiz and went to the Kentucky University at Lexington. There we find him a lad about seventeen years of age, hard at work ; studious, industrious, faithful and punctual in all his school duties, and as a reward for his thorough, faithful work, he was promoted to a Captaincy in the Second Session and had charge of the Military Department, and also received the appointment to West Point from the university as having the highest and best standing in his classes, but he declined to accept this high honor, and continued at the university as a student for two years longer, holding the position of Captain and noted for his competency and strict military discipline. He was also engaged as tutor in the university, by which means he was able to finish his education. Having completed his literary course in June, 1873, he went to teaching school and studying law ; he taught one year longer at Lexington and then took a course of law lectures at Kentucky University, and then returned to Cadiz and took charge of the high school, which position he ably filled as Principal for about eight years. In 1876 he was admitted to practice law in the courts of the State, since which time he has been actively engaged in the practice of his profession (even while teaching), and we predict for him a bright future. In August, 1883, he was elected County Attorney, which office he now honorably fills, and is said to be one of the most active, energetic and competent officers Trigg has had. He is a member of the Board of School Examiners, and also connected with the Society of Chosen Friends. Capt. Dabney was married June 14, 1876, to Miss Mattie, second daughter of J. W. Chappell, of Cadiz. Three bright children gladden their home. Capt. Dabney and wife are both devoted members of the Methodist Episcopal Church South. He has been Sunday-school Superintendent for the past six years.

WILLIAM L. DUNN was born in Robinson County, Tenn., May 8, 1858. He is a son of Samuel and Victoria (La Prade) Dunn, also natives of Robinson County, Tenn. At the breaking out of the war Samuel enlisted in the Confederate Army, and was killed at the battle of Chickamauga, aged twenty-eight years. The subject of this sketch was reared in his native county, and engaged in agricultural pursuits : there he continued to reside till January 1, 1883, when he came to Trigg County. He owns 178 acres where he now resides. Mr. Dunn was married December 10, 1879, to Miss Susie B., daughter of John F. White, one of the oldest and wealthiest settlers of Trigg County.

J. E. EDWARDS was born December 26, 1842, in Simpson County, Ky. He is a son of Henry M. and Susan (Travis) Edwards ; the former was born in North Carolina in 1811, died in 1866. Our subject at the age of two years was brought by his parents to Graves County, where he was reared. In 1863 he removed to Christian County ; engaged there in farming seven years. In 1870 he came to Cadiz—here kept a hotel four years. In 1876 he was elected Jailor ; held that office four years ;

then engaged in the sewing machine business three years. August, 1882, he was elected Assessor, which office he still holds. He owns a farm where he resides, one and one-half miles from Cadiz. He was married in December, 1864, to Alice B. Arbuckle, who was born in Christian County, by whom he had five children—two daughters and three sons. Mr. Edwards is a member of the Blue Lodge and Chapter, A. F. & A. M., K. of P. and Methodist Episcopal Church South.

RICHARD T. ELLIS was born November 10, 1844, in Cadiz. He is the only child of Ira A. and Elizabeth K. (Tyler) Ellis. The father was born in Christian County. He came to Cadiz in 1843; kept the Cadiz House about one year; he then removed to the iron works, where he kept books several years. He also held the office of Sheriff one term. In 1853 he was elected State Senator, and while a member of this body was taken sick and died in Cadiz in 1854. The mother was born on the farm now owned by our subject on March 15, 1825; she died in Cadiz May 1, 1846. Subject was married February 25, 1868, to Miranda E. Humphries. She was born in Trigg County. Two children bless this marriage—one son and one daughter. After living three years on this farm, in 1871, they removed to Golden Pond Precinct; there they remained one year, when they returned to this farm and occupied a house built on this land by his grandfather. In 1880 they removed to their present home. This is one of the oldest settled farms in the neighborhood, and originally contained 675 acres. Mr. Ellis now owns the homestead with 332½ acres. This farm is situated on the Cadiz and Hopkinsville road, and is considered one of the most desirable locations in this county. Mr. Ellis is a member of the I. O. O. F. He and wife are also members of the Methodist Episcopal Church.

HON. JAMES B. GARNETT was born on July 28, 1845, near Pembroke, Christian County; he is the youngest of five children born to Eldred and Frances A. (Pendleton) Garnett. The father was born in Abermarle County, Va., in 1813, and died on his farm in Christian County, Ky., in 1870. The mother was born in 1810 in Orange County, Va., and is now living in Christian County. Our subject has three brothers in Christian County, two engaged in merchandising at Pembroke, the other in farming and teaching school. His sister is the wife of Rev. R. W. Morehead, of Princeton, Ky. In 1866 Mr. Garnett commenced the study of law at the Lebanon Law School, and graduated at this college of learning in the class of 1868. Immediately after he came to Cadiz and located here, and since that time has been actively engaged in the practice of his profession. In 1870 he was elected County Attorney and served four years. During part of this time he was also Common School Commissioner for two years. In August, 1875, he was elected State Senator from the Third Senatorial District, which was composed of the counties of Trigg, Calloway, Lyon and Livingston. In 1880 he was elected Commonwealth's Attorney for the Second Judicial District, comprising the counties of Muhlenburg, Christian, Hopkins, Trigg, Caldwell and Lyon, for the term of six years; this office he still honorably fills. Mr. Garnett was a delegate to the National Democratic Convention at Baltimore in 1872, and at St. Louis in 1876; he was married in October, 1877, to Miss Virginia Hewell, of Tuscaloosa, Ala. This lady died on November 30, 1878.

JOHN J. GARTON was born in Christian County on July 5, 1827. He is the elder of two sons, now living, born to James C. and Frances (Londerman) Garton. The father was born in Kentucky, and died January 24, 1835, aged thirty-nine. The mother was a native of Virginia, and died December 3, 1854, aged fifty-three years. The subject of this sketch was raised on a farm. After attending the usual subscription school, at the age of fifteen he was apprenticed to the saddlery trade. He continued in this business until 1862, when he engaged in general merchandising. He first opened a store in Lafayette and afterward at Hopkinsville. In January, 1867, he came to Cadiz, where he has since been engaged in this business. He began at Lafayette with a stock of about $1,000, and now carries a stock of about $10,000. He has been acting as Postmaster at Cadiz for the past fourteen years. On February 15, 1854, Mr. Garton was married to Miss Fannie E. White, of Lafayette, Christian County. This lady died November 30, 1860, leaving three daughters. Mr. Garton was next married at Cadiz, on December 13, 1864, to Miss Bettie Lindsay, a native of Christian County. Mr. G. is a member of the Masonic fraternity, and of the Christian Church.

H. M. GARTON was born in Todd County, Ky., April 16, 1829. He is the third child of a family of four born to James C. and Frances Garton. After the death of his father, which occurred in 1840, his mother returned with her family to her father, John Londerman; there the subject of this sketch was reared. After attending school in Christian County, he commenced the study of dentistry, and attended the Baltimore Dental School in 1854–55. In 1856 he located in Cadiz, and opened his dental rooms. This business he continued till 1881. He with his brother, John J., in 1867, opened a general store here, and continued his interest in this business till the fall of 1878, when he sold out to his brother, and built his present spacious store-house, where he with his son, Henry H., is now engaged in the hardware and agricultural implement business. They are carrying a stock of about $5,000. His son, Henry H., was married October 7, 1880, to Miss Blanche, daughter of Col. Gentry. She was born in Trigg County. One daughter has blessed this union. Mr. Garton has held the office of Postmaster continuously since 1866.

W. D. GRACE was born January 24, 1813, in Caldwell, now Trigg County, Ky.; he is the second child of a family of four born to George and Nancy (Williams) Grace; they were born in North Carolina, and married in Montgomery County, Tenn.; the father was engaged in agriculture. On coming to Trigg County they settled on a farm of about 300 acres, three miles west of Canton; he died in 1850, aged sixty-five. Our subject at the age of nineteen bought a farm on Crooked Creek; lived there four years, then removed to Canton, where he lived about twenty-five years. He first kept hotel and later engaged in merchandising and commission, also engaged in pork-packing four seasons. In 1861 he removed to Cadiz; during his stay there he had raised three crops. January 1, 1867, he removed to their present farm which consisted at that time of about 1,300 acres; about 800 acres of this land have since been disposed of. Mr. Grace has been three times married; his first marriage, was July 15, 1832, to Mary Organ. She was born in Wilson County, Tenn.; died August 30, 1834. They had two children: Frances, wife of D. P. Austin, was born April 28, 1833; she died December 28, 1881; John R. was born May 27, 1834; he took up the study of law and graduated at the Louisville Law College, at the age of twenty-one; he then engaged in the practice of his profession, and soon after became a partner in the law firm of Mayes & Grace; he has held the office of County Judge, and now serving his third term as Judge of the Second Judicial District.

Mr. Grace was next married, June 11, 1839, to Elizabeth Gough; she was born February 20, 1820, in Stewart County, Tenn. She died July 6, 1849. They had four children—all deceased. His third marriage was on September 8, 1850, to Sarah Munday; she was born in Virginia. This union was blessed with two children, one living—Alex. H., who is now the owner of this farm. He was married, February 15, 1882, to Miss Eliza Wharton. She was born in Trigg County.

JUDGE JOHN R. GRACE was born May 27, 1834, in Trigg County, Ky. He is a son of William D. and Mary (Organ) Grace. The father was born in Caldwell, now Trigg County, January 24, 1813, and is now living on his farm, about three miles from Cadiz. The mother was a native of Wilson County, Tenn. She died August 30, 1834. John R. was reared in or near Canton, and attended the subscription schools of that locality, after which he attended the Lebanon High School one year. At about the age of nineteen he took up the study of law, under the preceptorship of Maj. Matthew Mayes, where he continued one year, after which he went to Louisville, and there entered the law department of the Transylvania College; there graduated in the class of 1855. He then came to Cadiz and engaged in the practice of his profession. In 1858 he was elected County Judge. Two years later he formed a partnership with Maj. Matthew Mayes, firm of Mayes & Grace. This partnership continued till 1865. He then formed a partnership with Henry C. Burnett, which continued till the death of the latter, which occurred in September, 1866. He continued the practice of this profession till 1868, when he was elected Curcuit Judge of the Second Judicial District, comprising the counties of Trigg, Christian, Hopkins, Caldwell and Lyon. He was re-elected in 1874, and again in 1880; this position he still honorably fills. In 1880 the county of Muhlenburg was added to this circuit. In October, 1882, he was nominated on the Democratic ticket for Congress, representing the First Congressional District, and was defeated by Oscar Turner, the Independent candidate, by a small majority. Judge Grace was married in 1859, to Miss Emeline, daughter of Abner Terry, of Trigg County. This lady died in January, 1861, aged twenty-four years.

WILLIAM W. GRAY was born in Christian County, on March 25, 1858, and is a son of James and L. (Brown) Gray. His father was a native of North Carolina. When young he removed to Kentucky, and engaged in merchandising at Wallonia. He continued business there until his death, which occurred in 1859. At the time of his death he was the owner of a large farm in Christian County, and two stores, one in Wallonia, the other in Christian County. The mother was a native of Virginia, and after her husband's death, she removed to her farm. In 1866 she was married to Frederick Routon, who was also a farmer. William W. was reared on his mother's farm. He continued to reside there until June, 1883, when he came to Cadiz. He is the owner of three farms in Christian County, and 250 acres in Trigg County. On January 8, 1881, he was married to Miss Lou Hancock, a native of this county. Two sons have blessed this union.

R. J. GRIGSBY was born February 20, 1834, in Logan County, Ky., and is a son of Jesse and Mary (Moseley) Grigsby. The former was born in Virginia, the latter in Logan County, Ky. The father of our subject when young learned the blacksmith's trade, which he followed most of his life. At about the age of twelve he was brought with his parents to this locality, where they settled on a farm; here he remained till the age of twenty-one. He then bought 200 acres of land where he now resides, and has since been engaged in farming. He has from time to time added other lands by purchase; he now owns from 600 to 700 acres embraced in two farms. He has held the office of Magistrate four years. Mr. Grigsby was married in September, 1866, to Tabitha Rogers. She was born in Trigg County. Two children bless this union—one son and one daughter.

THOMAS H. GRINTER, capitalist, was born in Logan County, Ky., September 12, 1823, and is the third of a family of nine children born to Samuel and Nancy (Hill) Grinter, natives of Virginia. His father was a farmer, and our subject grew to manhood on the latter's farm. When nineteen years old, on January 1, 1842, he came to Cadiz. Here he first clerked in Hiram Thompson's store for three years; he then bought out J. E. Thompson, and after various changes in the style of the firm, it finally became known as Thompson & Grinter. This partnership continued two years, and at the end of this time the latter sold out. He next purchased the office of Sheriff from James Garnett, which he held for two years; he then engaged in merchandising under the firm name of

Grinter & Baker; he remained in this business two years, then sold out, and again bought the office of Sheriff from Stanley Thomas. Since then he has been engaged attending to his private affairs, and managing estates for others, also acting as guardian for minors. Probably no other man in Trigg County has made or spent as much money as Mr. Grinter. Coming to Cadiz in 1842, with but $2, he is to day the richest man in Christian or Trigg County; his wealth in part consists of $120,000 in Government bonds; he also owns several stores and residences in Cadiz, among which might be mentioned the Cadiz House, erected in 1880. This building, including the ground on which it stands, cost $18,000. He is by far the largest tax payer of any one in Trigg County. Mr. Grinter was married, in 1850, to Mary, a daughter of William Redd, of Trigg County. This union has been blessed with seven children, two sons and five daughters. Mr. Grinter has been Town Treasurer, Trustee of the Jury Fund, and Master Commissioner of the Circuit Court. He is a member of the Masonic fraternity.

WESLEY GUNN, deceased, was born May 1, 1819, in Robinson County, Tenn. In 1854 he came to Cadiz, and engaged in the tobacco business; he also superintended the building of the present stemmery, now owned and operated by Mr. White; he afterward removed to a farm three miles distant from Cadiz; there he engaged in agricultural pursuits till his death, which occurred February 22, 1865. He was married, in 1856, to Miss Addie Grinter. She was born in 1837, in Logan County, Ky. Four children blessed this union—two sons and two daughters. The eldest son, S. Walker Gunn, now engaged with Torian & Barber, of Evansville, Ind. Thomas W. is now employed in the post office at Cadiz. Mrs. Gunn is a devoted member of the Methodist Episcopal Church South.

WALTER H. HANCOCK was born on August 24, 1850, in Campbell County, Va.; he is the eldest of a family of ten children born to D. M. Hancock, also a native of Virginia. When subject was six years old his father came to Trigg County, where he farmed. Subject remained at home with his father until he was twenty-six years old. In the meantime he held various local offices until 1882, among which might be mentioned Deputy Sheriff, and Constable. He next came to Cadiz, where he has since been engaged in the grocery and liquor business. Mr. Hancock was married on January 9, 1883, to Miss Ida M. Allen, daughter of William Allen, of Christian County, Ky. He is a member of the Methodist Episcopal Church South.

WILEY L. HILLMAN was born October 8, 1847, in Hopkinsville ; he is the third child of a family of four born to W. W. and Mary (Lindsay) Hillman ; the former was born in Louisa County, Va., in 1814, died on his farm near Cadiz in 1878, aged sixty-four; he moved to Christian County in 1832, where he lived till 1848, then came to Trigg County, carrying on his trade, that of contractor and builder; he built the Canton and Roaring Springs bridges at Cadiz, and various other improvements ; he bought a farm one and one-half miles southeast of Cadiz, where he lived till his death. His mother was a daughter of Dr. Lindsay, a native of Virginia. She died in 1849. When about the age of five our subject was brought by his father to Cadiz, where he was reared. In 1870 he went to Kansas ; there learned the boot and shoe trade, following this business there till January, 1877, when he returned to Cadiz and established his present business; he keeps on hand constantly a well selected stock of ready made boots and shoes, also manufactures to order ; he was married in 1879 to Fannie Falkner. She was born in Trigg County. They are members of the Christian Church, and he of the Masonic fraternity and K. of H.

JOHN G. JEFFERSON is the oldest native born white child now living in Cadiz ; he was born here on September 21, 1834, and is a son of Dr. Thomas B. and Martha A. (Graves) Jefferson. The father was born in Pittsylvania County, Va., on the 13th of April, 1805, and was a son of Peter F. and Elizabeth (Harrison) Jefferson. The former was a cousin of President Jefferson, the latter a cousin of President Harrison. When Thomas was six years old his father moved to Sumner County, Tenn. Here Dr. Jefferson obtained the rudiments of his education. At the age of eighteen he entered the office of Dr. Rawlings and commenced the study of medicine. After studying there one year he entered the Transylvania University at Lexington. At this institution he remained two terms, and graduated with honor to himself and credit to his preceptors. On his return from college he settled in the vicinity of Nashville, Tenn. After practicing medicine one year alone he entered into a co-partnership with Dr. Maxey, at Haysboro, Davidson Co., Tenn.

In 1830 he determined to go to St. Louis, and accordingly started for that place; he was delayed by a severe snowstorm at Hopkinsville, and while stopping there some of the citizens of Cadiz, among them William Cannon, then Clerk of the Circuit Court, petitioned him to settle at this point. Accordingly in the fall of 1831 he came to Cadiz, and cast his lot with the people of this county. In 1832, when the Asiatic cholera made its appearance in Kentucky, Salem, in Crittenden County, was smitten by the epidemic. The people of Cadiz, fearing this disease would appear at that point, solicited Dr. Jefferson to go and investigate the theory of the disease. With commendable zeal and fearlessness he started to Salem, but on his arrival at Princeton he found the scourge had already reached that point. Here the citizens stopped him and insisted that he should take charge of the case of Mr. Peter Simmerman, a merchant of that place, then pronounced by the home physicians to be in a hopeless condition. Our subject now has in his possession two letters concerning his father's treatment of this case; one written by N. S. Dalman, Esq., the other by Thomas Haynes, Esq., in which the courage, skill and firmness of Dr. Jefferson are spoken of in words of deep admiration. Simmerman although in a collapsed state when Dr. J. reached him, was cured, and as one of the letter writers remarked, " Dr. J. snatched an estimable citizen from the grave and restored him to the bosom of his fam￣ily." He continued to make tri-weekly visits to Princeton during the prevalence of the disease, and under the treatment of this physician the disease lost its terrors to some extent. From this time until his death Dr. Jefferson occupied a very high, if not the highest, rank in the medical profession of this and adjoining counties; he died on July 11, 1873, and his loss was severely felt in the community in which he had resided so long, especially by the poorer classes, for whom he had great sympathy. He loved the right, manly and the noble, and detested fraud, meanness and sham. The mother of subject was born in Davidson County, Tenn., and her death occurred in this county in April, 1853. The schools of the county furnished subject's education. When a youth he went to Eddyville, Lyon County, and there taught school for a while, then wrote in the County Clerk's office. While engaged in this latter occupation he also found time to read law some, and in 1855 he entered the Louisville Law School. From this institution he graduated in the class of 1856; he came to this county and practiced his profession for a few months, when he became book-keeper at Laura Furnace, where he remained until his marriage. During the war he spent most of the time in the South. In 1866 he returned to Cadiz and remained a short time; he then went to Texas, where he spent several months, and then returned to this county. In January, 1869, he was appointed County Court Clerk, and in the following August he was elected to the office for one year, and in August, 1870, he was re-elected for four years, and since that time has held the office continuously, being re-elected in 1874, 1878 and 1882; he is an insurance agent, and also does something in farming, having a tract of land near Cadiz. Mr. Jefferson was married near Nashville, Tenn., on May 17, 1861, to Miss Elizabeth S. Banks, a daughter of Samuel M. and Nancy R. (McCarty) Banks. Mrs. Jefferson was born in Fayette County, Mo., and is the mother of five children—one girl and four boys. Subject and family are all members of the Methodist Episcopal Church South. Mr. Jefferson is also a member of A. F. & A. M., I. O. O. F., K. of H. and Chosen Friends fraternities.

PETER S. JEFFERSON was born in Cadiz, Trigg County, on November 21, 1847, and is a son of Dr. Thomas B. Jefferson, whose sketch appears elsewhere in this work. Our subject's early education was received in Cadiz. At the age of fifteen he began to clerk for his brother William (now deceased). He remained with him for about three years. He next clerked for J. W. Chappell for about two years. He then went to Clarksville, and there acted as clerk in a warehouse for about seven months. He afterward returned to Cadiz, and has since been engaged in the grocery and liquor business. Mr. Jefferson was married on January 21, 1883, to Miss Corrie, daughter of Charles Baker, a son of one of the oldest settlers of Cadiz. This lady was born in Princeton.

L. LEWIS JOHNSON was born in Canton Precinct on April 23, 1860, and is a son of Levi L. and Mary (Vinson) Johnson. Subject is the sixth of seven children, of whom five are now living: Cyrus, in Lyon County; Alice, wife of J. M. Carr; Eliza, wife of Ricks Calhoun; Levi Lewis, and Cornelia, wife of Robert Randolph. The schools of the county furnished his education. He remained on the home farm until twenty-one. He then came to Cadiz, and engaged in the grocery business three years. Since then he has been engaged in farming; he is a member of Cadiz Lodge, No. 121, and in politics is a Republican.

GEORGE T. McCAIN was born November 25, 1852, in Trigg County; he is the third child of a family of five born to John A. and Caroline (Wharton) McCain; the former was born in North Carolina in 1816; he died in Graves County, Ky., in 1867; he had been engaged in merchandising since a boy, and was one of the oldest merchants of Wallonia; he was also largely engaged in the tobacco business; his mother was born in Paris, Tenn., in 1821; she died in 1860. The subject of this sketch, after attending school, entered his father's store as a clerk, where he remained till the death of his father. In the fall of 1876, he bought out T. W. Saffarans, who had been engaged in the grocery and liquor business in Cadiz; his stock amounted to about $1,200; since then this business has largely increased; he now carries a stock of about $4,000. Mr. McCain was married in 1878 to Miss Georgia Grinter, daughter of Thomas H. Grinter. She was born in Cadiz. Two children bless this union—one son and one daughter.

MAT McKINNEY, editor of the *Old Guard*. Samuel McKinney and Charlotte Walker Rowlette were both natives of the State of Virginia. The former was born in Charlotte County and the latter in Prince Edward. They were married in Halifax County in 1821. Mat McKinney, their son, subject of this sketch, was born near Appomattox Court House, the 26th day of December, 1825. He labored on a farm until he was a good stout boy, when he was placed in a mercantile establishment as salesman and book-keeper. His health giving way, his father required him to surrender his place in the house and seek employment in some other branch of industry. But little attention up to this time had been paid to his education, and feeling the necessity of a more intimate knowledge of books, desired first the advantages of a few years' schooling. His father being amply able to do so gave a ready and willing assent. He was consequently entered as a student in the male seminary at Cadiz, and afterward at Cumberland College, Princeton, Ky. He continued at school about two years, during which time he had pretty well mastered the Latin language, and made considerable progress in Greek and the higher branches of mathematics. Upon leaving school he commenced the study of law in Cadiz with Judge Collins D. Bradley. Remaining with him for the space of two years he was granted a law license, and commenced the practice. He de voted himself to the profession for about eighteen months, when a severe attack of hemorrhage of the lungs so discouraged him that he abandoned the pursuit of the profession forever. Soon after this resolution was taken we find him formally invested with the duties of an editor, which position he has occupied with occasional intermissions up to the present date. His paper has always been very popular with the masses, and his articles read with more than ordinary interest throughout the entire State. As a journalist, he was ever regarded as polite and conservative, but no one doubted his capacity in the use of harsh terms when the provocation was sufficient to justify them. He was a warm friend and admirer of George D. Prentice, and in turn very much beloved by him, and retains in his possession more than one invitation from him to take a position on the editorial staff of the old *Journal*. As a politician he is always firm, sometimes a little disorderly, but never fanatical, and would prefer to see the business interests of his town enhanced and the people of his county more prosperous and more happy than the success of all the parties and politicians in the world. He has never been an office-seeker, but was elected and served from 1861 to 1864 as Clerk of the County Court of Trigg County, and as a Representative in the Legislature from 1873 to 1877. He had at one time accumulated quite a handsome little fortune, the bulk of which he spent for negro property, and a few security debts relieved him of the residue. During his whole life it is said that he never refused a friend a favor when he was able to grant it. He is now poor, but, fortunately for himself, in society at least, his vivacity and cheerfulness have never forsaken him. He married Miss Jennie Bell Watson, a lady of great accomplishments and goodness, the 28th day of August, 1855. They have three children living: Mollie Walker, Charles Daniel and Jennie Watson. The elder daughter is married to Mr. G. B. Bingham, a most estimable young gentleman. The other two are still single. He is very proud of his wife, and has high expectations of his children. May the Great Dispenser of this world's pleasures grant him a full realization of all his hopes !

JOEL McKINNEY was born in Halifax County, Va., March 25, 1830. He is the fourth child of a family of eight born to Samuel and

Charlotte W. (Rowlette) McKinney. At about the age of three years he was brought with his parents to Kentucky. In 1837 his father, in company with Mr. Terry, engaged in merchandising in Wallonia, and later removed to Cadiz, where they continued this business several years. At about the age of seventeen Joel entered this store as a clerk, where he remained about eight years. In 1853 he removed to this farm, which consists of about 400 acres. This is one of the oldest farms in this county, and at one time was known as having the largest field of any farm between Canton and Hopkinsville. Mr. McKinney was married in 1872 to Miss Susan Crump. She was born in Trigg County. Six children have blessed this union—two sons and four daughters. Mr. and Mrs. McKinney are members of the Methodist Episcopal Church South.

R. W. MAJOR, Cadiz, was born January 13, 1842, in Trigg County. He is the second child of a family of eleven born to C. H. and Nancy (Wade) Major, both natives of Halifax County, Va. His father was born in 1817, and came to Trigg County in 1841; he first engaged in merchandising in Hopkinsville, where he continued about four years; he then removed to Trigg County and engaged in farming, continuing till 1875, at which time he moved to Canton, where he has since been engaged in the commission business. His mother died in 1849, aged thirty-two years. The subject of this sketch was reared on his father's farm, and afterward taught school; he enlisted in August, 1861, Company G, Fourth Kentucky Infantry; was mustered in Second Sergeant, and afterward promoted to Brevet Second Lieutenant, then Second Lieutenant, and later to First Lieutenant, and at the close of the war he had command of the company; he participated in the battle of Shiloh; was under fire at Vicksburg, battles of Baton Rouge, Murfreesboro, Jackson, Lookout Mountain, and all the battles to Dalton. There he was in command of the company, and the last to leave the field; his next engagement was the battle of Resaca; there he was wounded and was obliged to leave the field. In about forty days he returned to the army and took charge of the company; he then participated in the battles around Atlanta, and was wounded at Peach Tree Creek; also twice wounded at the battle of Jonesboro and then captured. After being out about twenty-five days he escaped and returned to his regiment, which was afterward mounted and sent to South Carolina. There they were engaged in a number of skirmishes. After the battle of Statesburg, on capitulated terms of surrender, they were paroled at Washington, Ga., and were the last troops that fired a gun east of the Chattahoochee. There they surrendered. He then returned to his father's farm, and soon after was appointed Deputy Sheriff, afterward twice elected Sheriff. Since this term of office expired he has been engaged in merchandising. He has held the office of Police Judge two terms. Is a member of the Masonic order and Chosen Friends. Mr. Major was married October 16, 1873, to Miss Emma Chappell. She was born in Trigg County. Four children bless this union—three sons and one daughter.

T. J. MITCHELL was born August 5, 1848, in Trigg County. He is a son of James and Martha (Alexander) Mitchell, who were also born in Trigg County. Mr. Mitchell, Sr., followed the cooper trade when young. T. J. took up this trade when a boy and still carries on this business; he is also operating a portable saw-mill and engaged in farming. In the fall of 1879 he removed to this farm, which he owns, consisting of 116 acres. Mr. Mitchell was married February 25, 1868, to Miss R. Bell Hawkins; she was born in Trigg County. Seven children have blessed this union—five sons and two daughters.

M. F. PETTY was born in February, 1822, in Morganfield, Union Co., Ky. He is the third child of a family of eight, born to George B. and Maria (Smith) Petty. They were natives of Virginia. The father of our subject learned the tailor trade when young; this business he carried on in Princeton, Caldwell County, until his death, which occurred in 1836. M. F. Petty was brought to Trigg County when a child, and has since lived on this farm which was settled by his grandfather Smith, and deeded to him by his Uncle William S. Smith, consisting of 300 acres. Mr. Petty was married in 1853 to Martha A. Gray. She was born in Trigg County. She died in October, 1854, aged twenty. Mr. Petty is a member of the Baptist church.

JAMES R. PREWETT was born October 7, 1854, in Caldwell County, Kentucky. He is the youngest of four children born to J. S. and Mary A. (Boyd) Prewett. The father was born in 1816, in Tennessee. He died January 12, 1855, in Caldwell County, Ky. The mother was born November 23, 1818, in Halifax County, Va. The family came to Trigg County, Ky., in 1838, remained twelve years, then returned to Caldwell County, Ky., where they lived until 1864, then returned to Trigg County and located on their present farm of 200 acres. Two of our subject's brothers now live in Texas, one of whom, John W., served eight months in the Confederate Army. The only sister, Mrs. Moseley, now lives in Christian County, Ky.

JOHN D. SHAW, Circuit Clerk, Cadiz, was born October 23, 1845, in Stewart County, Tenn; son of Capt. Thomas Shaw, one of the first men employed in running the Cumberland River; in later years he represented the State in the Legislature, and during the session he was taken sick and soon after its adjournment he died. The subject of our sketch received a common school education, and was first employed as clerk in a store, also in a warehouse; here he remained about two years; he then engaged a short time in merchandising in Henry County, Tenn., after which he came to Trigg County and engaged in farming. August, 1874, he was elected to his present position, and re-elected in 1880. He was married, in 1867, to Miss Ophelia, daughter of Jesse Wallis, and a native of Trigg County, Ky. This union has been blessed with four children—three sons and one daughter. Mr. Shaw is also Master Commissioner of the Circuit Court and Trustee of the Jury Fund of Trigg County. He is a member of the Masonic fraternity and Knights of Honor, and is Deputy Grand Master of Independent Order of Odd Fellows.

GEORGE J. SHOEMAKER was born November 30, 1813, in Adams County, Ohio, and is a son of Solomon and Nancy (Carr) Shoemaker; the former was born in Virginia, the latter in Ireland. Our subject was reared on his father's farm, where he remained till the age of twenty-one; he then removed to the Cumberland Iron Works; there worked five years. In 1839 he came to Trigg County, engaged in agricultural pursuits till 1878, when he was elected Jailor; he is now serving on his second term; he also held the office of Coroner four years. He was married, December 28, 1835, to Malinda Griffin, of Tennessee, Stewart County; she died in January, 1870, aged fifty-six; they had twelve children, seven living—three sons and four daughters. His second marriage was in November, 1870, to Eliza Pallomor, of Trigg County; four daughters bless this union.

JOHN L. STREET, merchant, Cadiz, was born July 7, 1818, in

Hanover County, Va.; son of the Hon. George Street, also a native of Virginia, and an early settler of this locality, coming to Trigg County in 1819, where he remained till his death, which occurred in 1831; he represented this county in the Legislature several terms. The subject of this sketch is the youngest child of a family of eight, he being the only remaining one living; he was raised on his father's farm, where he remained till the age of fifteen; after attending college in Illinois four years, in 1837 he came to Cadiz and was employed as clerk for John Hill two years; he then engaged in the tobacco business with his uncle, Spotswood Wilkinson, continuing this business till 1843 at which time he engaged in general merchandising, and which he has since continued, and is now the oldest merchant in Trigg County. On commencing business his sales amounted to about $30 a day; from this small beginning his business has increased to over three times this amount. Mr. Street has often acted as Town and School Trustee, and is a member of the Masonic fraternity. Since the age of twenty-one years he has been a member of the Christian Church, and is now the oldest male member of that denomination. Mr. Street has been twice married; his first union was blessed with three children—two sons and one daughter—his son, E. R. Street, being a partner in this business.

FRANK T. STREET was born in Trigg County, November 3, 1853. He is a son of John L. Street, the oldest merchant of Trigg County, and a resident of Cadiz. The subject of this sketch, at the age of sixteen, entered his father's store as a clerk; about six years later he was admitted as a partner; he continued a member of this firm about two and a half years. September 1, 1883, he bought a half interest in the Glenwood Mill and has since been engaged in this business. This mill is situated on Little River, and is the oldest mill site in the county. It was rebuilt in 1871, and is valued at about $10,000; it has a capacity of about fifty barrels in twenty-four hours. Mr. Street was married February 23, 1881, to Miss Gertrude Hart, who was born in Stewart County, Tenn., and raised in Memphis by her uncle, Capt. James Lee, one of the most successful men of Memphis. This union has been blessed with one child— James Lee. Mr. Street is a member of the Christian Church, and of the order of Chosen Friends.

J. E. SUMMERS was born September 24, 1828, in Christian County, Ky. He is the eldest child in a family of twelve born to William A. and Harriet A. (Anthony) Summers ; the father was born December 9, 1790, in Fairfax County, Va.; he came to Christian County in 1817 ; first engaged in teaching school. In 1829 he removed to his farm four miles west of Hopkinsville ; there he remained till his death which occurred April 27, 1857. The mother was born in August, 1809, in Sumner County, Tenn.; they were married November 22, 1827, in Montgomery County. The subject of this sketch was born on the farm now owned and occupied by his mother ; there he received his early education, and later attended school in Hopkinsville two terms. In 1854 he removed to Texas ; there engaged in farming. In 1857 he was called home on account of his father's death, and superintended this farm five years at a salary of $1,000 a year. During this time, by his judicious management, he made and divided out to the legatees of the estate $21,000. This farm contained about 500 acres improved, and gave employment to about sixteen hands ; this was considered one of the best farms in Christian County. In 1862 he commenced on his own account on a farm of 375 acres ; he later purchased other lands, making in all 750 acres. There he remained five years. In 1867 he sold part of his land and returned to his mother's farm, which he again took charge of, and where he remained four years. January, 1871, he removed to Cadiz, where he has since resided ; he now owns and occupies the residence formerly owned by the late Matthew Mayes, also a farm of 700 acres adjoining the corporation. Mr. Summers was married October 22, 1861, to Corinne Farley. She was born in Virginia ; she died April 4, 1866, aged twenty-five. Two daughters and one son blessed this union. His second marriage took place September 26, 1870, to Miss Mattie, daughter of J. F. Gill of Logan County, Ky. The result of this union is three children—one son and two daughters. Mr. and Mrs. Summers are life-long and devoted members of the Methodist Episcopal Church South.

F. G. TERRY was born in Christian County, Ky., April 28, 1838. He is the fifth of nine children born to Abner R. and Eleanor (Dyer) Terry, natives of Virginia. In 1839 his father engaged in merchandising at Wallonia, where he remained until 1844. He then came to Cadiz and continued in business here until his death, which occurred in 1847, aged forty. The subject of this sketch came to Cadiz with his parents when he was six years old. His education was received in the schools of this town. When fifteen he went to Princeton, where he sold goods for about six months. He then attended the naval school at Annapolis, Md., where he remained two years; he then went to Washington, D. C., and received the appointment of Clerk in the Third Auditor's office. This position he held until the breaking out of the war, when he returned to Cadiz. Soon after his arrival here he enlisted in Company G, of the Eighth Regiment, Kentucky Volunteer Infantry, C. S. A. Went out as Third Lieutenant, and in the fall of 1862 was elected Captain of company. He held this position until May, 1865, when he was paroled with his company. Among the battles in which he participated might be mentioned Fort Donelson, first siege of Vicksburg, Baton Rouge, Baker's Creek, Jackson, Miss., Guntown, Tupelo, Franklin, Tenn., and in all the engagements from that point on to the retreat of Hood's army to the Tennessee River. He then returned to Cadiz, opened a drug store, and has been engaged in this business ever since. Mr. Terry was married in 1868 to Miss Dannie, a daughter of Judge A. B. Dyer. This lady is a native of this county, and is the mother of two daughters. Among the offices which our subject has held are those of Town Trustee and Trustee of High School, which office he has held since the organization. Is a member of the Methodist Episcopal Church South, and of the K. of H. fraternity.

J. J. THOMAS was born March 19, 1833, in Trigg County; he is a son of Starkey Thomas, now deceased, whose sketch appears elsewhere in this volume. February, 1857, he settled on his present farm, which was deeded him by his father, consisting of 300 acres. Mr. Thomas was married in July, 1856, to Mary Cunningham; she was born in this county; this marriage has been blessed with nine children—six sons and three daughters.

ALFRED THOMAS was born April 29, 1835, in Trigg County; he is a son of Starkey Thomas, who died September 14, 1881, in his eighty-third year. Our subject was raised on his father's farm, where he remained till about the age of twenty-two; he then came to this land, which was deeded to him by his father, consisting of 248 acres; he now owns in all 1,600 acres, which are included in six farms; he also owns one house and lot in Cadiz; he employs about sixteen hands and is largely engaged in live stock. Mr. Thomas is one of the largest and most successful farmers in this county; he handles large quantities of tobacco and is the administrator of several estates, having served in this capacity the past eight years; he was married in 1863 to Eliza Martin; she was born in Trigg County; they have a family of four children—one son and three daughters.

F. M. THOMAS was born August 5, 1839, in Trigg County; he is the seventh child of a family of eleven born to Starkey and Mary (Bridges) Thomas; the former was born in North Carolina June 29, 1799; he died September 14, 1881; the latter was born in North Carolina, July 25, 1807, and now lives with her son Starkey at their old homestead. About 1806 the father of our subject was brought with his parents to Trigg County, where he remained till his death. They first settled on Donaldson Creek; there the family was reared. At about the age of twenty-three, F. M. Thomas settled on his present land, which was deeded him by his father, consisting of 400 acres. His father had owned over 2,000 acres; before his death it was divided among his children; he was married December 21, 1876, to Mary F. Rogers; she was born January 25, 1862, in Trigg County; four children have blessed this union—three sons and one daughter.

MOSES S. THOMPSON was born April 5, 1849, in Trigg County; he is the youngest child of a family of seven born to Moses and Clarissa H. (Smith) Thompson, who were both natives of Virginia. His mother was born in 1813, and when a child came to Trigg County with her parents, all coming here on horseback. They settled on a farm about three miles from Cadiz, where she has since lived. His father was born in 1807; he died March 16, 1884. When a boy he was apprenticed to the tanner's trade, and this business he followed through life; also engaged in agricultural pursuits. He owned previous to the war from thirty to forty slaves. Moses S. was reared on his father's farm. After receiving a common school education, at the age of fourteen he attended Asbury University, Indiana, and later the Georgetown College, Georgetown, Ky. After graduating at Eastman's Business College, Poughkeepsie, N. Y., he returned to Cadiz, and at the age of nineteen he engaged in merchandising on his own account. Commencing with a stock of about $3,500, he has since been continually in business here, doing a large and prosperous trade, carrying a stock of about $12,000. He occupies one of the finest store-rooms in Cadiz, located in the Hotel Block. This store is 23x90 feet, and well lighted from front and rear. Mr. Thompson was married in 1873 to Miss Nannie, daughter of Thomas H. Grinter. She was born in Cadiz. Five children gladden their home—three sons and two daughters.

THOMAS K. TORIAN was born January 31, 1845, in Cadiz, Ky., and is a son of George L. and E. E. (McCarty) Torian, who were natives of Halifax County, Va. His parents emigrated to this county in an early day; here the father kept hotel. After living here some time he moved to Christian County, and there settled on a farm. After residing there a few years, he sold out his farm and moved to Wallonia. There he bought a farm, but lived on it only about one year; he then returned to Cadiz. In 1869 he removed to Paducah, Ky., and there engaged in the tobacco business three years. In 1872 he returned to Cadiz and engaged in farming, but is at present living a retired life. Prior to the war Mr. Torian, Sr., was a large slave owner. Thomas K. has during the most of his life had charge of the farm which he has conducted for his father. In the spring of 1883, he opened a livery stable at Cadiz, and is at present still engaged in the business.

JESSE WALLIS was born January 7, 1813, in South Carolina. He is the son of James and Winnie (Jones) Wallis. The former was born October 10, 1786, in South Carolina; he died November 3, 1855. The latter was born August 19, 1791, also in South Carolina; she died December 17, 1855. The father of our subject learned the blacksmith trade when a boy; this he followed during life. Jesse remained with his father till the age of twenty-seven, also working at this trade. When they came to Cadiz his father opened a shop. Here he worked six years. In 1841 he went to Canton, there opened a shop and carried on this trade thirty-one years. While in Canton he was elected Town Marshal, and held the office two years. In 1882 he returned to Cadiz, and opened a confectionery and notion store, which he still continues. He was married in 1840, to Lucinda A. Moore. She was born in North Carolina; had six children, two living—one son and one daughter. On first coming to Cadiz, he was elected Captain of a military company which was formed here, and held that office as long as musters were kept up.

JESSE T. WALLIS was born July 26, 1816, in Trigg County. He is a son of William, Sr. and Ellen (Young) Wallis. They were born in South Carolina. His father followed school teaching, this being his principal occupation; he died in 1856, aged seventy. Our subject received his first schooling from Smith Martin, then from his father, and later from James B. Wallis. At the age of twenty-two he was placed as overseer for Beverly Dillard. · After remaining one year he bought a farm of 200 acres, where he remained about eight years, after which he removed to his present farm, consisting of 200 acres, where he has since lived. He was married, in 1846, to Mary E. Harris. She was born in Virginia, and partly reared in Christian County. This marriage has been blessed with eight children—three sons and five daughters: George, now living in Graves County, Ky., engaged in farming; Miner H. is a clerk in Little Rock; their youngest son, Charles is at home assisting on the farm.

C. H. WALLIS was born July 3, 1827, in Trigg County, about three miles south of Cadiz. He is the eldest of nine children born to William and Elizabeth (Wallis) Wallis. The father was born in South' Carolina, February 2, 1802. He came to Trigg County, in 1824, and now lives on the farm where he first settled. The mother was born April 30, 1809, in Trigg County. She died in 1849, and was buried on their farm. Our subject was brought up on his father's farm. There he remained till the age of twenty, when he removed to the Cumberland River; there he worked at the carpenter's trade about five years. In 1852, he went to Christian County, where he was overseer of a planta- tion about ten years. He then returned to Trigg County, and worked about three and one-half years in a still-house. In 1865, he removed to his present locality, and opened a wheel-wright shop, and has since been engaged at this business; he has also been toll-keeper at this point since coming here. Mr. Wallis was married in 1847, to Caroline Stokes. She was born in Tennessee; she died in 1877, aged forty-seven. They had a family of fourteen children, seven of whom are now living. Mr. Wallis is a member of the Masonic fraternity, and of the Methodist Epis- copal Church.

PROF. H. B. WAYLAND, Cadiz, was born July 18, 1820, in Mercer County, Ky. He is the only child of James and Fannie

(Burrus) Wayland. His father was born in 1795, in Madison County, Va. He died October, 1820. His mother died July 1, 1875. Our subject was reared by his grandfather, Nathaniel Burrus, who participated in the siege of Yorktown in 1781. He removed to Kentucky in 1785, and that year was married to Miss Mary Thelkeld. They lived together until her death, which occurred in 1853, making the remarkable length of their marriage sixty-eight years. Two years later Mr. Burrus died, aged ninety-two years ; our subject received a common school education, and later attended the South Hanover College ; there he graduated. After teaching school one year, he took up the study of law, also practiced a short time. In 1847 he resumed teaching and has since been engaged in this profession. His first teaching was under the direction of Trustees. The past ten years he has taught on his own premises, he having built a school-house on his own grounds and at his own expense. He owns seventy acres of land where he resides ; this he has improved with a very comfortable residence and out-buildings. These improvements cost, including the school-house, about $9,000. Mr. W. has taught in all thirty-six years, which exceeds all others in this county. He has taught twenty-four years where he now resides, and what is remarkable, there have been in this length of time twenty-four different teachers here, not connected with his school. Prof. Wayland was married in May, 1847, to Jacobina Stuart Drummond. She was born in Scotland ; she died October 30, 1883. Mrs. Wayland had charge of the musical department, and in 1863–64 taught as high as twenty-seven scholars at a time. Prof. H. B. Wayland is now Principal of the Cadiz High School. He is a member and Deacon of the Baptist Church. He has been for seventeen years successively, Clerk for the Little River Association.

GEORGE S. WHARTON was born in Trigg County, two miles east of Cadiz, April 22, 1828. He is the youngest child of a family of five, born to John and Eliza (Smith) Wharton. His father was born September 21, 1784, in Fauquier County, Va., he died on this farm May 1, 1872 ; he settled here in 1817, having bought about 700 acres land. At that time there was little or no timber in the country, that which is here now having grown since the coming of Mr. Wharton to this locality ; the timber used for the frame of their residence, which was built in 1854, was grown on this land. Deer, turkey and other wild game were in abundance, but have long since disappeared. Mr. Wharton was married November 5, 1867, to Miss Sallie, daughter of James E. Thompson, who, until the adoption of the new Constitution, long held the office of Circuit and County Clerk of Trigg County; he died October 5, 1881, aged seventy-six; their union has been blessed with five children—four sons and one daughter.

JOHN F. WHITE was born in Mecklenburg County, Va., on November 3, 1816, and is a son of Samuel B. and Nancy (Hester) White. When he was two years old his parents came to Montgomery County, Tenn., where they settled. In 1830 the parents came to Christian County and settled in Lafayette Precinct. There the father resided until his death in 1863. The mother died in 1834. John F. came to Trigg County in 1837, and settled on his present farm. He first purchased 150 acres, which he afterward increased to about 2,500. A portion of this has since been divided among his children. Starting with but little, Mr. White has, by his own endeavors, amassed one of the largest estates in the county. He began dealing in tobacco, buying and rehandling, about thirty-five years ago, and is to-day one of the most extensive buyers in the county. He has recently associated his son W. C., with him in this business, and the firm is now running a number of warehouses, one being located at Cadiz, another at Canton, another at Lamasco, and a fourth at Highland, Calloway County. When sixteen years old Mr. White joined the Methodist Church, and was licensed to preach. In 1841 he joined the Baptist Church, and has since then served faithfully as pastor at the Rocky Ridge Church. He has been thrice married, the first time being in Trigg County, in 1835, to Miss Susan Wharton, a daughter of John and Eliza Wharton. She was a native of Virginia, and to her were born five children—two sons and three daughters. This lady died in 1855. Mr. White was next married in Stewart County, Tenn., in December, 1858, to Miss Isabella Tate, of Lafayette, Christian County. She was the mother of three sons and one daughter, and her death occurred November 2, 1870. Mr. White's third marriage took place September 12, 1883, to Miss Cordelia Hanberry, a daughter of Thomas Hanberry, of Hopkinsville.

ROBERT WILFORD was born October 3, 1823, in Trigg County; he is the oldest child of Bennett and Sarah (Randolph) Wilford, the former was born in North Carolina, the latter in Tennessee. In about 1815 his father came to Trigg County, settled on a farm; here our subject was born and reared; at the age of twenty-one he was placed as overseer on the farm of Albert G. Dabney, where he remained one year; he then returned to his father's farm, where he remained two years; he then bought a farm of eighty acres, where he lived thirteen years; in 1865 he removed to Cadiz, where he has since resided and largely engaged in agricultural pursuits. His farm consists of 965 acres, adjoining the corporation, and is one of the best improved in the county. Ten hands are constantly employed on this farm. In 1870, he with his brother bought the Cadiz Mill; this they re-built at a cost of about $12,000. This mill has a capacity of about 150 bushels of wheat a day. Mr. Wilford had previously owned a mill at Little River, four miles east of Cadiz. He has owned as high as 3,500 acres of land; he now owns in all about 1,500 acres, and is one of the largest tax-payers in the county. He was married February 1, 1849, to Nancy, daughter of Cornelius Manning, who was born in 1774, in North Carolina; he died in Trigg County, in September, 1855. Her mother was born in 1778, in North Carolina; she died in Trigg County, in 1857.

W. W. WILSON was born May 13, 1860, in Trigg County. He is the eldest child of a family of seven, born to William A. and Cynthia (Young) Wilson; the former was born in August, 1832, near Kent's Bridge, Trigg County; he died April 15, 1878. The latter was born in Trigg County, in 1841; she died November 4, 1881. They owned at the time of their death about 900 acres; the subject of this sketch owns the homestead with 160 acres, and employs about seven hands and four teams on this farm.

A. T. WIMBERLY, editor, was born in Trigg County, September 1, 1847, son of Alfred and Maria (Savells) Wimberly. The former was born in North Carolina, the latter in Virginia. In about 1813 they were brought to this county with their parents. The father was engaged in agricultural pursuits; he died in 1873, aged seventy-three; the mother now lives with her son, the subject of this sketch, who was brought up on his father's farm; there remained till about the age of nineteen, then came to Cadiz; was clerk for Ragon & Baker about one year; then removed to Murray, Ky.; remained there one year, then returned and engaged in school teaching at Canton, where he remained about two years; then came to Cadiz and taught school one term. He held the office of Justice of Peace, and during this time took up the study of law; his father having died in the meantime he gave up the study of law and returned to teaching in Wallonia; there taught four years. In January, 1872, returned to Cadiz and at once established the *Kentucky Telephone*, and since has been identified with the paper. He married, May 4, 1882, Miss Lula Grasty, of Lyon County. One daughter blesses this marriage.

CANTON PRECINCT.

W. T. CUNNINGHAM was born in Rock Castle Precinct on March 30, 1838, and is a son of William and Virginia (Mitchell) Cunningham. Subject is the third of nine children, of whom eight are living. He remained at home until eighteen, then commenced life for himself, and settled down on a farm of 180 acres in that precinct. He resided there until 1868, when he came to Canton Precinct, and settled at the mouth of Little River. In December, 1883, he came to his present farm, where he now owns 200 acres. Subject was married, in 1868, to Miss Mattie Cameron, a daughter of John and Frances (Daniel) Cameron. Mrs. Cunningham was born in this county, and is the mother of five children—two sons and three daughters. Mr. Cunningham was a soldier in the late war, having enlisted in Company C, of the First Tennessee Cavalry, in the fall of 1861; remained in service three years; was taken prisoner at Gallatin, and was confined on Johnson's Island for seven months.

E. A. CUNNINGHAM was born in Rock Castle Precinct May 12, 1843, and is a son of William and Virginia (Mitchell) Cunningham. The father was born in Halifax County, Va., in 1800, and came to this county in 1817 with his father, William Cunningham. He made his home in this county until his death in the fall of 1880. E. A. Cunningham is the sixth of nine children, of whom eight are now living. He remained at home until he was of age, and then settled in the Canton Precinct, where he remained two years. He then moved to Cadiz Precinct; resided there five years, and afterward farmed in Rock Castle Precinct for eight years. In the fall of 1880, he came to his present farm, where he now owns about 300 acres. He devotes his attention mainly to tobacco growing. Mr. Cunningham was married in 1866 to Miss Margaret Hendrick, a daughter of George Hendrick. This lady was the mother of five sons, and died in January, 1877. In May following he was married to Miss Bettie Stalons, a daughter of Reuben Stalons of Cadiz Precinct. Two daughters bless this union. Mrs.

Cunningham died in February, 1881, and Mr. Cunningham was next married in April, 1881, to Miss Susan F. Robenson, a daughter of Charles Robenson, of Lyon County. One child blesses this union. Mr. and Mrs. Cunningham are members of the Baptist Church. Mr. Cunningham was a soldier in the Rebellion, having enlisted in Company G, of the Fourth Kentucky Regiment, Confederate States of America, on August 22, 1861. He served until May 22, 1865. He was a non-commissioned officer. Among the battles in which he participated might be mentioned Baton Rouge, Chickamauga, Dalton, Ga., and many others. He was shot through the knee at the battle of Chickamauga.

J. A. FOUTCH was born what is now De Kalb County (then Smith County) Tenn., on February 17, 1830, and is a son of William and Sallie (Welch) Foutch. The parents were both natives of North Carolina. Subject was next to the youngest of a family of six children. He remained at home until twenty-one, and then settled down in his native county. In 1860 he moved to Putnam County, Tenn. He remained there only one year, and then returned to his native county. In 1865 he came to Trigg County, and settled on his present farm. He now owns ninety-nine acres. Mr. Foutch was married, in 1852, to Miss Sarah Washer, a daughter of John and Frankie (Young) Washer. This lady was born in Smith County, Tenn., and was the mother of four (living) children—one son and three daughters. She died in October, 1880. Mr. Foutch was next married April 4, 1881, to Mrs. E. J. Wallace (*nee* Gresham), a daughter of James and Betsey (Dunn) Gresham, natives of this county. Mr. Foutch is a member of the Baptist Church. Mrs. Foutch of the Methodist. Mr. Foutch is a member of Canton Lodge, No. 242. Subject was a soldier in the late war, having enlisted in November, 1861, in Gordon's Battalion, Confederate States of America. He was taken prisoner in June, 1863, while on a furlough at home and subsequently confined at Louisville, Camp Chase and Fort Delaware. He remained in prison until February, 1865.

ANDREW C. HARRIS was born in this county on August 22, 1854, and is a son of James and Lurania (Cromwell) Harris; the parents are natives of Tennessee, came to this county about 1854, and are still living. Andrew C. is the fourth of nine children, of whom six are now living; he remained at home until 1881, helping his father, who is disabled; he then came to his present farm, where he now owns 109 acres; he pays especial attention to stock-raising, handling from twenty to thirty head of cattle per year. Mr. Harris was married on January 5, 1881, to Miss Queen V. Peal, a daughter of Bayley and Frances (Prescott) Peal. Two daughters—Effie May and Arminda—bless this union. Mr. and Mrs. Harris are members of the Mt. Pleasant Baptist Church.

JAMES A. HOLLAND was born in Golden Pond Precinct June 7, 1848, and is a son of William and Mary (Jones) Holland; the father was also a native of this county, his grandfather, Basil Holland, having come to this county from North Carolina as early as 1805. The mother was also born in this county, and her people were immigrants from South Carolina. When subject was about a year old his parents came to this precinct, and here the father died in 1882; the mother is still living. Subject is the oldest of four children; he remained at home until twenty-one, and then went to Missouri, where he remained two years; he next returned to this county and engaged in carpentering. In 1879 he went to Cerulean Springs, where he learned the trade of blacksmith and wagon-maker; he remained there two years, and then came to this county; here he has since followed his trade; he also does something in farming. He was married in 1870 to Miss Margaret Holland, a daughter of Whitmel Holland. This marriage has resulted in five children, two of whom are living: Pearlie M. and Julia A. Mr. Holland and wife are members of the Baptist Church. He has been identified with the Good Templar organization.

JOSHUA HOPSON, deceased, was born in Halifax County, Va., on January 5, 1812, and was a son of Morgan and Nancy J. (Boyd) Hopson. The father was a son of Joseph Hopson, and was also born in Virginia; he read law in that State and practiced some. In 1813 he came to Christian County and settled near Garrettsburg. There Joseph Hopson died. The father represented Christian County in the Legislature in 1816–17. In 1831 he came to what is now Trigg County, and settled in Canton Precinct; here he resided until his death, in 1858. Our subject remained at home until he became of age and then settled down in the Canton Precinct, about three miles from the town. There he resided until 1848, and then moved to within a mile of Canton. In 1853 he removed to Golden Pond Precinct, and resided there until 1865; he then moved back to Canton Precinct and remained there until his death on March 18, 1877.   He was one of the most extensive farmers in the county, and at one time owned about 2,500 acres, which he divided among his children prior to his death.   In 1855 he began to run a ferry across Cumberland River at Canton.   At first he owned only a half interest, but afterward purchased the whole; his widow still has charge of the ferry.   Mr. Hopson was married in 1832 to Miss Leah Wade, a daughter of Hampton and Jane (Simmons) Wade, natives of Virginia. This lady was born in Virginia, and was the mother of six children, three dead and three living—two sons and a daughter.   She died in 1846, and Mr. Hopson was next married to Miss Mira Moore, a daughter of Jefferson and Mary (Dulin) Moore, natives of Virginia and early settlers of Christian County.   Mrs. Hopson was born in Christian County, and is the mother of four living children—one son and three daughters.   Mrs. Hopson is a member of the Canton Christian Church, as was also Mr. Hopson prior to his death.

MORGAN HOPSON was born in this county October 29, 1833, and is a son of Joshua and Leah (Wade) Hopson.   Subject is the eldest of six children, of whom three are now living.   He remained at home until the age of sixteen, and then clerked in a store at Canton for about two years; he next went to Garrettsburg, and clerked one year.   In 1853 he moved to Mississippi, and there he engaged in agricultural pursuits until 1864; he then returned to Trigg County, and settled on his present farm.   He first inherited 800 acres, and at present owns about 2,500 acres in this county, and 1,000 acres in Mississippi.   Of the whole there are about 1,600 acres in cultivation.   He pays considerable attention to stock-raising and trading.   Mr. Hopson was married in Mississippi, January 14, 1858, to Miss Virginia L. Allen, a daughter of David B. Allen.   Mrs. Hopson was born in Mississippi, and is the mother of ten living children—five sons and five daughters.   Mr. Hopson and family are members of the Baptist Church; he is a member of the Knights of Honor.

THOMAS N. INGRAM was born in Hickman County, Tenn., on March 11, 1815, and is a son of Thomas and Susannah (Gee) Ingram. The parents were natives of Virginia, and came to Tennessee in an early day.   The father was a soldier in the war of 1812, and was among the soldiers sent to New Orleans to meet Gen. Pakenham; while there he was taken sick and died. The mother died in Hickman County, in 1828. Thomas N. is the youngest of four children. His earlier education was received in Carroll County. In 1832 he went to Mississippi, and remained in the State two years clerking and farming. In January, 1835, he returned to Kentucky and settled in Calloway County. There he engaged in merchandising until 1839, when he came to Canton. Here he first sold goods in the building now occupied by W. C. Major as a hotel. He engaged in this business three years, and then bought a farm, which he ran four years. He was then elected Constable, and served in that capacity eight years; he afterward engaged in driving horses and mules to the South for some time. In 1874 he was elected Magistrate, and is still holding that office. Mr. Ingram was married in Calloway County, in 1838, to Miss Nancy J. Martin, a daughter of James Martin. Mrs. Ingram was born in Hopkins County, Ky., and is the mother of ten children, four of whom are now living—two sons and two daughters. He has been Secretary of Canton Lodge, No. 242, A. F. & A. M., since 1854. In 1857 he and Mr. Young Linn edited a paper at Canton, called the *Canton Dispatch*. This paper continued in circulation for about one year, and was well patronized. In 1859 he and his son, J. T. Ingram, one of the firm of J. S. Spiceland & Co., who were publishing the *Southern Yeoman* in Canton at that time, bought the interest of J. S. Spiceland, and published the *Southern Yeoman* until the fall of 1860; sold a half interest to C. C. Coulter, and moved the publication place to the city of Mayfield, where they continued the publication until 1861, when it was suspended on account of the ravages of the war.

DR. GEORGE H. JEFFERSON was born in Cadiz, Trigg Co., Ky., on August 31, 1831, and is a son of Dr. Thomas B. and Martha A. (Graves) Jefferson. Subject was the second of a family of eight children, of whom six are living. His education was received in Cadiz. When sixteen years of age he commenced reading medicine with his father, and attended lectures at Louisville in 1851 and 1852. Returning to Cadiz he entered into partnership with his father, and remained with him three years. He then came to Canton, where he has had a very extensive practice. He owns about 800 acres, and has farming carried on for him. Dr. Jefferson was married, October 18, 1855, to Miss Nancy J. Hopson, a daughter of Joshua and Leah (Wade) Hopson. Mrs. Jefferson was born in this county, in 1838, and is the mother of eleven children, of whom six are now living. Subject has been identified with the Canton Masonic Lodge. Is a member of the Trigg County Medical Society, and has served as President of that organization one year.

LEVI L. JOHNSON was born in Linton Precinct January 13, 1828, and is a son of Wiley and Margaret (Craig) Johnson. The father was also born in this county; his father, Randle Johnson, having come here from South Carolina at a very early day. The latter died here in about 1842. Mr. Wiley Johnson died in 1834 when subject was but six years old. The mother died in 1879. Subject was the second of a family of five children, of whom four are now living. At the age of thirteen he was apprenticed to Mr. C. B. Senseney, at Linton, to learn the tanner's trade. Remained with him about four and a half years. He then came home and resided with his mother until 1847. In that year he came to his present farm, where he built a tan-yard. This he ran until about 1875 when he was compelled to give it up; he also has paid some attention to farming, and now owns about 500 acres. Mr. Johnson was married in January, 1849, to Miss Mary Vinson, a daughter of Ezekiel and Mary (Wallace) Vinson, natives of South Carolina. Mrs. Johnson was born in this county and was the mother of seven children, of whom five are now living—two sons and three daughters. This lady died November 23, 1881, and subject was next married November 30, 1882, to Miss Georgia McEntyre, a daughter of Henry and Jane (Middleton) McEntyre. She is a native of this county and the mother of one child. Subject is a member of Cruson Council, No. 5, Chosen Friends. Before the war he was identified with the Whig party; since then he has given his support to the Republicans.

DR. J. H. LACKEY was born in Logan County, Ky., May 26, 1838, and is the son of Edward A. W. and Lucy (Cash) Lackey. The father was a native of Bedford County, Va., the mother of Amherst County. Both are still living in Canton. Subject is the oldest of nine children; his education was received in the schools of Logan County. In 1868 he began reading medicine with his uncle, Dr. T. J. Lackey, of Logan County. After three years' study he attended the Louisville Medical College, also the Cincinnati Medical College, graduating from the latter institution in the class of 1874. He began practicing in Logan

County, but came to Canton in 1871. Here he first clerked in Mr. Fuqua's drug store, but afterward turned his attention to the practice of his profession, and he has since been engaged in it. In 1882 he attended another course of lectures at Louisville. He is a member of the County Medical Society. Dr. Lackey was married in 1873 to Miss Mollie Major, a daughter of C. H. and Mary Jane (Clark) Major. Mrs. Lackey is a native of this county, and is the mother of five living children—three sons and two daughters. Subject is a member of Methodist Episcopal Church South ; also of Canton Lodge, No. 242, A. F. & A. M., and Cruson Council, Chosen Friends, No. 5. In politics is a Democrat.

F. M. McATEE was born in Logan County, Ky., December 30, 1833, and is a son of Charles M. and Mary (Brashear) McAtee. The father was a native of Kentucky, the mother of Maryland. The father died in this county in 1860, the mother in 1861. F. M. is the second of seven children. He remained at home until twenty-one, then commenced farming for himself; he has resided on several farms in this and Christian County. In 1881 he came to his present place; he also pays some attention to stock-raising. Mr. McAtee was married, in this county, in 1858, to Miss Margaret Francis, a daughter of James and Ann (Gore) Francis. Eight children have blessed this union, of whom five are now living—four sons and one daughter. Mrs. McAtee is a member of the Christian Church.

C. H. MAJOR, SR., was born in Madison County, Va., on September 17, 1817, and is a son of Charles and Mary (Sims) Major. The parents were of Welsh descent. Subject was next to the youngest of a family of nine children, and of this number only two are now living: James, in Missouri, and C. H. When the latter was nine years old the father came to Kentucky, and settled in Christian County eight miles southeast of Hopkinsville. There he resided until his death in 1857. The mother died in 1820. Subject remained at home until eighteen, and then commenced life as a clerk in Hopkinsville. At the end of five years he began merchandising for himself, and was engaged in this business five years. In 1841 he came to Trigg County and began farming, settling on the Cadiz pike. He owned about 1,000 acres, of which 450 acres were in cultivation. In 1873 he lost one of his limbs by falling on a mowing-machine, and in 1879 he sold his farm and came to Canton. Here he opened a commission house. He buys and rehandles tobacco, and also acts as forwarding agent for freight. Mr. Major was married in 1839 to Miss Nancy J. Wade, a daughter of Hampton and Jane (Simmons) Wade, natives of Halifax County, Va. This lady was born in Virginia, and came to this county in 1818 with her parents. To her husband were born three sons, all of whom are now living. Her death occurred in 1848. In Christian County, in 1849, Mr. Major was married to his second wife, Miss Mary J. Clark, a daughter of Thomas P. and Eleanor (Rawlins) Clark, natives of Maryland and Virginia. Mrs. Major was born in Christian County, and is the mother of eight children—five sons and three daughters. Mr. Major and family are members of the Baptist Church. He is also a member of the Grange fraternity. Previous to the war he was an old-time Whig; since that time he has been identified with the Democratic party.

MAJOR NOEL was born in this precinct on September 27, 1839, and is a son of Thomas and Nancy (Dew) Noel. The parents were natives of Virginia, and came to this county in about 1810. The father is still living; the mother died in 1880. Subject was the eldest of three children. The commom schools of this precinct and Russellville College furnished his education. In 1858 he went to Marshall County, and clerked in a grocery store for about twelve months. He then went to Hickman County, and taught school, after which he returned to Trigg County and settled on his present farm. He now owns about 300 acres, 175 acres of which are in cultivation. He also pays some attention to stock-raising. Mr. Noel was married in 1859 to Miss Helen Cunningham, a daughter of James and Sallie (Wimberly) Cunningham, of this county. Mrs. Noel was born in this county, and is the mother of eight children—six sons and two daughters. Mrs. Noel is a member of the Mount Pleasant Baptist Church.

EDMUND ROSS was born in Laura Furnace Precinct February 3, 1839, and is a son of Jonathan and Narcissa (Stubblefield) Ross. The parents were natives of Henry County, Tenn., and came to this county in an early day. The mother died in 1862. The father afterward came to this precinct, and resided here until his death in February, 1884. Subject is the third of eight children, of whom four are now living. He assisted on the home farm until the age of twenty-one, and then began farming for himself in Laura Furnace Precinct. He remained in that precinct nine years, and then came to his present farm, where he now owns about 500 acres, with 200 acres in cultivation. In April, 1878, he began merchandising, and continued in business for five years. For the past ten years he has been extensively engaged in buying and rehandling tobacco. In 1877 he put up a saw and grist-mill, which is still in operation. Was married in 1861 to Miss Tempie Feutrell, a daughter of Perry Feutrell. Fifteen children have blessed this union, of whom six are still living, all daughters.

PEYTON THOMAS was born in this precinct April 6, 1820, and is a son of Cullen and Elizabeth (Feutrell) Thomas. The father was born in Bertie County, N. C., in 1790, and came to this county with his father, James Thomas, in 1805. The grandfather settled on the farm now occupied by Peyton Thomas, where he died in September, 1832. The father grew to manhood here, and settled on a farm to the south of his father. He first inherited seventy-five acres, and by his own exertions finally increased it to 1,000 acres; he was Magistrate of the county for a number of years under the old Constitution, and held the office of Sheriff for two years by seniority. His death occurred June 8, 1862, the mother's in 1844. Subject was the second of six children, and is the only one now living; he worked on the home farm until twenty-one, and then came to his present farm; he now owns about 400 acres, of which 100 acres are in cultivation. At the age of eighteen he began black-smithing, and worked at the trade himself for a number of years. Afterward hired hands and had the business carried on. In 1855 he sold goods for one year, and in 1858 he commenced merchandising again, engaging in it until 1862. In April, 1883, he opened his present store, and now carries a stock of about $1,500. In 1865 he began to keep the county poor, and with the exception of seven years he had charge of them up until December, 1883. Mr. Thomas was married December 2, 1841, to Miss Sallie Ethridge, a daughter of David T. Ethridge, of Davidson County, Tenn. Mrs. Thomas was born in the same county, and is the mother of ten children. Of this number nine are now living—four sons and five daughters. Subject and family are members of the Baptist Church, and he has held the office of Church Clerk for many years; he was Magistrate of the county for twelve years. From 1858 to 1860 he was

Postmaster at Donelson Postoffice; he is a member of Canton Lodge, No. 242, A. F. & A. M.   Peyton Thomas had one married sister, who gave birth to two children and then died of consumption ; his mother died in 1844, and about a year later his father married Drusilla Carter, who bore him two children, who died within four years.   James Thomas, brother of our subject, served through the Mexican war.   He was subsequently elected Major of the Kentucky State Militia, and then ranked as Colonel of Trigg County.   He once ran for the Legislature on the Whig ticket, but was defeated through the machinations of the Sons of Temperance.   An incident rather unusual occurred in the deaths of James Thomas (brother of subject) and his father, Cullen Thomas, which occurred respectively at ten minutes past 12 o'clock P. M., June 8, 1881, and June 8, 1882.

WILLIAM F. TURNER was born in Dixon County, Tenn., on September 19, 1819, and is a son of William and Nancy (Hyde) Turner. The father was born in Baltimore, Md., the mother near Nashville, Tenn. In 1833 the parents came to this county, and first settled in Canton Precinct, where they lived thirty years, and then moved to Bethesda Precinct, where the father died in 1864.   The mother died in 1865.   Subject was the third of five children, of whom three are now living ; he commenced life for himself when twenty-five years old, and settled in Canton Precinct.   At the breaking out of the war he moved to Stewart County, Tenn., and there resided twelve years ; he then moved to Linton Precinct, this county, and in the fall of 1883 came to his present farm, where he now owns 162 acres.   Mr. Turner was married in 1843 to Miss Elizabeth Carr, a daughter of John Carr.   Mrs. Turner was born in this county, and is the mother of eleven children.   Of this number four sons and three daughters are living.

QUINTUS M. TYLER was born in Caroline County, Va., August 6, 1816, and is a son of John D. and Harriet (Redd) Tyler.   The parents were natives of Virginia, and were of English descent.   In the fall of 1818 they came to Montgomery County, Tenn.   There the father taught school most of his life-time, and his reputation as a teacher was very distinguished.   He represented Montgomery County in both Houses of the Tennessee Legislature.   He died May 20, 1860.   The mother died October 18, 1820.   Subject was the second of three children, of whom two are living: Mary, widow of Henry H. Bryan, and Quintus. The latter's education was received under the tutorage of his father; he remained at home until twenty years of age and then commenced life as a salesman in a store at Port Royal. In 1839 he went to Dover, Stewart Co., Tenn., where he also clerked. On January 1, 1840, he returned to Montgomery County and assumed control of his father's business. Here he remained until 1846; he then commenced teaching school at the Spring Creek Church and taught three years. In January, 1849, he came to Cadiz, Trigg Co., and taught at this point with the exception of one session until June, 1860. Returning to Montgomery County, he acted as administrator of his father's estate and also taught school. In this county he remained four years and then spent one year in travel. In September, 1866, he went to Garrettsburg, Christian Co., and opening a school there taught until June, 1870. He then taught one session at Glendale, Logan Co. In 1871 he came to Canton, Ky., and entered the mercantile business with John D. Tyler. In this he was engaged five years. In March, 1878, he began teaching again, and has since followed that profession. Mr. Tyler has in his life-time been one of the most successful teachers in the State. He has taught over fifty different terms, and to him have gone about 670 young ladies and young gentlemen. He was married on January 12, 1843, to Miss Emily B. Waller, a daughter of Richard and Eliza Waller, natives of Virginia. Mrs. Tyler was born on December 19, 1816, and died on August 26, 1851. Mr. Tyler is an Episcopalian in principle; he is a member of Cadiz Lodge, No. 121, A. F. & A. M., Swigert Chapter, No. 40, Eddyville Council and Paducah Commandery, No. 11, Knights Templar; he has been a member of the Masonic fraternity since 1845; has been representative to the Grand Lodge, and has served as Grand Marshal of the State.

FERGUSON SPRINGS PRECINCT.

WILLIAM M. GILLAHAN, farmer, was born in Trigg County, Ky., June 2, 1818, and is a son of James and Elizabeth (Baker) Gillahan. Subject's grandparents came from North Carolina, and were among the first settlers in Trigg County. His father lived and died near what was the site of the old Empire Furnace; his mother died in the fall of 1861 by the hand of one of her slaves (Easter Gillahan), whom she had reared from childhood. William M., our subject, has made farming his sole occupation. On Christmas, 1859, he settled on the farm which he now owns, and which is one of the best in Ferguson Springs Precinct. In 1843 he married Cecelia Ferguson, a native of Kentucky, by whom he had eight children; two sons and one daughter are living. Mrs. Gillahan departed this life in March, 1861, and in November, 1862, Mr. G. married Margaret Choat; to this union have been born eight children, seven of whom are living. Three of his children by his first wife and one by his last are married. K. P. was married to Nancy F. Choat March 27, 1863; they have two daughters. Robin was married May 9, 1880, to Martha B. McWatters; they have one son and one daughter. S. R. married Martha Lampkins March 8, 1883; Cecelia was married, December 21, 1882, to J. H. Smith; they have one daughter. The children at home are: R., J. Margaret G., R. M., Christian L., Robert L. and Ellen T. Three grandchildren—Lillie Gillahan, William P. and Florence, the last two, orphans of J. C. Gillahan, also make their home with our subject. Mr. Gillahan's aunt was the first white child born in Christian County. K. P. Gillahan's wife and his father's wife are sisters.

W. C. HOLLAND, worker in iron, was born in Trigg County, Ky., November 17, 1825, and is a son of A. W. and Jane (Rhodes) Holland; the former was born in Kentucky and died in 1857, aged fifty-seven. His father (and grandfather of our subject) came to this locality about the year 1790, and settled where Cadiz now stands. Subject's maternal grandfather, Ephraim Rhodes, settled on the land now occupied by W. D.

Grace, and here the mother of our subject was born in 1810 and died July 20, 1846. Subject was reared on his father's farm, and attended the schools of the neighborhood. At the age of nineteen he engaged in the saw-mill business for William H. Martin; later he was employed by W. D. Grace for three or four years. In 1852 he went to Texas and remained until 1856, when he returned. Since that time he has been employed by D. Hillman, D. Hillman & Sons, and now by J. H. Hillman, of Center Furnace, and also superintends his farming interests in Tennessee. Mr. Holland was married, May 16, 1858, to Maria Clements, a daughter of W. C. Clements, of Huntsville, Ala. To them were born eight children, of whom seven are living. Mr. H. held the office of Justice of the Peace in Calloway County; he is a member of the I. O. O. F., and a consistent member of the Baptist Church.

LAURA FURNACE PRECINCT.

C. C. FLORA was born February 28, 1837, in Granger County, Tenn ; he was a son of Daniel and Hannah (Blair) Flora. The father was born in Tennessee in 1818; he died November 6, 1871. The mother died in Granger County, Tenn., aged thirty-seven. In November, 1844, the family came to Trigg County, and settled in Golden Pond Precinct ; they bought 140 acres of land from George Grace, and engaged in farming. The father was also Postmaster at this point, and held the office from 1853 to 1855. Our subject served as Deputy, and at the age of sixteen opened a grocery store. This business he continued two years, after which he moved to Canton and was clerk in the dry goods store of E. C. Spiceland one year. The business then changed hands; A. G. Cobb became proprietor. After continuing one year, subject and E. C. Spiceland bought out the business, and after various changes he moved to Roaring Springs Precinct and engaged in farming one year; he then returned to Canton and again clerked for E. C. Spiceland one year. In 1861 he returned to Golden Pond, and was engaged in farming until 1863. In the spring of 1864 he opened a store on these premises, and soon after was robbed by guerrillas of both stock and cash. He soon opened a general store at Linton, which he continued until 1867 ; he then carried on business about two miles north of his late locality. In 1877 he moved to his farm, which consists of 200 acres. In 1881 he opened a general store on this farm, and was appointed Postmaster ; the office is known as Deason Postoffice. In August, 1878, he was elected Justice of the Peace, and was in his second term when he died, July 24, 1884. Mr. Flora was married on December 31, 1857, to Mary H., daughter of J. M. Darnell, of Roaring Springs. Their union was blessed with eight children—four boys and four girls. Mrs. Flora has been a life-long member of the Methodist Episcopal Church, and still resides with five of her children at the old home. Mr. Flora lived and died in the Methodist faith.

PHILIP REDD was born October 19, 1819, in Trigg County, Ky. He is the fourth child of a family of eight born to William and Frances (Hackett) Redd, who were reared in Caroline County, Va. The father immigrated to Christian, now Trigg County, in 1818; he engaged in farming. Our subject at the age of eighteen was employed as manager on his father's farm—a position he held for three years. In 1840 he went to Eddyville, Caldwell Co., and with his brother, George K., engaged in the tanning business. In 1844 they came to Mr. Redd's present location and purchased about 3,600 acres of land and at once commenced the erection of a tannery. This business they carried on with great success. His brother died in December, 1883, aged seventy-one. Mr. Redd then bought out the entire business, which consists of tannery, saw and grist-mill, a blacksmith-shop and shoe-shop, all of which are inclosed with a substantial board fence twelve feet high. He is also engaged in the cultivation of fish, having a pond for this purpose on his premises. His tanning business at times has been quite extensive, having sold as high as $23,000 worth of leather in a year; he is also largely engaged in farming, employing from twelve to fifteen hands. His residence was built in 1852 at a cost of about $2,000. Mr. Redd is one of the earliest settlers of this locality.

LINTON PRECINCT.

J. S. McNICHOLS was born in Montgomery County, Tenn., on October 10, 1828, and is the son of Samuel and Mary (Dycus) McNichols. The father came from Scotland in 1799, and settled in Montgomery County. J. S. remained at home until his father's death, in March, 1846; he then attended school in Whitley County for one year and afterward continued his studies in Montgomery County until 1853; he then went to Roaring Springs, Trigg County, where he merchandised until 1855; he next went to Lyonport, Tenn., where he remained until 1859. In October of that year he came to Canton and formed a partnership with Dr. J. C. Whitlock. The firm erected a warehouse and store. In 1882 Dr. Whitlock sold his interest to Frank Macrae, and the firm is now doing business under the name of McNichols, Macrae & Co. They now handle about $5,000 worth of merchandise per year, and also deal extensively in tobacco. Mr. McNichols was married at Cadiz, in November, 1857, to Miss Cornelia Wilkinson, a daughter of Judge J. H. and Joyce (Tillotson) Wilkinson, natives of Virginia. Mrs. McNichols was born in Montgomery County in 1857. She and husband are members of the Linton Methodist Episcopal Church. Mr. McNichols is a member of Linton Lodge, No. 575, A. F. & A. M.; he has served as School Trustee for the precinct. Mr. and Mrs. McNichols are parents of seven children—four sons and three daughters.

ELIAS A. NUNN was born in Smith County, Tenn., November 16, 1833, and is a son of Lindsey and Rachel (Coleman) Nunn, natives of Shenandoah County, Va. The father came to the county in 1848, and settled three miles west of Canton, where the mother died in 1852. In 1854 the father moved to Henry County, Tenn., where he died in 1881. Subject is the fourth of seven living children. He began life for himself when twenty years old, and settled at Linton. Here he engaged in the saw-milling business with Messrs. Gentry & Whitlock, 1865, under the title of Gentry, Nunn & Co. He remained in this business until

1882. He came to his present farm in 1870, where he now owns about 1,800 acres ; has about 200 acres in cultivation. Mr. Nunn was married in 1865 to Miss Margaret Martin, a daughter of John Martin, of Trigg County. Mrs. Nunn is a native of this county, and is the mother of five children—two sons and three daughters. Subject is a member of Linton Lodge No. 575, A. F. & A. M. In politics he is an Independent.

E. C. SPICELAND was born in Stewart County, Tenn., June 1, 1826, and is a son of Sanford and M. (Copeland) Spiceland, natives of Northampton County, N. C. In 1845 our subject went to Canton, and kept the ferry for one year; the following year he ran a saloon. In 1847, he enlisted in the Mexican War and remained about three months ; served, while out, in the Quartermaster Department. On his return to Canton he clerked for W. D. Grace. In 1850 he moved to Cadiz and there clerked for William Sorey & Co. After remaining there one year, he returned to Canton, where he clerked in a warehouse. In 1854 he began merchandising for himself, and remained in business at that point until the breaking out of the war. In 1862, he enlisted in Company L, of the Eighth Kentucky Cavalry. He went out as Lieutenant, and was afterward made Regimental Quartermaster. He returned to Canton in September, 1863, and in partnership with John D. Tyler ran a warehouse. On January 1, 1866, he came to Linton, and began merchandising. At this place he has since been engaged in business. In 1875 he took his son, S. I. Spiceland, into the business as partner. The firm now carry a stock of about $10,000. Soon after he came to Linton, he was appointed Postmaster and held the office until about 1875. Since that time the position has been filled by his son. Mr. Spiceland was married in 1848 to Miss Martha Ross, a daughter of Kenneth Ross, of Tennessee. She was born in Stewart County, and died in April, 1866. She left three children— one son and two daughters. Mr. S. was next married in July, 1866, to Miss Mary Scudder, a daughter of P. P. Scudder. She died in 1871, and in 1872 Mr. Spiceland married Miss Martha Barte, a daughter of A. J. Barte ; they have five children living—two sons and three daughters. Subject is a member of the Baptist Church ; has served as Magistrate of the county. In politics he is identified with the Republican party.

WILLIAM S. TINSLEY was born in Roaring Springs Precinct on March 10, 1824, and is a son of James and Elizabeth (Scott) Tinsley.

The father was a native of North Carolina, and came to Todd County in 1816. He soon after came to this county, where he died in 1868. The mother was born in Virginia, and died here in October, 1883. Subject was the third of eleven children. He remained at home until twenty one, when he went to Todd County and remained six years and then settled on Salina Creek, in Roaring Springs Precinct. He lived there until March, 1879, when he moved to McPherson County, Kas. He remained there only about sixteen months, and then returned to Kentucky, and settled in Graves County. There he resided until November, 1883, when he came to his present farm where he now owns 316 acres. Mr. Tinsley was married in 1855 to Miss Elizabeth J. Carr, a daughter of William and Ann (Rogers) Carr. The following children blessed the marriage: Alice A., James N., Ann, Leemina E., Martha E., Ophelia E. and William S. Mrs. Tinsley died August 10, 1878. Mr. Tinsley and family are members of the Baptist Church.

JOHN L. TURNER was born in this precinct and county, on April 9, 1846. He is the second child born to William and Elizabeth (Carr) Turner, who are still living in Canton Precinct. John L. remained at home until the age of nineteen, when he settled in Canton Precinct and began life for himself. In the fall of 1879 he came to his present farm where he has since resided. He now owns about 250 acres, about 80 of which are in cultivation. In 1883 he was appointed Overseer of the Poor and still holds that position. The farm now contains about twenty-five inmates. Mr. Turner was married in the fall of 1864, to Miss Faith Carr, a daughter of Jackson Carr. She is a native of Stewart County, Tenn., and is the mother of five children—three sons and two daughters. Mr. and Mrs. Turner are both members of the Baptist Church.

JOHN H. WOLFE was born in Livingston County, Ky., on June 7, 1836, and is a son of Henry and Julia (Harmon) Wolfe. The father was a native of Columbia, Penn., the mother of Livingston Co., Ky. Subject is the third of four children of whom three are now living. He remained at home until fourteen years of age, and then began life as an engineer on a steamboat. He followed this occupation for about twenty-six years, on boats plying between Nashville and New Orleans. During most of this time he held a license as a first-class engineer. Mr. Wolfe followed engineering until February, 1884, when he came to this county, and has since been giving his attention to farming. Subject is what might be called a self-made man. His first schooling was obtained at Louisa College when he was twenty-one years of age. He remained there seven months, and has since prosecuted his studies by himself. He was married on January 28, 1879, to Mrs. Molly B. Rogers (*nee* Watwood), daughter of J. F. and Mary A. (Yates) Watwood, natives of Tennessee. Mrs. Rogers is a native of Montgomery County, being born there in 1842. This marriage has resulted in one child : Nep B. Mrs. Wolfe is a member of the Oak Grove Baptist Church. Mr. Wolfe is a member of Liverpool Lodge, No. 175, I. O. O. F.

ROARING SPRINGS PRECINCT.

CHARLES A. BACON was born in Charlotte County, Va., on February 15, 1807, and is a son of Lyddall and Margaret (Crenshaw) Bacon. The parents were also natives of Charlotte County, and were of English descent. In that county they resided until their death. The father was drafted into the war of 1812, but being a man of family, his place was taken by his brother William. Charles A. remained at home until about twenty-two, and then spent some fifteen months in traveling in the South. Returning to Virginia, he taught school for some five years, and in December, 1832, came to Tennessee. He settled in Montgomery County, on a farm which at that time contained the first blockhouse ever erected in that region. He remained there only one year, and then came to Christian County, Ky. He first settled near Lafayette, and lived there about two years. He next went to Garrettsburg just as the town was being laid out. He remained there until 1838, and then moved to Beverly, where he farmed until the fall of 1839. At that time he sold out his farm and came to Lafayette, where he merchandised until 1842. He then moved to Garrettsburg and sold goods there until 1846. In that year he came to Roaring Springs (this county), and put up the first store ever built here. He merchandised here until 1854, when he sold out his stock and turned his attention to farming. He had prior to this purchased about 100 acres adjoining the town, which he afterward increased to 295. Here he has since resided. Mr. Bacon was married in Halifax County, Va., on February 12, 1832, to Miss Susan Rowlett, a daughter of Matthew J. and Martha (Pleasants) Rowlett, natives of Lunenburg County, Va. Mrs. Bacon was born in Halifax County, Va., on February 15, 1808, and to her were born five children. Of this number three are now living, viz.: Dr. Thomas L. Bacon, in Cadiz; Lyddall Bacon, a merchant in Memphis, and Dr. C. P. Bacon in Evansville. This lady died on October 11, 1841, and Mr. Bacon was next married on December 17, 1844, to Mrs. Margaret Gaines Ratcliff (*nee*

Gibson), a daughter of Pitman and Susan Gibson. This lady was born in Christian County on June 7, 1823, and to her were born three children, all of whom are living: Malcolm M., John A. and Hillery (in Evansville). Mrs. Bacon died on November 13, 1880. The farm is at present carried on by John A. Bacon, who is also devoting some attention to stock-raising, making a specialty of fine Berkshire hogs. This gentleman was married on December 21, 1881, to Miss Lelia Sallee, a daughter of Henry and Bettie (Crenshaw) Sallee. Our subject has been identified with the Baptist Church since 1830. Is also a member of Roaring Springs Lodge, No. 221. In politics he has been a Whig since he cast his first vote, but has of late years been voting with the Democratic party.

JOSEPH BOYD, SR., was born in Trigg County on August 2, 1829, and is a son of Ebenezer and Mary (Sparkham) Boyd. The parents were natives of North Carolina. The father came to this State in 1800 with his parents, who first settled near Lexington. In 1810 they came to this county, where the grandmother died. The grandfather moved to Mississippi, where he died in about 1825. In this precinct the father grew to manhood, and settled in the southwest part of it. He lived there until his death, which occurred in April, 1874. He was a member of the Presbyterian Church. The mother died on July 4, 1846. Subject is the sixth of eight children, and of this number but four are living: Elizabeth J. (wife of Martin Campbell, of Christian County); Matthew H., in Davidson County, Tenn.; Martha C., wife of Jesse Stamper, of Lafayette, and Joseph. Joseph commenced to learn the carpenter's trade when seventeen years old, and followed it for about fifteen years in Christian, Stewart, Montgomery and Trigg Counties. When about thirty years of age he turned his attention to farming, and settled on his present farm, where he has since resided. He owns about 220 acres, of which 130 acres are in cultivation. Mr. Boyd was married in Christian County on August 14, 1851, to Miss Mary F. Pratt, of Hopkinsville, a daughter of W. S. Pratt, who was a native of Madison County, Va. This lady was born in Christian County in 1830, and is the mother of five children, of whom four are living: Willie, in Lafayette; Charles H., Joseph Jr. and Frank C. Mr. Boyd is now acting as trustee of the Lafayette High School, which position he has held for the past ten years.

Mrs. Boyd is a member of the Christian Church. Mr. Boyd is a member of Lafayette Masonic Lodge, and is identified with the Democratic party in politics.

CHARLES R. CLARK was born in Sussex County, Va., March 10, 1823, and is a son of F. H. and Nancy (Judkins) Clark. They were also natives of Virginia, and came to Stewart County, Tenn., in 1832. There the father died May 20, 1860, the mother August 29, 1851. Subject is the eldest of three living children: Charles R., Marcus L. and Ann E., widow of W. H. A. Pugh, of Stewart County, Tenn. Charles R. remained at home until about the age of twenty-two; he then came to Trigg County, and settled near the farm on which he now resides. In January, 1857, he came to his present farm, where he now owns about 350 acres. He has about 250 acres in cultivation and ten acres in orchard; he also pays some attention to stock-raising. Mr. Clark was married in Stewart County, Tenn., on December 14, 1851, to Miss Amanda Cherry, a daughter of Daniel and Rebecca (Stancell) Cherry, of North Carolina. Mrs. Clark is the mother of eleven living children: Thomas H., Jesse H., James M., William M., Amalgus G., M. W., Yateman G., Charles W., Alonzo, Silas W. and Woodsey. Mrs. Clark is a member of the Baptist Church.

ELBRIDGE A. COLEMAN was born in what is now Caledonia Precinct, Trigg County, February 6, 1833. He was a son of James and Nancy (Wooton) Coleman. The parents were natives of Virginia, and came here at an early date. The father died in this county in about 1838, the mother in 1848. Elbridge A. is the second of four children, of whom two are now living: Mrs. Mary F. Wooton, of Caledonia Precinct, and Elbridge, our subject. The latter commenced life for himself at about twenty-one years of age, and settled down in Caledonia Precinct. He lived there until 1877, when he purchased the Lindsey Mill in this precinct, and moved to his present location. The mill, which is now known as "Echo Vale" Mill, is one of the best mills in the county, and is now valued at about $5,000. To the mill Mr. Coleman devotes most of his attention; he, however, owns a farm of about 675 acres in this and Caledonia Precinct, and has farming carried on for him. He was married in this county on August 27, 1863, to Miss Mary J. Carter, a daughter of Jesse and Emeline (Sallee) Carter. The father was a native

of Virginia, the mother of Montgomery County, Tenn. Her father was
of French descent, and settled first in Christian County, but afterward
came to Trigg, where he died in 1875. The mother is still living with
her daughter. Mrs. Coleman was born in Christian County on May 17,
1845, and to her and husband have been born twelve children, of whom
eight are now living : Alva (wife of Dr. J. A. Miller), James D., Emma
A., Anne I., Jesse C., Thomas F., Maud B. and Bettie L. Mr. and
Mrs. Coleman are both members of the Little River Baptist Church.
In politics he has been identified with the Democratic party.

THOMAS CRENSHAW was born in this precinct and county on
June 10, 1820 ; he is the only living one of three children born to Cornelius and Nancy (Kent) Crenshaw. The parents were natives of Halifax County, Va., and emigrated to this county in 1819. The father soon
after his arrival here purchased about 440 acres at $5 per acre (the
land now forms part of the farm owned by subject), and there resided
until his death. In his life-time he was a consistent church member,
having been at first identified with the United Baptist denomination,
afterward with the Christian Church, to which he belonged at the time of
his death. He was a soldier in the war of 1812, having gone out in a
Virginia company ; he was stationed at Norfolk and was an officer in the
ranks. Our subject at the age of twenty-five assumed control of the home
farm for his father, and continued the management of it until the latter's
death. He inherited his father's estate of about 440 acres, which he has
since increased to about 1,000 acres. Of this there are about 600 acres
in cultivation. He also does something in stock-raising, handling about
100 head yearly. In farming he makes nothing a specialty, but raises all
the cereals and also tobacco. Mr. Crenshaw was married in this county
on September 22, 1840, to Miss Eliza Ann Greenwade. This lady was
a daughter of John and Annie (Thomas) Greenwade, the father being a
native of Maryland, the mother of Bourbon County, Ky. This lady was
born in Trigg County in 1823, and to her were born eight children, seven
of whom are living, viz.: Elizabeth R., wife of Thomas Cochran; Susan
B., wife of Henry Richards ; Malcolm B.; Nancy E., wife of E. M. Jones ;
Thomas E., Robert C. in Christian County, and Millard F., in Hopkinsville. Her death occurred on December 30, 1858, and Mr. Crenshaw was
married on May 17, 1860, to Miss Cynthia A. Carland, a daughter of

Hugh and Nancy (Richards) Carland.   The father was a native of Pennsylvania, the mother of Maryland.   Both lived and died in New Brighton, Penn.   Mrs. Crenshaw's ancestors were of a patriotic stock.   Two of her greatuncles were soldiers in the Revolution, and were killed at the battle of Bunker Hill, and her maternal grandfather was a soldier in the war of 1812, and was killed at the battle of Chippewa.   Mrs. Crenshaw was born in Sharon, Penn., on December 30, 1830, and is the mother of one child—Hugh C.   Most of Mr. Crenshaw's life has been spent in farming ; he has, however, devoted some attention to merchandising, and has also dealt some in commission business.   In politics Mr. Crenshaw was first an old line Whig, during the war a Union man, and since that time he has been identified with the Democratic party.   Mr. and Mrs. Crenshaw and family are members of the Christian Church.

ALBERT CRENSHAW was born in Trigg County on June 10, 1840, and is a son of Robenson and Mary (Walden) Crenshaw.   The father was born in Halifax County, Va., in September, 1816.   He was a son of Cornelius and Nancy (Kent) Crenshaw, who came here in 1819. The father grew to manhood in this county, and resided here until his death on February 12, 1853.   The mother was also born in this county on September 22, 1820, and died here on December 31, 1851.   The parents were both members of the Christian Church.   Subject is the eldest of six children, all of whom are living, viz.: Albert, James, born June 22, 1842, now in Hopkins County ; William B., born November 18, 1844, now in Oxford, Kas.; Robenson, born June 4, 1847, now in Cadiz; John W., born September 27, 1849, also in Cadiz, and Cornelius, born November 6, 1851, and now in Texas.   The common schools of this county and Christian furnished his education.   After his father's death he made his home with his uncle, Thomas Crenshaw.   At the age of nineteen he began clerking in a dry goods store at Roaring Springs, and remained there three years.   He next turned his attention to farming and settled in the northwestern part of the precinct, where he resided until 1870.   In that year he came to his present farm, where he now owns about 270 acres, of which there are about 250 acres in cultivation.   Mr. Crenshaw was married on October 31, 1861, in this county, to Miss Emma Rasco, a daughter of J. M. and Sarah (Johnson) Rasco.   The father was a native of this county, the mother of Christian.   Mrs. Crenshaw was born in this county on October 26, 1844, and is the mother of nine children, of whom six are now living: Mary F., born January 6, 1863 (now the wife of C. F. Miller); Sallie R., born January 24, 1865; Ernest L., born May 24, 1866; Emma, born September 30, 1875; Albert W., born Febuary 14, 1878; Myrtle, born September 14, 1879. Of the deceased ones: James M., born March 20, 1868, died October 11, 1874; George S., born December 14, 1871, died October 10, 1874; Robert, born March 20, 1873, died April 23, 1874. In politics Mr. Crenshaw supports the Democratic party. Both Mr. and Mrs. Crenshaw are members of the Christian Church, and Mr. Crenshaw is now an Elder in that denomination.

SAMUEL J. DAWSON is descended from one of the earliest pioneer families of the county. He was born in this precinct on January 14, 1837, and is a son of Samuel and Maria (Masonfrith) Dawson. The father was born in Bourbon County, Ky., on August 14, 1800; his father, John Dawson, was born in Virginia, and was of English descent. The latter came to this county in 1817, with his son, and settled on the head waters of Casey Creek. There he died in about 1832; his wife in about 1841. Samuel Dawson grew to manhood in this county, and in 1827, he was married to Miss Masonfrith, who was a native of Bedford County, Va., and was born there on May 16, 1805. He inherited 200 acres from his father, and settled down about two miles northwest of Roaring Springs; he afterward increased the farm to 455 acres, and continued to reside there until his death, which occurred on June 28, 1863. For a short time he served as Constable of the county. He was identified with the Sons of Temperance. He was a man of fair education for his day and time, was well read on all subjects; was possessed of a fine memory, and was regarded as an authority by his neighbors on all subjects of dispute. The mother is still living on the old home farm. Samuel J. (subject) is the youngest of four living children: Susan E., widow of J. A. Miller; Rhoda M., John W. and Samuel J. The latter commenced life for himself when about twenty-five years of age, and soon after settled on his present farm. He now owns 175 acres; has 140 acres in cultivation. Mr. Dawson was married in Lafayette, Christian Co., on April 22, 1862, to Miss Margaret Clardy, a daughter of John H. and Ann Eliza (Watkins) Clardy. The father was born in Mecklenburg County, Va., but was reared principally in North Carolina; the mother was born in Warren County, N. C. Mrs. Dawson was born on October 24, 1843, and to her and husband have been born three living children: Marion, Blanche and Samuel. Mrs. Dawson is a member of the Christian Church. During the war Mr. Dawson was a strong Union man, but since that time he has been identified with the Democratic party.

WICKLIFFE DAWSON was born in this county on March 1, 1853, and is a son of Greenup and Susan J. (Calloway) Dawson. Subject is the youngest living child ; his education was received in the schools of the county. He remained at home until twenty-six, and in 1879, he moved to Roaring Springs where he remained till November, 1881, when he came to his present farm, which consists of 240 acres, of which there are about 160 acres in cultivation. Mr. Dawson was married in Clarksville, Montgomery Co., Tenn., on October 29, 1878, to Miss Belle Nance, a daughter of E. T. and Sallie (Snow) Nance, natives of Virginia. Three children have blessed this union, two of whom are now living: Idyle and Effie. Mrs. Dawson is a member of the Christian Church. In politics, Mr. Dawson is identified with the Democratic party.

MOSCO GARNETT was born in this precinct on October 8, 1827, and is a son of James and Polly (Brown) Garnett. The father was born in Virginia, on February 23, 1787. He came to Woodford County with his parents in an early day, and in 1823 he settled in this precinct. Here he died on November 5, 1870; he was a member of the Baptist Church. Under the old constitution he was Magistrate of the precinct, and finally, by virtue of priority became Sheriff of the county. The mother died in this county on August 11, 1869. Mosco is the youngest of ten children, of whom four are now living: Fannie, widow of Charles Humphreys; Charles W., in Graves County; Susan, wife of Isaac Dabney, and now in Texas; and Mosco. The latter remained at home until about the age of twenty-three, and then commencing life for himself, settling on his present farm; he now owns about 250 acres, of which there are 200 acres in cultivation. Mr. Garnett was married in this county October 20, 1853, to Miss Susan Savells, a daughter of Absalom and Lurana (Savells) Savells. The parents were natives of Norfolk County, Va., and were early settlers of Cadiz Precinct. Mrs. Garnett was born in this county February 25, 1823. This union has resulted in eight children, five of whom are now living, viz.: Cornelia, wife of G. P. Carloss ; Mary E.; Henry O.; Susan Dabney, wife of Lesley Tuggle, of Cadiz Precinct, and Lulu. Mr. and Mrs. Garnett are members of the Locust Grove Baptist Church. He is a member of the Masonic fraternity, and is identified with the Democratic party.

J. W. HAYES, SR., was born in Garrettsburg Precinct, Christian County, May 28, 1824, and is a son of John T. and Elizabeth (Brame) Hayes. The parents were natives of Mecklenburg County, Va., and came to Christian County in 1823. There the mother died when subject was but an infant, and the father came to Trigg County soon after this event. He settled one mile south of Roaring Springs, and remained there until his death, which occurred January 19, 1849. Subject is the only living child. He remained at home until twenty-one, and then went to Williamson County, Tenn., where he worked at the blacksmith trade for six months, and then returned to the home farm, where he remained two years; he commenced for himself by settling on a farm about one mile west of Roaring Springs. In 1856 he came to his present farm; he first bought 170 acres, now has about 590 acres, and is at present paying some attention to stock-raising. Mr. Hayes was married in this county, October 21, 1848, to Miss Jane Nance, a daughter of L. and Onie (Sims) Nance, natives of Virginia. This lady was born in Trigg County, June, 1827, and died on July 29, 1851. Subject's second marriage took place October 21, 1852, to Miss Lucy A. Ledford, a daughter of Andrew and Martha S. (Lewis) Ledford, both natives of Virginia, and early settlers in the county. Mrs. Hayes was born in this county April 23, 1837, and seven children have been born to her and husband, viz.: Mary L., wife of W. E. Thacker; Martha E., wife of Albert Rasco; James A., John W., Jennie L., Henry T. and Titia C. Mr. Hayes and family are members of the Christian Church. He is a member of the Masonic fraternity, and in politics a Democrat.

DR. H. L. J. HILLE was born in Oldenburg, Germany, August 26, 1850, and is a son of William and Mary (Lotze) Hille. The father was born in Austria, the mother in Oldenburg, Germany. A brother of hers, Herman Lotze, has achieved considerable notoriety as an author. The parents came to this country in 1842, and first settled in New Orleans. From there they went to West Virginia, and there the father first followed merchandising, afterward saw-milling. The parents were on a visit to Germany when subject was born, and they returned to this country soon after the latter event. The father continued to reside in West Virginia until his death, which occurred November 3, 1876. The mother died at Roaring Springs December 17, 1883. Subject is the sixth of fifteen children, of whom but five are now living, viz.: Henry (subject), Anna, Dora (wife of Robert Camp, in Texas), Adolph (in Hopkinsville), and Fannie (wife of Dr. Greenwade, of Texas). Our subject's education was received in the schools of Putnam and Mason Counties, W. Va., and at the Gallipolis (Ohio) Academy. He commenced the study of medicine when seventeen years old with Dr. A. R. Barbee, of Point Pleasant, W. Va.; he read with this gentleman four years, and then attended the medical department at the University of Michigan at Ann Arbor. From this institution he graduated in the class of 1871; he began the practice of his profession immediately afterward, and first settled in Kanawha County, W. Va.; he remained at this point two years, and then went to Sherman, Grayson Co., Tex.; there he remained four years, and then came to Kentucky; he immediately made Roaring Springs his place of residence, and has since had a fair share of the practice of this part of the country. Dr. Hille was married at Dover, Tenn., October 25, 1875, to Miss Camille Walter, a daughter of Bernard Walter, of Dover, Tenn.; she was born February 18, 1855, and is the mother of five children, of whom three are now living—Mary, Henry and Mabel. In politics the Doctor votes the Democratic ticket.

GARLAND W. JONES was born in Mecklenburg County, Va., July 21, 1837, and is a son of Col. J. T. and Louisa A. (Yancey) Jones; the father was a native of North Carolina, the mother of Virginia; they came to Kentucky in 1847, and settled in Montgomery County in 1848; in the following year they came to Trigg County, and settled one mile north of Roaring Springs; there he resided until he died, July 19, 1874; when he came to the county he first purchased 200 acres, which he afterward increased to about 1,000, which after his death was divided and a part of it sold. He was a member of the Methodist Episcopal Church; the mother is still living on part of the home farm. Subject is the eldest of five living children: Garland W., Amos K. (in Graves County), Malinda E. (wife of D. A. McKennon, of Paducah, Ky.), Tillman G. and

Carrie V. (wife of Lee Hutchingson); he remained at home until twenty-one; he then received about 280 acres from his father, and commenced life for himself; this farm he afterward increased to 430 acres, on which he now resides. Mr. Jones was married, in Graves County, Ky., October 21, 1880, to Miss Bettie Houston, a daughter of George and Louisa (Moore) Houston. The father was a native of Virginia, the mother of Todd County, Ky.; both parents are still living in this precinct. Mrs. Jones was born in Todd County September 20, 1857; this union was blessed with two children, one of whom, Garland H., is living. Mr. Jones was a soldier in the late war. He enlisted in November, 1862, in Col. Woodward's regiment, but was only out a short time. Mr. and Mrs. Jones are both members of the Methodist Church. In politics Mr. Jones gives his support to the Democratic party.

TILLMAN G. JONES was born in Pearson County, N. C., on February 9, 1845, and is the sixth of nine children, born to Col. J. T. and Louisa A. (Yancey) Jones. Tillman G. remained at home until the age of twenty-two, and then began clerking for Richards, Crenshaw & Co., at Roaring Springs. He remained there about six months, and then came to Cadiz and clerked a short time. He next bought tobacco for parties at Newburg, Tenn. In 1868 he was appointed Deputy Sheriff, and served for about three months under Sheriff Dyer. He then returned home, and taking charge of his father's business managed it until the latter's death. He then ran the farm for four ·years for his mother, and in 1878 came to his present location. He now owns 190 acres, cultivates about 140 acres, and is also doing considerable in stock-raising. Mr. Jones was married in this county on Oct. 14, 1874, to Miss Julia Greenwade, a daughter of Isaac and Elizabeth (Kane) Greenwade. This family was one of the earliest pioneer families in the county. Isaac Greenwade was born here, and his father John Greenwade came from Virginia in a very early day. His people were of English descent. Mrs. Greenwade was also a native of this county, and is still living at Lafayette. Mrs. Jones was born in this county on July 14, 1846, and to her and husband have been born six children, of whom four are now living: Herbert C., Bertha M., James G. and Coatney E. Mr. Jones is a member of the Methodist Church; his wife of the Christian Church. In politics Mr. Jones is a Democrat.

JOSEPH LEDFORD was born in this precinct and county on February 16, 1816, and was a son of Joseph, Sr., and Jane (Smith) Ledford. The parents were natives of South Carolina, and came to this county in the fall of 1815. Here the father resided until his death, which occurred in October, 1845. He was a member of the Baptist Church. Joseph Ledford is the third of six children, and is the only one now living. He remained at home until about twenty-five and then settled on his present farm. He now owns about 800 acres, and has about 400 acres in cultivation. Mr. Ledford was married in this county on December 7, 1843, to Miss Onie D. Nance, a daughter of Peyton and Nellie (Sims) Nance. The parents were natives of Virginia, and came to this county in 1826. Mrs. Ledford was born in Virginia on August 2, 1824, and was the mother of five children: T. P. D., Alice E. L. (wife of W. A. Ledford), George, E. J. A., and Annie. Mrs. Ledford died on March 2, 1862. Mr. Ledford was a Union man during the war, and is at present identified with the Democratic party.

W. W. LEWIS was born in Lafayette Precinct, Christian County, on November 28, 1849, and is a son of P. M. and M. J. (Ledford) Lewis. The father was born in Charlotte County, N. C., on May 2, 1812, and was of English and Welsh descent; he came to Lexington, Ky., in 1812, with his parents; he came to Christian County in 1820 and resided there until 1853, when he came to Trigg County. In this county he lived until his death, which occurred on January 14, 1884; he was a Mason and a member of the Christian Church. The mother was born in Trigg County on July 30, 1820, and died here on November 20, 1876. Subject is the oldest of five children, four of whom are now living: William W., Mattie J., George P. and Henry. Subject was educated in the common schools of the county, and also attended the academy at Elkton, Todd County, for a short time. He commenced farming on the home place in 1870, and now owns 200 acres. Has about 125 acres in cultivation; he is a member of the Christian Church, and of Roaring Springs Lodge, No. 221, A. F. & A. M. In politics he is a Democrat.

G. W. McCRAW was born in Montgomery County, Tenn., on February 22, 1848, and is a son of William and Thetus (Hill) McCraw. The father is a native of Charlotte County, Va., the mother of Montgomery County, Tenn. They came to this county in 1859, and are still living here. Subject is the fifth of thirteen children, of whom nine are now living. When twenty-two years of age he began working at the saddler's trade, but only followed this industry about twelve months ; he next turned his attention to farming, and first settled near Fairview, Todd County. From there he moved to Christian County, settled near Lafayette, and in 1877 he came to his present farm. He now owns about seventy-three acres. Mr. McCraw was married in Todd County on December 10, 1872, to Miss Mary E. Fulcher, a daughter of Joseph and Mary A. (Nichols) Fulcher. Mrs. McCraw was born in Todd County on May 10, 1843, and is the mother of four living children: Jennie B., Mack H., Joseph R. and Bennie. Mr. McCraw is a member of the Methodist Church.

WILLIAM ROBERTS was born on July 18, 1810, on Little River in what was then Christian County, now Cadiz Precinct, Trigg Co. He is a son of John and Nancy (Atkins) Roberts. The father was born in Buckingham County, Va., in 1759. His father died when he was quite young. At the age of sixteen John Roberts volunteered to go as a guard to a party who were coming West. The party came to what is now Nashville, Tenn., and Mr. Roberts was one of a number who helped erect the block-house that stood where the capitol building now stands. He lived at this point for some time, and there his first wife was killed and scalped by the Indians. He came to this county in 1804, and settled near Cerulean Springs. In the early part of the year 1814 he came to Little River, and purchased a tract of land from David McKee, and which is now included in the Cadiz Precinct. Here he resided until his death which occurred on January 7, 1833. The mother died here on October 7, 1837. She was a member of the Cumberland Presbyterian Church. Our subject was the eldest of four brothers : William, Robert R., David L. and Phineas E. Of this number, David L., now in Mississippi, and William (subject), are the only ones living. William remained at home until after his mother's death and then commenced life for himself and settled on Little River in this precinct. In 1841 he came to his present farm, where he has since resided. He now owns 220 acres, of which eighty-five are in cultivation. Mr. Roberts was married on July 9, 1833, to Miss Nancy Malone, a daughter of Booth and Martha A. (Darnell) Malone, natives of Montgomery County, Tenn. Mrs. Roberts was born in that county in 1813. To her and husband have been born eight children, of whom three are now living: John W. (at home), Richard R. Roberts (a merchant in St. Louis, Mo.), and Susan A. (wife of Irving Branden, of Wallonia). Mrs. Roberts died on January 7, 1859, and subject was next married to Mrs. Medas J. Nelson, a daughter of Mahala and Rebecca (Randolph) Ingram. Mrs. Roberts was born in Claiborne County, Miss., on August 15, 1822. Mr. Roberts is a member of Roaring Springs Lodge, A. F. M., also a member of the Methodist Church. He cast his first vote for Andrew Jackson for President, and has since then been a strong Democrat.

WILLIAM S. ROGERS was born in this precinct on October 29, 1824, and is a son of John and Martha (Scott) Rogers. The grandfather, John Rogers Sr., came here at an early date and settled on the farm now owned by subject, where he died. There the father was probably born, and died in about 1841. The mother was a daughter of William Scott, who came here from Virginia. She died in about .1876. Subject is the fourth of six children, of whom but two are now living: Mrs. Telitha J. Sholer and William S. (subject). The latter remained at home until about twenty-five, and then settled on the farm where he now resides; he owns 279 acres, of which about 160 are in cultivation; he was married in this county on January 15, 1846, to Matilda Tart, a daughter of James and Mary (Lawrence) Tart, natives of North Carolina. Mrs. Rogers is a native of this county, and is the mother of eleven children, of whom seven are now living: Joseph G., in Texas; William H., Cyrus W., in Texas; Mary E., wife of J. P. Joiner, of Texas; Franklin H., Freeman T., in Texas; Ira B. William S. is a member of the Baptist Church. In politics he is a Republican.

U. L. ROGERS was born in this county on September 14, 1846, and is the next to the youngest of a family of six children born to Benjamin S. and Polly (Lancaster) Rogers. The father was a native of North Carolina. The mother was born in this county; her people were also from North Carolina. The father died in 1849, but the mother is still living with subject. The latter took charge of the home farm in 1865, which now contains about 400 acres, of which 250 are in cultivation. He also does something in stock-rasing. He is a member of Linton Lodge, No. 575, A. F. & A. M.

SAMUEL SUMNER was born in Canton Precinct, Trigg County, on May 27, 1845. He is a son of Joel and Catherine (Miles) Sumner. His grandfather, Isaac Sumner, was one of the first settlers of the county. He came here from North Carolina in an early day, and made a settlement on Donaldson Creek. There the father of subject was born, and lived until his death in the spring of 1852. The mother was also a native of this county, and died here in May, 1863. Subject is the youngest of eleven children, of whom six are now living: James, in Canton Precinct; Alfred, in the same precinct; Green, in Stewart County, Tenn.; Ben, in Texas; Mary E., wife of Lafayette Ricks; and Samuel, our subject. The latter remained at home until the age of eighteen, and then, soon after the breaking-out of the war, he enlisted in Capt. Slaughter's company of Col. Woodward's regiment. He had been out about four months when he was taken prisoner, and sent to Louisville. After being confined there for some little time he took the oath of allegience and was permitted to return home. He next began working at the carpenter's trade, and followed it in Canton and vicinity for about eighteen months. He then began farming near the home place. In 1872 he came to his present farm, where he now owns about 210 acres, of which about eighty-five acres are in cultivation. On November 3, 1863, Mr. Sumner was married to Miss Lucy L. Rogers, a daughter of Joseph Rogers, one of the pioneer settlers here. Mrs. Sumner was born in this county, and is the mother of seven children, of whom five are now living, viz.: Elizabeth C., Joseph A., Jesse F., Addison B. and Olive T. Both Mr. and Mrs. Sumner are members of the Baptist Church. Mr. Sumner is an ordained preacher of this church, and is at present acting as pastor of the Baptist Church; is also a member of Canton Lodge, No. 242, A. F. & A. M. He has served as Coroner of the county for four years. In politics he is a Democrat.

DR. J. A. WHITLOCK was born in Union Schoolhouse Precinct, Christian County, on May 1, 1850, and is a son of Dr. J. C. and Maria F. (Withrow) Whitlock. The father was a native of Louisa County, Va.; was born there in 1818, and was of English descent. He came to this county when a boy, and lived in Caledonia Precinct. He took up the study of medicine and graduated at the Philadelphia Medical College. Returning to this State, he settled in Union Schoolhouse Precinct, and is to-day one of the most successful practitioners of Christian County. The mother is also still living. Our subject is the second of a family of five children, three of whom are now living, viz.: Lucy, Kate (wife of Alfred Wallace) and John A. The latter received his literary education at the Washington College at Lexington. Returning to this county, he began the study of medicine with his father; he read with him two years, and then attended the University of Medicine at Louisville. From this institution he graduated in the class of 1873. He returned to Christian County and first settled at Newstead; he remained there five years, and then came to Caledonia, Trigg Co.; he resided at this point one year and next moved to Bennettstown, Christian Co. There he remained two years, and then went to Pee Dee, Christian Co. On October, 1883, he came to Roaring Springs, where he now has a fair practice. On July 13, 1873, Dr. Whitlock was married in Christian County to Miss Mary L. McReynolds, a daughter of O. G. and Sarah L. (McCallister) McReynolds, natives of Virginia and early settlers of Christian County. Mrs. Whitlock was born in that county on April 13, 1853. Dr. Whitlock is a member of the State Medical Society, and of the Christian County Medical Society. Is also a member of the Presbyterian Church, his wife of the Christian. Subject is a member of James Moore Lodge, No. 230, A. F. & A. M., and Locust Grove, No. 127, I. O. O. F. In politics he is identified with the Democratic party.

GOLDEN POND PRECINCT.

JOSEPH AHART was born May 28, 1837, in Smith County, Tenn.; he is the eldest child of a family of six born to George and Sarah (Hankins) Ahart. The father was born in Virginia in 1808; he died in Trigg County in 1876. The mother was born in east Tennessee in 1814; she died in March, 1882. On coming to this county they settled two miles west of Canton; there our subject was reared; at the age of twenty-two he commenced farming on land given him by his father; this he afterward sold to his brother. In the fall of 1863 he came to this farm, which he rents, consisting of about 100 acres, and where he has since resided. He enlisted in August, 1862, in Company L, Eighth Kentucky Cavalry (Union), and served his enlistment. He was married in February, 1859, to Nancy E. Bell; she was born May 12, 1845, in this county; she died August 31, 1883, leaving three children: James M., Henry J. and Martha L. Mr. Ahart's second marriage was on January 13, 1884, to Mrs. Mary U. Ricks. She was born in this county; she has three children by a former marriage: George R., Leona A. and Fredonia A. Ricks. Mr. Ahart is the agent of the Fungo Landing for all shipments for Golden Pond; he is a member of the Masonic order.

CHARLES C. BOGARD, deceased, was born in Stewart County, Tenn., in 1814; he came to Golden Pond, Ky., in 1841, and engaged in farming and trading extensively till his death, which occurred in 1855. He was married to Elitha Griffin, January 12, 1840. She was born in Hampton County, N. C., February 27, 1819; she came with her parents when an infant to Tennessee. There she was reared. They have had seven children, five of whom are now living: William A., Hester A., Z. T., Sarah E. and Mary A. John D. died in 1882, aged forty-two. Joseph B. died in 1864, aged eighteen. Mrs. Bogard now owns over 400 acres of land, part of which she has rented out.

J. M. CRASS was born April 5, 1854, in Trigg County. He is a son of Elisha Crass and Sallie Ross. His parents came to Trigg County in about 1824; they died in 1859. Subject was reared by his brother-in-law, W. D. Vickers. At the age of eighteen he commenced selling groceries and farming; after selling goods two years, he secured a contract to carry the mail from Aurora to Cadiz; this contract continued two years. Later he engaged in milling and ran a steam ferry. In 1880 he built his present corn-mill, which has a capacity of 150 bushels a day. Mr. Crass took up preaching in 1880, in connection with the Christian Union Church, and in October of the same year he was ordained a minister of that denomination. He has charge of Averett's Chapel, Walnut Grove Church, and Flint Valley Church, Calloway County; he also preaches at the Cumberland Presbyterian Church in Calloway and Marshall Counties. Mr. Crass was married, in 1870, to Mrs. Mary F. Burrow, of Todd County. Mr. Crass was a member of the first Christian Union Council held in Trigg County, October, 1878. He was also a member of the first Christian Union Council held in Illinois, in Fayette County. It was held at Bethel Church, twelve miles south of Nokomis. Mr. Crass is still a Christian Union Preacher, and his prayer is that all Christians may be united in Christian union upon the grand principle of the Bible. There are now 130,000 souls united on the grand principle of union, taking the Bible for their rule of faith and practice, renouncing all creeds and confession of faith.

PERRY FUTRELL, farmer, was born in Trigg County, Ky., October 23, 1814, and is a son of John and Elizabeth (Deloach) Futrell, both natives of North Carolina and of English descent. John Futrell emigrated to Kentucky about the year 1800, and settled on Donaldson Creek. He was a farmer; was engaged in the Indian war in Indiana; was a devoted member of the Baptist Church, and died about the year 1873. Perry Futrell was educated in Trigg County, and remained with his parents until 1836, when he was married to Elizabeth Colson, a native of Kentucky. Eleven children were born to this union, of whom seven are living. Mr. Futrell has followed farming all his life. He began life with nothing, and now owns 280 acres, 120 of which are under cultivation. Mr. Futrell is one of the oldest and most highly esteemed citizens of the precinct and county.

SOLOMON D. FUTRELL was born June 4, 1820, in Trigg County. He is a son of John and Elizabeth (Deloach) Futrell; his parents were born in North Carolina; there they were married and came to Christian, now Trigg County, at an early date. The father died in 1873, at the advanced age of ninety-four. The mother died in 1828, aged forty-five. On coming here the courts in Hopkinsville were held in black jack poles. From Hopkinsville to Donaldson's Creek there was no growth of timber; a riding switch could not even be obtained. On their arrival at Nashvile there were but three stores, and but one in Hopkinsville. Our subject, at the age of twenty-one rented a farm, and there he remained eight years. He then bought eighty acres of land, which he improved and sold. He now owns 213 acres largely improved, all of which he has acquired by his attention to business and judicious management. He married, in 1846, Clarissa Futrell. She was born in Trigg County. They have had ten children, seven of whom are now living—four sons and three daughters.

CASWELL FUTRELL was born April 30, 1830, in Trigg County. He is a son of Perry and Betsey (Colson) Futrell. The father and mother were both born in Trigg County. Our subject was reared on his father's farm. On arriving at his majority he bought a farm of 106 acres; he has since increased this to 154 acres, well improved, all of which has been done by his own industry. Mr. Futrell was married to Caroline Colson. She was born in Trigg County. He enlisted in 1862 in Company D, Second Kentucky Cavalry, and served his enlistment.

WILLIAM G. GORDON was born in Rome County, Tenn., in 1839. At about the age of six years he came with his parents to Trigg County, where he has since lived. He first purchased $212\frac{1}{2}$ acres of land, and now owns about 310 acres, largely improved. He was married in 1861 to Eliza J. Choat. She was born in Stewart County, Tenn. They have one son—William J.—who was born in 1863, and works this farm with his father. He was married in 1880 to Mattie Wallace. She was born in Trigg County. They have two children—one son and one daughter.

DR. J. W. JOHNSON was born November 6, 1850, in Robertson County, Tenn. He is a son of William and Polly (Dunnington) Johnson. The parents are natives of Tennessee. The former was born in 1812, and is now living on his farm in Robertson County. The latter died in 1877, aged sixty years. Our subject was reared on his father's farm, and attended the subscription schools of that locality. At the age of fifteen he entered the Neaphogen College, Cross Plains, Tenn., where he remained four years. He then attended the East Tennessee University one term, and the Stonewall College one term, after which he came to Crittenden County. There he studied medicine under the preceptorship of Dr. J. R. Clark two years. He then moved to Lyon County, where he practiced medicine about seven months. Then removed to Golden Pond, where he has since been engaged in the practice of his profession, except one term spent at the Medical Department of the Louisville University. In 1883 the Doctor was a candidate for the Legislature, and was defeated by 39 votes.

A. D. MATHENY was born May 25, 1823, in East Tennessee. He is the son of James and Elizabeth (Deatherage) Matheny. Subject was reared on his father's farm. In 1845 he tramped to Trigg County, and settled in Golden Pond Precinct, where he remained till his marriage in 1850. He then lived in the Canton District seven years, then returned to the Golden Pond District where he still lives on the farm he first purchased. He has since added other lands, and now owns 600 acres of poor land, all of which he has acquired by strict attention to business and hard work. Mr. Matheny was married in 1850 to Miss L. A. C. Ross, of Trigg County, born in Stewart County, Tenn., May 25, 1826. To them have been born seven children, of whom six are living—four boys and two girls.

DAVID MAYES was born November 6, 1826, in Granger County, east Tenn. He is the ninth of a family of ten children born to John and Nancy (Mayes) Mayes. The father was born in Virginia; he died in Granger County, Tenn., in 1850, aged seventy-six. The mother was born in Granger County. She died in about 1834, aged sixty. In 1846 our subject came to Trigg County, and worked at various kinds of employments till 1852, when he bought 119 acres where he now resides; he has since increased this to 211 acres. This farm lies on Turkey Creek bottom, and is one of the finest and most productive farms in the county, and by far surpasses any other farm between the rivers. Mr. Mayes was married August 5, 1853, to Catharine Vinson. She was born in Trigg County on December 8, 1836. This union has been blessed with eight children, six of whom are living: Fathey E., wife of Albert Calhoun;

Caroline, now Mrs. Miller; Nancy J., now Mrs. William May; Josephus; Rebecca, now Mrs. Flinn and Rufus; John D., died November 13, 1880, aged sixteen; Bedie Ann, died in October, 1869, aged two years. Mr. and Mrs. Mayes are life-long and devoted members of the Missionary Baptist Church.

J. W. ROSS was born May 3, 1829, in Henry County, Tenn. He is a son of Jonathan and Narcissa (Stubblefield) Ross, both natives of Tennessee. In 1830 he was brought with his parents to Trigg County, where he has since lived. The father died November, 1883, aged eighty years. The mother died in 1861, aged sixty. Subject was reared on his father's farm. He owns 200 acres of land, and is engaged in agricultural pursuits; also owns and operates a saw-mill on his land; he was engaged in merchandising from 1876–78, at Golden Pond and Maple Grove, Ky. He enlisted in 1862 in Company L, Eighth Kentucky Cavalry; served about six months, and was discharged on account of physical disability. He was married in 1848, to Mrs. Mary A. Ritch, of Rome County, Tenn.; they have one daughter—Martha A., now Mrs. Ahart. Mrs. Ross has two children by a former marriage.

C. H. SMITH was born June 20, 1820, in Wilson County, middle Tenn. He is the son of James and Martha (Johnson) Smith. The parents were also natives of the same county and State; the father died in 1876, aged seventy-five; the mother died in 1855, aged forty-nine. Subject was reared on his father's farm. He enlisted in 1846, in the Mexican war; served part of two years. He then returned to Wilson County, and in the fall of 1847, he was married to Miss Matilda Vaughn. She was born in the same county. This marriage has been blessed with five children—two daughters and three sons. In 1859 they moved to Trigg County, and settled where they now live on the Tennessee River. Mr. Smith owns 300 acres of land, about 150 acres of which are improved. Since coming to this land he has placed himself in comfortable circumstances by his constant and strict attention to business.

RICHARD T. SOLOMON was born August 27, 1857, in Trigg County, He is the fourth of a family of eight children born to John and Sallie (Meredith) Solomon. The father was born in Granger County, east Tenn., and served in the Mexican war. The mother died in 1866, aged about thirty-five. Our subject commenced working out at about the age of twelve, and since this time has taken care of himself. He was married, in 1877, to Mrs. Polly Joyce, of Granger County. Three children have blessed this marriage: Cora, Josie and_Oscar. Mrs. Solomon has six children by a former marriage: Mary, Manda, John, Eliza, Elfie and Allie.

DR. A. THOMAS was born in Trigg County, Ky., April 8, 1822. He is a son of Perry and Elizabeth (Bridges) Thomas. The father was born in Bertie County, N. C.; came with his parents to Christian, now Trigg County, in 1806, and is still living in Canton Precinct, at the advanced age of eighty-eight years. He still enjoys remarkably good health. The mother is also living and enjoying good health, now in her eightieth year. Subject at the age of twenty-one took up the study of medicine under the preceptorship of Dr. Thomas B. Jefferson. After studying four years he attended the Medical Department of the Louisville University, and graduated in the class of 1848. He then returned to Trigg County, where he has since been engaged in the practice of his profession. The Doctor is the oldest practicing physician now in this county. He practiced at the Stacker Iron Works five years, and two years in Canton. In 1856 he came to Golden Pond, where he has since resided, except the two years he was Assistant Surgeon in the Union Army, stationed at Smithland, Ky. On his return from the army he was appointed Postmaster, which office he still holds. He was married, in 1866, to Mrs. Mary J. Frazelle, a native of Trigg County.

JOHN B. WILLIAMS, farmer, was born in Trigg County, Ky., May 16, 1832, and is a son of Futrell and Frances E. (Craig) Williams; the former a native of North Carolina, and of Scotch descent; the latter a native of South Carolina, and of Irish descent. Futrell Williams, in youth learned the wagon-maker's trade, and followed it in connection with farming. He emigrated to Kentucky in the year 1807, with his parents. John Craig, grandfather of our subject, came to Kentucky in 1799, landed at Donaldson Creek, and built his camp-fire against a small cottonwood tree. It is now one of the largest trees in the county, and still bears the marks of his camp-fire. It stands near the mouth of Craig's Branch, named in honor of John Craig, the pioneer. Futrell Williams, subject's father, was born in 1805, and died in 1862. His wife Frances was born August 27, 1797, and died 1878; she was a consistant member of the Missionary Baptist Church. John B. Williams received his education in his native county. He remained with his parents until March 4, 1852, when he was married to Temperance E. Ricks, daughter of John and Charity Ricks, and a native of Kentucky. To Mr. and Mrs. Williams were born ten children, of whom six sons and one daughter are living. Mr. Williams has held the office of Constable and Magistrate. He belongs to the Blue Lodge, A. F. & A. M., No. 567, at Golden Pond, and was connected with the P. of H. He is a member of the Baptist Church.

DR. G. P. YARBROUGH was born July 21, 1851, in Golden Pond Precinct. He is a son of Asa and Temperence (McGregor) Yarbrough. The parents were natives of Stewart County, Tenn. The father died May 19, 1872, aged fifty-eight years. The mother died in August, 1883, aged fifty-nine. Our subject was reared on his father's farm. At the age of twenty he engaged in school teaching, and during this time he studied medicine. After teaching about ten months he studied under the preceptership of Dr. Benj. Franklin three years. During the winter of 1872 and 1873 he took a course of lectures at the Medical Department of the University of Tennessee, after which he returned home and raised a crop on his father's farm. In June, 1874, he received a certificate from the Judicial Medical Board at Hopkinsville, and since that time has been actively engaged in the practice of his profession at this point. He was married, in 1876, to Sarah H. Malone. She was born in Ferguson Springs Precinct, a daughter of W. B. Malone, now engaged in the tobacco business at Canton.

ROCK CASTLE PRECINCT.

BLAKE BAKER, Jr., farmer, was born in Trigg County, Ky., February 19, 1837, and is a son of Blake and Edna (Gressham) Baker; the former a native of North Carolina and of English descent, the latter a native of Virginia and of Scotch descent. Blake Baker, Sr., was educated in Kentucky, to which State he removed when quite young. He made farming his sole occupation. He first settled in Lyon County, then Caldwell County, and finally located in Trigg County, where he died August 29, 1852. He was a member of the Baptist Church, and served as Magistrate for a number of years. Blake Baker, Jr., remained at the homestead until January 30, 1859, when he was married to Elizabeth J. Grasty, a native of Kentucky. Seven children bless their union— four sons and three daughters. Mr. Baker has filled the office of Magistrate since 1872, and is a Democrat in politics. He owns and operates a farm in Rock Castle Precinct, Trigg County. Mr. and Mrs. Baker are devoted members of the Baptist Church.

SAMUEL F. BAKER, farmer, was born in Trigg County, Ky., May 17, 1842, and is a son of Blake and Clarinda E. (Standrod) Baker, both natives of Kentucky and of Scotch-English descent. The former died about the year 1845. S. F. Baker received a good education in the schools of his locality; his father died when he (Samuel) was very young, and he was taken and reared by his grandfather Standrod, with whom he remained until his marriage, which took place February 15, 1861, to Sarah A. Hendrick, a native of Kentucky. To them were born three children, of whom one son and one daughter are living. Mrs. Baker died in September, 1865. Mr. Baker's second marriage was on October 15, 1868, to Sarah A. Thomas, a native of Kentucky. Seven children were born to this union, of whom two sons and three daughters are living: Margaret E., Mark S., Nancy I., Lulu B. and Zee. Mr. Baker has followed farming all his life, and at present fills the office of Magistrate for the precinct. He owns and operates a farm near Rock Castle Precinct. Mrs. B. is a devoted member of the Baptist Church.

J. R. BURNAM was born in North Carolina, October 4, 1823, and is a son of Wilson and Elizabeth (Gambrel) Burnam, both natives of North Carolina and of English descent, respectively. Wilson Burnam emigrated to Kentucky about the year 1830, and settled in Trigg County; he was a carpenter, and worked at his trade in connection with farming until his death in 1877. J. R. Burnam was educated in Trigg County and remained with his parents until 1850, when he was married to Sarah J. Holly, a native of Kentucky; to them were born two sons and one daughter. Mrs. Burnam died some seventeen years ago, and Mr. B. next married Lucy Hyden, a native of Tennessee. Two children bless this union—one son and one daughter. Mr. Burnam is by trade a brick-layer, and follows this business in connection with farming. He is a member of the I. O. O. F. at Rock Castle, also of the Blue Lodge, A. F. & A. M. at Parkersville, Ky., and is one of the leading men of the precinct and county.

JOHN F. CAMPBELL was born in Trigg County, Ky., December 17, 1830, and is a son of William and Sarah Campbell. John F. remained with his parents until twenty years of age, when he entered the employ of Hillman, Van Lear & Co., as book-keeper and salesman; with them he remained four years, and after spending some time at home, again entered their employ. In 1860 he began business for himself at Rock Castle; one year later he began farming, which he has since followed, with the exception of three years, when he was engaged in the milling business. At present he resides near Rock Castle, west of the Cumberland. Mr. Campbell was married February 14, 1861, to Sarah Cunningham, a native of Tennessee. To them were born eight children, of whom Joseph N., William J., James S., Charles, Alice B. and George G. are living. Mr. C. is a member of the Blue Lodge, A. F. & A. M., Joppa, No. 167. He owns one of the best farms between the Cumberland and Tennessee Rivers; he is one of the leading citizens of the precinct and county.

WILLIAM M. CAMPBELL was born in Trigg County, Ky., October 3, 1842, and is a son of William and Sarah J. (Baker) Campbell, both natives of Kentucky, the former of Scotch and the latter of French descent. William Campbell, Sr., was born in Bourbon County, Ky., October 26, 1797, where he lived for some time, then removed to Tennessee, where he spent one year, then came to Christian County, and thence to Trigg County, where he still resides at the advanced age of eighty-seven years, the oldest man in Rock Castle Precinct and the second oldest in the county. When Mr. Campbell came to Trigg County it was unoccupied save by wolves, bears and wild game. In youth he learned the tanner's trade, but made farming his occupation instead. William M. Campbell (our subject) received a good common school education, but was forced to leave school early owing to ill health. At the beginning of the war troubles, though barely old enough for enrollment, he was elected Captain of Company A, First Regiment Kentucky Volunteers. In September, 1861, he enlisted in Capt. T. G. Woodward's squadron, Kentucky Cavalry, C. S. A., which subsequently composed Companies A and B, First Kentucky Cavalry, commanded by Gen. Ben Hardin Helm. Mr. Campbell served throughout the war, rising through successive grades from private to Lieutenant commanding company. He was desperately wounded in front of Columbia, S. C., on the 15th of February, 1865. After the war he taught school one year. He was married, November 16, 1865, to Rebecca C. Holland, a native of Kentucky, by whom he has had nine children, of whom Nannie, John S. David W., William M., Jr., and Richard G. are living. After his marriage Mr. Campbell engaged in merchandising; later was employed as head salesman for Hillman & Son's Iron Works, and at present is head salesman for Ewald & Co.'s store (iron works), and also superintends his farm. He is a member of the P. of H. and A. F. & A. M., and of the Missionary Baptist Church. Has served as Sheriff of Trigg County four years; has also figured conspicuously in politics, and is one of the leading influential business men of the county.

THOMAS W. FINLEY, farmer, was born in De Kalb County, Tenn., January 10, 1847, and is a son of Henry and Permelia Finley, natives respectively of Tennessee and Georgia, and of Irish descent. Thomas W. remained on the homestead until August 14, 1864, when he was married to Meridian Walker, a native of Tennessee. They had five children, of whom two sons and two daughters are living. In 1867 Mr. Finley emigrated to Kentucky, settled in Trigg County and followed farming; December 16, 1875, his wife died, and June 11, 1876, he married Mary Powell, a native of Kentucky; to them were born two children. His third marriage was December 20, 1881, to Nancy Keil, a native of Tennessee. Mr. Finley is a member of the Baptist Church; he owns and operates a farm in Rock Castle Precinct, where he is a representative citizen.

DANIEL HILLMAN, proprietor of a smelting furnace and rolling-mill, was born in New Jersey, February 26, 1807, and is a son of Daniel and Grace (Huston) Hillman. They were natives of New Jersey and are supposed to be of English descent. Daniel Hillman, Sr., was largely engaged in the iron business in New Jersey, and also engaged in the same business for eight or nine years in Greenupsburg, Ky., after his removal to that place; there also Mrs. Hillman died. Some years after, Mr. Hillman, in company with another party, built the first smelting furnace in the neighborhood of Birmingham, Ala. Daniel Hillman, Jr., received a good common school education in Kentucky, to which State he came with his parents, when he was quite young. He went into business with Van Lear at Cumberland Furnace, Dixon Co., Tenn.; from there he came to Empire Furnace in Trigg County, Ky., and entered into partnership with Dr. Watson. While at the Cumberland Furnace he was married to a daughter of Dr. J. Hart Marible, member of Congress. To their union were born four children—two sons and two daughters—all of whom are living. While engaged at the Empire Furnace, he built the Fulton Furnace in Trigg County, moved the rolling mill from Nashville to Lyon County, and put it up across the river from the Empire Furnace. On the death of his partner, he bought the latter's interest and controlled the business. He afterward took his two brothers as partners, and the firm was known as D. Hillman & Bros. He had large commission houses all over the country, and before the war, built what is known as Center Furnace, which is now operated by one of his sons; he also owned a furnace in Hickman County, Tenn. At the breaking out of the war these furnaces were closed, the Center Furnace being now the only one in operation. Before the war Mr. Hillman was also owner of 72,000 acres of land. In 1870 or 1871 he purchased property in Alabama, both coal and iron—the Alice Furnace Company which is now consolidated with the Pratt Coal Company. The Trigg Furnace was built in 1871 and was operated for some three and a half years, when Mr. Hillman's health began to fail, and it is now idle. Mrs. Hillman died in 1861. His second marriage, took place in the fall of 1865, to

Mary A. Gentry, a daughter of Meredith P. Gentry, Member of Congress from Tennessee. To this union have been born four sons, three of whom are living. Mr. Hillman is a member of the Nashville, Tenn., Lodge, A. F. & A. M., also a Knight Templar. Since the failing of his health, he has sold some of his property. He is one of the leading, influential citizens and business men of Trigg County.

SAMUEL M. HOLLAND was born in Trigg County, Ky., November 7, 1857, and is a son of J. A. and Minerva (Standrod) Holland, the former a native of Virginia, and the latter a native of Kentucky, of English descent respectively; the father emigrated to Kentucky at an early age, and settled in what was then Caldwell County, but now Trigg County; he was a farmer; he was married October 10, 1844; he was a member of the Blue Lodge, A. F. & A. M., Joppa, No. 167, in Lyon County, Ky. Mr. and Mrs. Holland were life-long members of the Baptist Church; the former died February 15, 1877, the latter January 31, 1884. Samuel M., our subject, remained with his parents on the homestead until November 4, 1880, when he was married to Lucy K. Baker, a native of Kentucky. To them have been born two children: Albert B. and Pearl. In connection with farming Mr. Holland owns and operates a cotton-gin, grist-mill, smith and wagon-shop. He owns a beautiful farm in Rock Castle, Trigg County, where he resides; he is one of the influential men of the county.

WILLIAM LITCHFIELD, farmer, was born in Lyon County (then Caldwell) November 20, 1820, and is a son of James and Nancy (Wimberly) Litchfield, the former a native of Virginia, and the latter of North Carolina, and were of English descent respectively. James Litchfield migrated to Kentucky in 1818, his first wife having died some time before. His second marriage was to the mother of our subject; he purchased a farm in Lyon County, then Caldwell County, Ky., where he died at the advanced age of ninety-four. William Litchfield remained with his parents in youth, and in 1844 was married to Elizabeth Oliver, a native of Kentucky. Five children bless their union, two sons and three daughter, all living. Mrs. L. died some years ago. She was a member of the Methodist Church. Mr. L. next married Mrs. Alzadie M. Dunn, a native of Kentucky, on March 3, 1880. They have one child—Carrie M. M. R. M. Dunn. Mr. Litchfield is a Democrat in politics, and is one of the pioneer citizens of the county. In religion he is a Baptist.

EPHRAIM D. OSBURN, farmer, was born in Trigg County, Ky., May 4, 1842, and is a son of Miles and Margaret (Sanders) Osburn, the former a native of Mississippi, the latter a native of Kentucky, of English descent, respectively. Miles Osburn came to Kentucky when quite young; was reared by his half-brother, and remained with him till he was married; he then settled in Rock Castle Precinct, and followed farming; he remained there till the fall of 1883, when he sold out and moved to Illinois, where he now resides; he is a member of the church, and one of the leading citizens of Trigg County. Ephraim D. Osburn remained with his parents until January 16, 1864, when he was married to Sarah E. Luttrell, a native of Kentucky. Nine children blessed their union, of whom five sons and one daughter are living. At about the age of eighteen Mr. Osburn learned the carpenter trade, and follows it in connection with farming, his principal occupation. In 1862 he enlisted in the Eighth Kentucky Regiment, Company B, and served three years. Mr. Osburn is a firm believer in the doctrines of the Baptist Church; he owns a farm in Rock Castle Precinct, and is one of the representative men in the county. Politically he is a Democrat.

WILEY PEAL, farmer, was born in Trigg County, Ky., November 19, 1849, and is a son of Harvey and Emily Creekmore) Peal, both natives of Trigg County. Harvey Peal was born July 11, 1820, in Trigg County, and owns the farm on which he now resides in Rock Castle Precinct. Wiley Peal remained with his parents until February 8, 1872, when he was married to Mattie Merrifield, a native of Kentucky. Three children bless their union: Anna, William R. and Daisy D. Mr. Peal follows farming, and frequently teaches school in the winter season, and for a time was clerk in the Tennessee Rolling Mills. He has held the office of Town Trustee. Mr. and Mrs. Peal are devoted members of the Baptist Church.

WILLIAM M. PEAL, farmer, was born in Trigg County, Ky., November 13, 1857, and is a son of Harvey and Emily Peal. He remained on the farm with his parents until March 7, 1876, when he was married to Sarah E. Creekmore, a daughter of George Creekmore, and a native of Kentucky. They have one child—Ida Lee. After his marriage Mr. Peal purchased a farm, on which he resides. In politics he is Republican, and leads the quiet but industrious life of a farmer in Rock Castle Precinct, where he is one of the representative citizens.

DRURY W. STANDROD, farmer, was born in Trigg County, Ky., February 23, 1822, and is a son of Bazzel and Rebecca (Rogers) Standrod, the former of German descent, the latter not known; the former died March 11, 1869; the latter March 28 1867. Drury W. Standrod was educated at the subscription schools of his native county; he was married October 14, 1853, to Catherine F. Campbell, a native of Kentucky. To them were born seven children, of whom three are living: Rebecca Frances, Samuel Ewing and Mary Elizabeth. Mr. Standrod followed farming until 1847, when he engaged in the mercantile business at Rock Castle; continued in the same until 1870, during which time he was and is still connected with the warehouse. He has held the office of Postmaster almost continuously since 1854; he is a member of the Blue Lodge, A. F. & A. M. Since 1870 he has principally been engaged in farming, and owns a farm of 225 acres, 175 of which are in cultivation. Mr. Standrod is one of the highly respected citizens of Rock Castle Precinct. The original family were all members of the Lutheran order of Baptists, and died in that faith, in which Mr. Standrod is also a believer.

S. E. STANDROD, physician, was born in Rock Castle, Trigg Co., Ky., June 7, 1857, and is a son of D. W. and C. F. Standrod. S. E. Standrod received a good education in his native county; he then attended the Nashville and Vanderbilt University of Medicine, where he will graduate this year. He is one of the promising young men of the county, is a devoted member of the Baptist Church, and bids fair to soon appear among the leading men of his chosen profession.

JOHN JAMES WALLACE, farmer, was born in Trigg County, Ky., and is a son of J. L. and Caroline (Prescott) Wallace, the former a native of Stewart County, Tenn., and the latter a native of Kentucky. J. L. Wallace began life at the age of thirteen, working by the month on a farm for very small wages. In 1839 he came to Kentucky, and in 1854 purchased a farm in Trigg County, which he still owns. He spent some three years in Texas, one year in Arkansas, then returned to Trigg County, where he now resides. He was married April 1, 1850. He is a member of the Blue Lodge, A. F. & A. M., Joppa, No. 167, and is a believer in the doctrines of the Baptist Church. J. J. Wallace, our subject, received a good education in youth in his native county. He remained with his parents, engaged on the farm until December 16, 1876, when he was married to Jane McConnell, a native of Kentucky. To them were born four children, of whom two sons and one daughter are yet living. Mr. Wallace owns a nice farm, and bids fair to become one of the leading farmers of the county.

ALVIN G. WALLACE was born in Trigg County, April 28, 1861, and is a son of James and Martha (Whithurst) Wallace, both natives of Tennessee, and of English descent. James Wallace was by trade a cabinet-maker, at which he worked in connection with farming. In 1856 he emigrated to Trigg County, Ky., where he bought a farm on which he resided during the remainder of his life. He served some two years in the Confederate Army during the late war. He was a member of the Blue Lodge, A. F. & A. M., Joppa, No. 167, in Lyon County. Mr. and Mrs. Wallace were life-long members of the Baptist Church. Mr. W. died October 26, 1879, loved by all who knew him. Alvin G., our subject, has always lived on the farm which he operates since the death of his father, and takes care of his only sister—Mary C. and his widowed mother. Mr. Wallace is twenty-three years old, a man of good habits, enterprising, industrious, and one of the promising young men of the county.

WALLONIA PRECINCT.

RICHARD BLANKS was born September 10, 1818, in Mecklenburg County, Va. He is a son of James and Sallie Blanks. The father was born in the same county and State January 15, 1769; he died July 10, 1852, at the mature age of eighty-three years, five months and twenty-five days. The mother was born in Mecklenburg County, Va.; she died July 5, 1859, aged eighty-five years, three months and eight days. In 1835 the family came to Trigg County; they settled on the farm now owned by subject; it consists of 156 acres of land; he also owns forty-eight and one-half acres on the Muddy Fork. Mr. Blanks was married on November 13, 1851, to Lucy Falkner. She was born in Trigg County. This marriage has been blessed with two daughters.

JOHN M. BOYD was born April 2, 1846, in Trigg County. He is the eldest of a family of nine children born to William and Harriet (Gray) Boyd. The father was born in Halifax County, Va.; he died November 18, 1877, aged sixty-three. The mother was born in 1826, in Tennessee, and is now living in this precinct. John M., in 1869, secured a position as clerk in a warehouse at Canton, where he remained about one year. He then bought an interest in a saw-mill in Canton, and operated it about four years; after which, a grist-mill was attached and run about three years. He then engaged in merchandising about four years. In September, 1882, he removed to his present locality, having built a grist-mill that fall at a cost of about $6,000. Mr. Boyd was married, in 1871, to Miss Marion Hopson, of Trigg County. This union has been blessed with two daughters. Mr. and Mrs. Boyd are members of the Baptist Church.

GEORGE W. BOYD was born in Christian County on August 3, 1846, and is a son of John W. and Polly (Anderson) Boyd. The father was born in Halifax County, Va., in 1813; he died in Christian County in 1865. The mother was born in Christian County, and died in 1854. Our subject at the age of nineteen secured employment in the County Clerk's office, also in the Circuit Clerk's office, and later engaged in school teaching; the latter position he held about ten years. He then engaged in farming, which he still continues. He owns a farm of 200 acres, located about one and a half miles southwest of Wallonia. Mr. Boyd was married in 1871 to Virginia Wall. This lady was born in this county. Their union has been blessed with one son—Walter S. Mr. Boyd is a member of the Christian Church.

ED. BRANDON, firm of Brandon Brothers, proprietors of saw-mill, and merchants, was born January 10, 1842, in Trigg County. He is the fifth child of a family of seven born to John L. and Eliza A. (Howell) Brandon; the former was born October 22, 1810, in Halifax County, Va. At about the age of seventeen, he came with his parents to Trigg County, and is now living with his sons. Mrs. Eliza A. Brandon was born in North Carolina in 1809. She died in May, 1874. Our subject was brought up on his father's farm; he followed farming till March, 1883, when he engaged in his present business. In the spring of 1879, he was appointed County Surveyor, and in August, 1879, he was elected to this office to fill an unexpired term, and again re-elected in 1883. He, with his brother, in 1879, bought what was known as the Larkin's saw-mill and which they have since operated. Mr. Brandon was married, June 4, 1863, to Louisa A. Larkins. She was born in Trigg County and is a daughter of William Larkins who died September, 1875, aged seventy-six.

L. S. DUNNING was born on the Muddy Fork of Little River, Trigg County, Ky., December 25, 1839, and is the ninth child of a family of thirteen born to Levi and Jeanette M. (Carney) Dunning. This family are of English origin; they immigrated to North Carolina at an early day. Shadrach Dunning, the great-grandfather of our subject came to Kentucky. He settled in what is now Trigg County, as early as 1803, and selected for his home a tract of land lying on the Muddy Fork of Little River, where he followed the vocation of a farmer until the time of his death. After coming to this county his descendants became scattered, part of them going to Missouri and part to Texas. The father of subject was born in Bertie County, N. C., October 3, 1797, and died in Trigg County, April 16, 1853. The mother was born in the same county and State, on the 24th of November, 1803, and died in Trigg County on her farm April 3, 1877. In many respects

Mrs. Dunning was a very remarkable woman. Left in moderate circumstances at the death of her husband, she, by close application to business,
succeeded in a few years in acquiring a competency; confining her attention to agricultural pursuits, she increased the original homestead from
about 600 or 800 acres to over 1,500 acres, and was considered the most
successful woman in the county. Mr. L. S. Dunning enlisted in 1862,
in Company B, Eighth Kentucky Regiment, Confederate Army, and
served till May, 1865; he participated in the siege of Vicksburg, Jackson,
Guntown and in the charge on Paducah, where Col. Thompson lost his
life, and served in other engagements. At the close of the war he
returned to his mother's farm, where he remained several years. In 1871
he removed to his present farm, which at that time contained 120 acres;
this he has increased to over 600 acres and is one of the best improved farms
in the neighborhood, and speaks well for his success as an agriculturist.
Mr. Dunning was married in 1871 to Miss Henrie, daughter of the late
Dr. L. D. Shelton, of Christian County. They have a family of four
children—three sons and one daughter.

JAMES H. GLOVER was born August 19, 1847, in Appomattox
County, Va. He is a son of A. P. and Mary (Dickerson) Glover, also
natives of Virginia. The father of subject owned a farm of 452 acres in
Virginia; this he disposed of, and in 1869 removed to Christian County,
where he now resides. Our subject came to this farm in 1881, having
purchased it from W. W. Carney. It consists of 240 acres; he formerly
owned a farm in Caldwell County where he resided about twelve years.
He was married in 1872 to Miss Sallie E. Terry; she was born in Halifax County, Va. This marriage has been blessed with five children,
three sons and two daughters.

W. J. GRAY was born July 29, 1839, in Caldwell County, Ky. He
is a son of Nathan and Lydia (Green) Gray. The father was born in
Caldwell County; he died in 1867, aged fifty-four. The mother was born
in the same county and State; she died in 1857, aged thirty-eight. Our
subject came to this farm in 1872; it consists of 207 acres of land. Mr.
Gray was married March 16, 1862, to Martha E. Kanedy. She was
born on this farm. Their union has been blessed with seven children—
three sons and four daughters. Mr. Gray is a life-long and devoted
member of the Baptist Church. He is a member of the Masonic fraternity and Chosen Friends.

W. C. HAYDON was born April 12, 1826, in Trigg County. He is a son of Dr. William C. Haydon who was born in 1782 in Virginia, and was brought with his parents to Clark County, Ky., when quite young; there he grew to manhood; he then attended the Philadelphia Medical College, and graduated from that school of learning. On his return to Clark County, he engaged in the practice of his profession. He married in Mt. Sterling, Ky. Soon after moved to Princeton; while practicing he secured the contract and built the first courthouse erected in Princeton. After a residence of a few years there, he removed to Trigg County, where he engaged in the practice of his profession till death. He also engaged in agricultural pursuits. He had served as magistrate several years, and held the office of Sheriff two years. The Doctor was usually called upon to prepare deeds, mortgages and other legal instruments, and was recognized as one of the leading men of this locality. Our subject now owns and occupies the homestead where he was born, consisting of 420 acres. He was married in January, 1855, to Miss Eliza A. Robertson. She was born in Virginia. Nine children have blessed this union —three sons and six daughters.

DR. W. A. LINDSEY was born at Lindsey's Mills, Trigg County, March 24, 1857; he is the son of James A. and Mary E. (Garnett) Lindsey. The father was born in 1833, also at these mills, which had been erected by his father, S. S. Lindsey, at an early day. James A. died in 1860, aged twenty-seven years; he had opened a store at the mills, where he was engaged in merchandising at the time of his death. The mother was born in 1838, on Little River, in this county, and now lives with her son in Wallonia. At the age of twenty-three, subject took up the study of medicine, under the preceptorship of Dr. J. W. Crenshaw, of Cadiz. In 1881 he attended the Louisville Medical College; he graduated from this school of learning in the class of 1883; he then went to Roaring Springs, where he practiced a short time. In May, 1883, he located at Wallonia, where he is now actively engaged in the practice of his profession. The Doctor is a member of the Trigg County Medical Society.

W. J. MOORE was born in Mecklenburg County, Va., August 24, 1835. He is the third child of a family of six born to Henderson and Margaret (Owen) Moore. The former was born September 6, 1806, in

Mecklenburg County, Va.; he died in 1878, in Trigg County. The latter was born in the same locality, January 6, 1807, and is now living in this county with her son, James H. Moore. Our subject was reared on his father's farm; at the age of twenty he secured employment as clerk in a store; he continued in this capacity till 1875, when he established himself in business; he continued merchandising till March 1, 1883, at which time he retired, and is now settling up his book and other accounts.

DR. A. G. P'POOL was born February 27, 1849, in Mecklenburg County, Va. He is a son of Dr. E. F. and Sarah (Gregory) P'Pool. The father was born November 6, 1814, in the same county. He there followed the medical profession, and was also a planter till 1857, when he removed to Nashville, and engaged in the publishing of the *Tennessee Baptist*, and later attended the Nashville Medical College, from which he graduated in 1861 or 1862. He then resumed the practice of medicine, and continued this profession till his death, which occurred in May, 1880. The mother was born in 1820, and now lives in Nashville, Tenn. Our subject in 1868 commenced the study of medicine, under the preceptorship of his brother, Dr. E. S. P'Pool, after which he attended the Louisville Medical College. He graduated from the University of Nashville in the class of 1872, and at once commenced the practice of his profession at Nashville, and in the fall of 1872 removed to Caldwell County, where he continued his practice till 1877; he then came to Wallonia. Here he remained till 1880, when he returned to Nashville, Tenn., on account of the death of his father. In Nashville he practiced but a short time, and again returned to Wallonia, where he has since been actively engaged at his profession. He now occupies the premises formerly owned by his brother. He was married in 1874 to Susan M., daughter of E. M. Wood, of Caldwell County. Five children bless this union—three sons and two daughters. The Doctor is a member of the Trigg County Medical Society. Was Vice-President of this body in 1883.

ROBERT WADE was born December 29, 1824, in Montgomery County, Tenn. He is the seventh child of a family of twelve born to Peter and Elizabeth (Wortham) Wade. The former was born in Halifax County, Va.; he died in October, 1860, aged seventy-two. The mother was born in the same county and State in 1796; she died in 1866. Our

subject was brought to this county with his parents in 1832. He assisted
on their farm till the age of twenty-one, since which time he has been
carrying on business on his own account. He lived on a rented farm
from 1860 to 1863, and then bought his present farm, which consists of
216½ acres. Mr. Wade was married in September, 1861, to Miss Nancy
J. Brandon. She was born in Trigg County. They have four children
—three sons and one daughter. They lost William Lee September 1,
1883, aged seventeen. Lucy Jane died in 1881. Mr. Wade is a member of the Masonic fraternity, and a life-long and devoted member of the
Methodist Episcopal Church South.

ABITHAL WALLACE was born March 18, 1839, in Stewart
County, Tenn. He is the eldest child of a family of ten born to James
Wallace and Martha Whitehurst; the former was born in 1815, in Stewart County, Tenn. He died in 1880, aged sixty-three. The latter is
the daughter of Joshua Whitehurst, who was born in Martin County,
N. C., in 1776, and now a resident of Stewart County, Tenn.,
where he is enjoying a reasonable degree of health, at the advanced age
of one hundred and eight years. Our subject came with his parents to
Trigg County, in 1855. He assisted on their farm till the age of twenty-
one, since which time he has been engaged at contracting and building.
In 1860, he built a residence in Cadiz, now occupied by W. C. White.
He owns a store room in Wallonia, and other property in the village. He
in company with Maj. Bingham built several bridges in this county.
From 1876 to 1882 he was engaged in merchandising in Wallonia. He
now has an interest in a drug store in Princeton, Ky. Mr. Wallace
enlisted in 1862, Company D, Col. Woodard's Second Regiment of Cavalry; served about nine months, after which the regiment was disbanded
near Columbia, Tenn. He was married February 7, 1861, to Mary D.
Cameron. She was born in this county; two sons bless this union—
Alexander and James D. Wallace.

E. E. WASH was born April 3, 1843, in Simpson County, Ky.
He is a son of W. O. and Frances B. (Goodlette) Wash. The former
was born in 1808, in Kentucky; he died November 21, 1880. The
latter was also born in Kentucky. She died January 17, 1876, in Wallonia, aged sixty-one. Our subject was brought to Trigg County with his
parents when young, and on attaining his majority, engaged in agricult-

ural pursuits on his own account. In 1876 he came to his present farm, consisting then of 125 acres. He has since added to these possessions as his circumstances would admit, and now owns about 400 acres, and is considered one of the best farmers in the precinct. Mr. Wash was married May 2, 1877, to Miss Nannie Boyd, daughter of William Boyd. This union has been blessed with two children.

J. R. WATKINS was born in Trigg County June 1, 1828; he is the eldest of a family of fifteen children born to H. B. and Diana F. (Wade) Watkins. The father was born November 1, 1806, in Montgomery County, Tenn.; he died November 27, 1874. The mother was born in Halifax County, Va., November 27, 1807 ; she died April 2, 1868. They immigrated to Trigg County in December, 1827. Our subject was reared on his father's farm, and from 1850 to 1870 he held the position of overseer; he then bought a farm, which he has since improved and where he now resides. He owns in all 380 acres. Mr. Watkins was married, in 1873, to Miss Mildred Husk. She was born in Trigg County.

S. M. WATKINS was born December 11, 1848, in Christian County; he is a son of Samuel M. and Sarah (Hawkins) Watkins; the former was born in Tennessee, and died in August, 1873, aged fifty-six; the latter was born in Christian County in 1821. Our subject after arriving at manhood removed to the Purchase, where he remained one year; he then came to Trigg County and worked for his uncle, Hezekiah T. Watkins, from 1870 to 1874, when he was married to Susan A., daughter of S. J. Watkins. He then lived on his father-in-law's farm one year, and then returned to his uncle's farm, where he worked two years. In the fall of 1877 he came to his present farm, consisting of 100 acres. Mr. and Mrs. Watkins have four bright children—three sons and one daughter. The parents are members of the Methodist Episcopal Church South.

CERULEAN SPRINGS PRECINCT.

M. E. BAREFIELD was born in Campbell County, Ga., December 26, 1845; he is the fourteenth child in a family of fifteen children born to John and Anna (Parker) Barefield. The father was born in Georgia, and died December 27, 1883, at the advanced age of ninety-six years. The mother was born in North Carolina, and is now living in Georgia with one of her sons. Our subject enlisted, in 1863, in Company K, Thirtieth Georgia Regiment, Capt. H. B. Morris. He served until the close of the war. In 1867 he came to his present farm; his first purchase was 100 acres. By his economy, good management and industry he has increased this farm to 278 acres; his farm is well improved, with a comfortable residence, which he built at a cost of about $1,500; his other buildings cost about $300. He was married, in 1868, to Mary E. Ladd, of this county. Two sons have blessed this marriage. Mr. Barefield is a member of the Missionary Baptist Church.

DR. JOHN J. BLAKELEY was born March 26, 1834, in Trigg County; he is the second of a family of nine children born to William S. and Louisa (Haggard) Blakeley. The father was born in North Carolina in 1801, and died in Trigg County, Ky., in 1865; the mother was a native of Virginia, and was born in 1811. They were among the earliest settlers of this county. Our subject, at about the age of thirty-three, commenced the study of medicine under the preceptorship of his brother, Dr. W. H. Blakeley; having studied four years, he went to Cincinnati and attended the Pulte Medical College, after which he went to St. Louis and attended the Hahnemann Medical College, and graduated in the class of 1872; he then returned to Trigg County, at which time his brother, Dr. Blakeley, removed to Bowling Green; he at once assumed his brother's practice, and has since been engaged in the practice of his chosen profession. He owns a farm of 125 acres, where he now resides, and is also engaged in agriculture. He was married in June, 1858, to Almira E. Blakeley, a native of Trigg County. Four children have blessed this union—two sons and two daughters.   He is a member of the Masonic fraternity, also a member of the Baptist Church.

C. M. COX was born February 2, 1855, in Cerulean Springs Precinct, Trigg County.   He is a son of C. M. R. and Nancy C. (Moore) Cox, both natives of Mecklenburg County, Va.   The father was born March 18, 1818; at the age of seventeen he started on foot for Kentucky, with $20 in his pocket.   Trigg County was his first stopping place; here he remained three years, when he returned to his native State and county, and was married in 1838, after which he returned to Trigg County, and bought a farm of 100 acres, which he afterward sold.   After serving as overseer for four years he bought his present farm of 100 acres.   Our subject also owns 100 acres which he cultivates in connection with his father's.   He has recently completed a comfortable house at a cost of about $1,400, also a barn at a cost of $250.   Mr. C. M. Cox was married in 1872 to Miss Frances Ladd, of Trigg County.   Their union has been blessed with three children—one son and two daughters.   His uncle, Lanson Cox, is still carrying on his farm in Mecklenburg County, Va., at the advanced age of ninety-one years.

A. B. CULLOM, M. D., was born in Davidson County, Tenn., July 16, 1839.   His parents were Jesse P. and Susan A. (Hooper) Cullom, the former born in same county and State in 1815, and died March 28, 1851, in Lexington, Mo.   The mother was born in Dixon County, Tenn., August 29, 1815, and is now living with her son, Dr. Cullom, who at the age of sixteen commenced the watch-making trade, which he followed five years.   He enlisted in 1861 in Capt. Crenshaw's company, under Gen. Price, of Missouri.   He served until the close of the war. Soon after enlistment he was commissioned First Lieutenant and participated in the battles of Carthage, Springfield and Pea Ridge.   He was then detailed on scout duty in which he continued until the close of the war, when he returned to Nashville and followed his former trade one year.   He then secured a position as clerk in the dry goods store of J. M. Hooper, where he continued one year, after which he took up the study of medicine under the preceptorship of Dr. J. P. Cullom.   He remained with the Doctor three years.   He then attended the Medical Department of the Nashville University and graduated in the class of 1870.   He then moved to Calloway County and commenced the practice of medicine.   In

1879 he moved to Cerulian Springs, where he has since been engaged in the practice of his profession with good success. He was married November 9, 1876, to Miss S. A. Brown, of Calloway County, Ky. Three children have blessed this union. The Doctor is a member of the Masonic fraternity, Blue Lodge, and Chapter at Murray, Ky.; also is a member of the Baptist Church, and has been Superintendent of the Sunday-school of that place since his arrival here in 1879.

DR. B. F. FELIX was born in Wayne County, Ill., November 29, 1844. His parents are D. K. and Susan Ann (Mansfield) Felix; the father is a native of Ohio County, Ky., and now lives on his farm in Wayne County, Ill. The mother was born in Logan County, Ky. Our subject was reared on his father's farm, and attended the district schools of the county. In 1876 he commenced the study of medicine; two years he continued under the preceptorship of Dr. P. J. Puckett, of White County, Ill. He then attended the Pulte Medical College at Cincinnati, during the fall and winter of 1877 and 1878, and after leaving college moved to Stewart County, Tenn., where he practiced but a short time, then went to Elkton in Todd County, Ky., and entered into practice with Dr. C. T. Lewis, continuing about six months. March 5, 1879, he came to Cerulean Springs, where he has since been engaged in the practice of his chosen profession. He was married October 5, 1864, to Miss Olive Butler, a native of Wayne County, Ill. She was born September 21, 1848, and died May 17, 1877, leaving three daughters. His second marriage occurred December 11, 1879, to Miss Jennie Hester, a native of Caldwell County, Ky. They are members of the Missionary Baptist Church.

W. S. GOODWIN was born on this farm July 18, 1823; he is the fifth child of a family of six born to Samuel and Mary (Griffith) Goodwin. The father was born in South Carolina September 2, 1785; when a child, Jesse Goodwin, his father, moved to Nashville, Tenn., and after raising one crop removed to Christian, now Trigg County, Ky., and located near Cerulean Springs—the Goodwin family being the earliest settlers of the county. This farm, now owned by subject, was deeded to his father, Samuel, by his grandfather in 1804; here he continued to reside till his death, which occurred December 5, 1862, at the age of seventy-eight. This farm now consists of 200 acres and is very pleasantly situated about one mile from Cerulean Springs. Mr. W. S. Goodwin was married, May 4, 1848, to Miss Martha Wilson. She was born in Caldwell County, June 3, 1823, and reared in Trigg County. This marriage was blessed with nine children; six are now living—three sons and three daughters. Mr. Goodwin was Deputy Sheriff from 1844 to 1848; he is also a member of the Masonic fraternity, and he, with Mrs. Goodwin, are life-long and devoted members of the Baptist Church. The land where the Baptist Church now stands was deeded to this denomination by Jesse Goodwin, and is the oldest church in this part of the State.

B. F. GOODWIN was born September 8, 1850, in Trigg County; he is a son of Robert S. and Nancy (Blakely) Goodwin. The father was born March 29, 1811, in Christian, now Trigg County, and is a son of Samuel and Sarah (Brown) Goodwin. They emigrated from North Carolina to Nashville, Tenn., in 1782; then soon after removed to what is now Trigg County, and were the earliest settlers of the county. Samuel Goodwin died here, July 26, 1844, in his seventy-eighth year; his wife died in February, 1842, aged sixty-seven. Robert S. Goodwin now resides on and owns part of the land which was entered by his father, and for which he holds a patent from the United States. Our subject received his early education at the subscription schools of this locality, after which he went to Cadiz and continued his studies under Prof. Wayland; he then secured a position as clerk for G. W. Lindsey, where he remained six years; and later with G. T. McCain, with whom he clerked two years. In 1882, he, with J. T. Harper, opened a general store at Cerulean Springs, and is doing a business of about $10,000 a year. Mr. Goodwin is Postmaster at this point, having been appointed in January, 1882.

J. T. HARPER was born July 7, 1831, in Pittsylvania County, Va.; his parents were L. B. and Lucy (Stamps) Harper. The father was a native of South Carolina, and died in Trigg County in 1859; the mother was born in Pittsylvania County, Va., and died in this county in 1855, at the age of sixty-two years. Our subject, in 1848, came with his parents to Trigg County and engaged in farming; in 1860 he settled on a farm of 420 acres in Cadiz Precinct, which he has since owned and improved. He recently bought the Cerulean Springs Hotel and grounds, where he now acts as "mine host." A notice of these springs will be found in the general history of Cerulean Springs, in this work. He owns, in company with Mr. J. F. White, 140 acres adjoining the Springs. Mr. Harper is also engaged in general merchandising with Mr. B. F. Goodwin, at Cerulean Springs. In 1857 he married Miss Eliza, daughter of John F. White, who is well and favorably known. To them were born two children—a son and daughter. The parents are life-long members of the Baptist Church. Mr. Harper is a member of the K. of H.

WILLIAM B. LADD was born August 11, 1830, in Trigg County, Ky.; he is the seventh child in a family of eight children born to John and Mary (Jones) Ladd. The father was born in North Carolina in 1793, and died in Trigg County in 1868. The mother was born in South Carolina, and died December 10, 1880, at the advanced age of ninety-three years. In 1852 subject bought 100 acres of land where his residence now stands. He has since increased this farm until he now owns 360 acres; he has cleared about 160 acres of this farm; in 1878 he built his present residence, which is one of the finest in the precinct, at a cost of about $2,000; he has placed other buildings on the farm at a cost of about $800; he has a nice farm, and is numbered among the most industrious and worthy men of his precinct; he also owns a farm of 123 acres of well-improved land in Caldwell County, which is now rented. He was married, in 1852, to Mary Dyer, a native of Trigg County; these parents have seven children—five sons and two daughters. The parents and six of the children are members of the Baptist Church.

ELIJAH LADD was born on the farm where he now resides March 10, 1857; he is the eldest child and only son in a family of four children born to W. H. and Jemima (Guthrie) Ladd; the parents are both natives of this county; the father was born on this farm in 1826; he died here in 1881; the mother was born in 1827, and now resides on the home farm. Our subject owns 360 acres of land which was formerly a part of his father's farm; about 200 acres of his land is well improved. He was married, March 8, 1883, to Miss Celia Mitchell, a native of Trigg County, Ky.

WILLIAM D. LANDER (deceased) was born December 13, 1818, in Christian County, Ky.; his death occurred November 5, 1878, at Cerulian Springs; he went to Graves County, Ky., in 1858; two years later he moved to Trigg County; in 1862 he located on this farm consisting of about 400 acres; he was largely engaged in buying and shipping live stock, in which business and farming he was eminently successful; he was landlord of the Cerulean Springs at the time of his death. His marriage occurred November 5, 1843, to Annie W., daughter of Robert and Dicey (Baker) Rogers. Mr. Rogers was born in Virginia, and died in 1852, aged fifty-four years; Mrs. Rogers was born in Caldwell County, Ky., and died in 1850, aged fifty-two. Our subject has two children—Julia P. (now Mrs. John D. Gardner) and Robert Short (now in the livery business in Eddyville).

W. F. READ was born in Caldwell County, Ky., June 30, 1849; his parents are James and Frances (Headspeth) Read, both natives of Taylor County, Ky. The former was born in 1830, the latter in 1832. Subject was brought up on his father's farm, where he received an education from subscription schools. In October, 1882, he opened a store at Friendship, Caldwell County, and continued it about a year, when he moved to Cerulean Springs, where he keeps a store and carries a stock of about $3,000, and is doing a fair and increasing business. He was married in 1870 to Miss Jennie Goodwin, a native of Trigg County. This union has been blessed with five children: Edgar L., born October 22, 1871; James G., March 13, 1873; Viola, September 23, 1876; Neville, September 3, 1878; Blanche, August 17, 1881.

JOHN H. ROGERS was born in Trigg County, May 21, 1823; he is the eldest of four children born to Robert and Nancy (Baker) Rogers. The father was born in 1798 in Virginia, and died in Christian County, Ky., in 1852. The mother was born in 1802, in Caldwell County, Ky.; she died in Christian County in 1854. Our subject was reared on his father's farm, and at the age of twenty-three rented a farm in Christian County where he remained three years. After the death of his father he bought out the heirs and took possession of the farm, where he remained four years. He then moved to Graves County, Ky., and remained five years. In 1863 he removed to Trigg County and lived on a rented farm near the Springs one year. He then returned to Christian County and farmed there two years. In 1881 he came to his present farm of 125 acres, which he rents. He was married January 1, 1846, to Elizabeth H. Hicks, a native of Springfield, Robinson Co., Tenn. This lady died May 22, 1875, aged forty-six years. Ten children (five boys and five girls) have blessed this union. Mr. Rogers is a member of the Masonic fraternity.

HEZEKIAH SMITH was born September 19, 1830, in Hopkins County, Ky. His parents were Austin P. and Myra (Sisk) Smith, both natives of North Carolina ; the former died in 1875, at the age of seventy-six years; the latter was born in May, 1801, and died in Hopkins County, Ky., in 1866. Hezekiah was reared on his father's farm, where he remained until 1852, when he bought a farm of 115 acres in Hopkins County where he resided until 1869, when he sold his farm and moved to his present location ; he owns 165 acres 110 of which are improved. For the past twenty years he has been engaged in preaching for the Baptist Church, and for the past fourteen years has had charge of the church at Muddy Fork, of the same denomination. He was married in 1854 to Dorcas Stanley of Hopkins County, Ky. Mr. and Mrs. Smith had ten children, eight of whom are living. Their son, Eden H., died in August, 1883, at the age of twenty-four; he had recently graduated with distinguished honors from the Jefferson Medical College, and was about entering upon the duties of his chosen profession, with bright prospects, when death, who " always likes a shining mark," claimed him as a victim.

J. F. SMITH was born July 12, 1832, in Williamson County, Tenn. His parents are B. and Rebecca (Boyd) Smith ; they were born in east Tennessee ; the former in 1802, the latter in 1798 ; she died in Christian County March 8, 1882. In December, 1859, our subject came to Christian County and lived on a leased farm there for ten years. In 1869 he moved to Trigg County and rented a farm from Mrs. West for two years. In 1871 he purchased 129 acres where he now lives; he has since increased this farm to 195 acres, about 115 of which he has cleared. On his coming here he found it a dense wood. Mr. Smith was married January 8, 1857, to Miss Martha E. McPeak, who was born in Bedford County, Tenn. To them were born twelve children, of whom six daughters and four sons are living. Mr. S. is a member of the Masonic fraternity.

ANDERSON STEWART was born September 8, 1837, in Trigg County, Ky. He is the eighth in a family of nine children born to James and Jemima (Good) Stewart. The father was born in Virginia, September 30, 1799, and died February 2, 1872. The mother was born in Virginia, January 2, 1800, and died October 4, 1876. She is the daughter of John S. Wood. James Stewart came with his family to Trigg County in 1822. Anderson Stewart was married December 27, 1859, to Lucy Wood, a native of Georgia. These parents have two sons and two daughters. After marriage Mr. Stewart worked on a farm, receiving part of the crop as his compensation. He then lived on a rented farm for three years. In 1864 he removed to his present farm consisting of 274 acres and is known as the " Wiley Wilson " farm. Mr. Stewart is a self-made man, having no advantages in early life for education. He began without means, but by his industry and close attention to duty, has placed himself in very comfortable circumstances, and is one of the leading farmers in the community where he lives. His residence is one of the finest of his neighborhood, and his farm is well stocked; his out-buildings are commodious and well arranged; his farm is located one and a half miles from Cerulean Springs.

T. R. STEWART was born September 8, 1845, in Trigg County. He is a son of Johnson and Susan (Good) Stewart, both natives of Virginia. In July, 1824, they moved to Christian County, remained there but one year, then came to Trigg County, where the father died in April, 1883, at the advanced age of eighty years. The mother is now living with her son Mitchell in Cerulean Springs Precinct. Our subject owns an interest in 150 acres of land; part is included in the John McGhee farm where he now resides; also part of the old homestead formerly owned by his father. Mr. Stewart was married, in 1878, to Eliza J. Warren, a native of Christian County. These parents have three children—two sons and one daughter. Mr. Stewart has also one son by a former marriage. Mr. Stewart is a member of the Baptist Church.

ROBERT R. TURNER was born in Christian (now Trigg) County, Ky., February 8, 1812, and died August 9, 1884; he was the second child in a family of eleven, born to James W. and Jane (Rogers) Turner. The father was born in South Carolina. Our subject's grandfather and two uncles served the in Revolutionary War. James W. emigrated to Christian County from South Carolina about the year 1808, and located about one and one-half miles from Cerulean Springs, on a farm, where he died in 1856, at the age of seventy-seven years. His wife was born in Virginia. She died in 1864, aged seventy-two. Our subject was married, in 1834, to Leah Goodwin. She was born on this farm in 1809, and is a daughter of the late John Goodwin of this county. Our subject has nine children, six of whom are now living. His son, Robert P., enlisted in the late war, and died in the hospital at Hopkinsville soon after enlistment. John J. served throughout the war. David R. enlisted and served about seven weeks, when he was discharged on account of physical disability. Mr. Turner held the office of Magistrate continuously for forty years. His continuous re-election evinced the high esteem in which his services were held by his constituency; his term expired June, 1883, when he positively declined a re-election. He was a life-long and devoted member of the Baptist Church.

MONTGOMERY PRECINCT.

CAPT. EDMUND BACON (deceased) was born March 28, 1785, within a few miles of the old home of Thomas Jefferson. His father was a descendant of one of the best families in Virginia. His brother William had the management of Jefferson's estate during his four years' absence as Minister to France, and so satisfactory was his management, that upon the latter's election to the presidency, he naturally turned to the same family to find one capable of managing his large estate. Notwithstanding our subject's youth he was selected for the difficult task, and during his twenty years in that position he was Jefferson's adviser in all things pertaining to his finances, and often went to Washington to consult him and he frequently received long letters from him. He moved Mr. Jefferson to the capital and at the expiration of his term of office, moved him back to Monticello. Capt. Bacon was familiar with the appearance of many of the prominent men connected with the early history of the country, such as Patrick Henry, Madison, Monroe, the Leighs, Barbours and Randolphs, who were frequent visitors at Monticello. Mr. Jefferson's two daughters were fond of visiting Capt. Bacon's house and were as much at home there as at Monticello. He purchased the land upon which the University of Virginia stands, and assisted Mr. Jefferson in laying off the site for that institution. In 1818, seeing that Mr. Jefferson's financial ruin was only a question of a few months and knowing he could be of no further service to him, he determined upon emigrating to the West. Accordingly in August, of that year, he started upon his journey, stopping at the Warm Springs to pay a visit to Mr. Jefferson, who was sojourning there at the time. Upon his departure Mr. Jefferson gave him the following letter:

WARM SPRINGS, August 18, 1818.

The bearer, Mr. E. Bacon, has lived with me a number of years as manager of my farm at Monticello. He goes to Missouri to look out for lands to which he means to remove. He is an honest, correct man in his conduct and worthy of confidence in his engagements. Any information or instruction which any person may give him, will be worthily bestowed, and if he should apply particularly to Gov. Clark on his way, the Governor will especially oblige me by imparting to him his information and advice.

THOMAS JEFFERSON.

On his journey he passed through Louisville, then an insignificant settlement, also Vincennes, Ind., and arrived at St. Louis where he met Gov. Clark. The Governor wished him to settle there, but he was not very favorably impressed with the country. He therefore returned to Virginia, and again had charge of Mr. Jefferson's farm for a year or two, after which he again visited Missouri, but at last decided to settle in Kentucky, and accordingly bought 1,000 acres of land, at $2 per acre, in Trigg County, where he spent the remainder of his life. Here he gave almost his entire attention to stock-raising, and was recognized as one of the most successful stock-raisers in the country. He had but three sons : Thomas, Fielding and William, all of whom preceded him to the grave. He was kind, courteous and agreeable to everybody, was much beloved by his neighbors and would have attracted the attention of a stranger as a remarkable man and a specimen of a perfect gentleman. He died in February, 1866.

WILLIAM J. BACON, grandson of the above, and one of the heirs to his estate, was born September 16, 1832, in Christian County, Ky., and is a son of Fielding W. and Sicily (Radford) Bacon. He received his education in the schools of his native county ; he remained at home until attaining his majority ; he then began life for himself by engaging in the tobacco business and farming, which he continued until 1863, when he went to New York City and entered into the firm of Bacon, Clardy & Co., of which he was the senior member. At this time there were 116 firms engaged in the business (tobacco and cotton commission), and at the end of two years Bacon, Clardy & Co. stood first in the amount of the former article handled. At this time, during the busy season, their acceptances averaged $750,000 per month. In 1867, on account of the failure of Mr. Clardy's health, the firm dissolved partnership, and Mr. Bacon returned to Trigg County, where he has since been engaged in farming and stock-raising. He gives the greater part of his attention to breeding and training trotting and fancy road horses. He has been the owner of several that have attained national celebrity, such as Exchequer, Lucille, Rigolette and others. Mr. Bacon was married November 13, 1867, to Miss Delia, daughter of Col. Joseph L. Carrington, of Richmond,

Va. Eight children have been born to them, three of whom—Carrington, William J. and Ada M. are living.

HENRY BLANE, M. D. Among the skilled members of the medical profession in Trigg County, we would mention the name at the head of this sketch. He was born September 27, 1837, in Halifax County, Va., and is a son of John and Sarah (Tilson) Blane, both of Scotch-Irish descent, and natives of Virginia. In 1838 they removed to Tennessee, where the former still lives. His wife died in December, 1881. Subject received his early education in the common schools. In 1859 he entered the Shelby Medical College, at Nashville, Tenn., from which he graduated, standing first in a large class. In May, 1861, he entered Company D, Fourteenth Tennessee Regiment, as Assistant Surgeon, with which regiment he served nine months. He then began the practice of his profession in Stewart County, Tenn., where he remained until 1866, since which time he has been in Trigg County, the past two years at Montgomery, where he has a large and increasing practice. Dr. Blane was married, October 15, 1863, to Alpha Griffin, of Stewart County, Tenn., who died December 25, 1868, leaving two children: Robert L. and Aurelius. The Doctor was next married, December 21, 1871, to Lucy B. Dyer, of Trigg County, and daughter of John Dyer. Three children have been born to them: Homer, Plomer and Verner, all of whom are living. Dr. Blane is a member of the Masonic order, and of the Knights of Honor. He has ever been a strong advocate of temperance principles, and holds a high place in the confidence of the people, both as a man and a physician.

JOHN E. RICKETTS, a native of Montgomery, Trigg Co., Ky., was born November 26, 1851. He is the only child of G. W. and Elvira (Lewis) Ricketts. The former was born in Maryland, September 27, 1822. When about one year old he came with his parents to Christian County, where he grew to manhood. He came to Trigg County in 1850. He was married January 28, 1850, and soon after bought a farm, a part of which our subject still owns. By untiring energy and close attention to business, he accumulated a large fortune, owning at the time of his death over 1,300 acres of as good land as there is in the State. He was a member of the Baptist Church and the Masonic order. John E. received his early education in the common schools and afterward took a classical course at Bethel College, which he entered in 1864.   He also attended the Commercial College at Louisville, Ky.; he then kept books for a short time in that city.   In 1882 he went to Cadiz and engaged in the grocery business, which at the death of his father he sold out and took charge of the farm, which business he still continues.

BETHESDA PRECINCT.

FRANCIS M. ATWOOD was born December 4, 1851, in Trigg County, Ky. John H. and Martha (Forguson) Atwood, are his parents. The father is a native of Tennessee ; he came to this county in boyhood and settled on a farm ; he served as private in the late war under Gen. Huel and others ; he is living on the farm with Francis and is fifty-five years of age ; he is a member of the United Baptist Church. The mother was a native of Kentucky. She died in 1871, aged thirty-five years. She was also a member of the Baptist Church. These parents had eight children, five brothers still living. Farming has always been the occupation of our subject, and he has been very successful in business. He now owns 250 acres of land, 125 of which are well improved. He raises principally corn, tobacco, wheat and potatoes. He deals moderately in stock, having at present thirty-five head of cattle, fifty head each of hogs and sheep, besides five mules and horses Altogether his outlook is encouraging. He was married December 16, 1874, to Miss Martha A. Jones, of this county. She is daughter of Pressly and Sallie (Mitchell) Jones. The latter's father and mother are still living. Martha A. Jones' great-grandmother, Sallie Mitchell, died the past August aged eighty-six years. This family is noted for its longevity. Henry P. Atwood, our subject's eldest son, has seen his mother, his grandmother, his great-grandmother, and his great-great-grandmother all at the same time. To Francis and Martha A. Atwood were born five children, viz.: Henry P., Julian L., Nora B., Naomi L. and Flora B. Both parents are members of the United Baptist Church.

JAMES B. HOLLOMAN was born October 2, 1827, in Obion County, Tenn. His parents are J. B. and Sarah Holloman, both natives of Kentucky. They went to Tennessee after marriage. The father was one of the most extensive farmers of the neighborhood. His death took place in 1865, on his sixty-fifth birthday. He was a devoted and life-long member of the Cumberland Presbyterian Church. The mother is still living in Tennessee at the advanced age of eighty-two. These parents had seven children—four boys and three girls. Four of the children are yet living. Our subject was married November 6, 1849, to Ailcy M. Osborn, of Kentucky. After marriage he began farming for himself. He had but a small start in beginning, but by industry, economy and good management he has secured a nice home of 100 acres, seventy-five of which are improved. He has been reasonably successful in business. His children were : Isam (deceased), Lucy A., Mary W. (deceased), Sarah (died the past February at the age of twenty-five years ; she was for twelve years a devoted member of the Methodist Episcopal Church South), William B. (living in Texas), Susan C., Robert L., James I. (deceased). Both parents are members of the Methodist Episcopal Church South.

SAMUEL LARKINS was born January 24, 1822, in Graves County, Ky. He is a son of William and Penelope (Hollowell) Larkins, both natives of North Carolina. The father came to this county from Caldwell County in 1841, and settled on 1,100 acres of land. He was married in Trigg County about the year 1819. These parents had eleven children, nine of whom are now living. The father died in 1866, at the age of seventy-seven years. The mother's death occurred at the age of sixty-eight. Both parents were for many years zealous and influential members of the Methodist Episcopal Church South. They reared eleven children, who reached the years of maturity, and before the parents died, they had the pleasure of seeing their children all members of the church of their choice. Our subject began for himself at the age of twenty-one years. He has been quite successful in business. He was Magistrate of this county for fourteen years. He was a member of the State Legislature from 1863 to 1865. He has held other county and precinct offices, quite to the satisfaction of his constituency. He was commissioned by Gov. Powell, Major of Kentucky Militia. He now owns 300 acres of land, about one-half of which is improved. The Hollowell marble monument cost $2,500, is twenty-five feet high, and is upon Mr. Larkin's farm. His land is perhaps among the best in the precinct. He raises corn, wheat and tobacco, and can raise almost anything that can be grown in this latitude. He was married in 1853, to Josephine Brandon, of this county. Severn J., Mattie A., Mollie J., Robert S., Anna E. P. and Charles T., are their children. Miss Anna E. is a teacher of experience ;

her services are in good demand in that calling. Both parents are prominent members of the Methodist Episcopal Church South. Mr. Larkin was County Elector on the Fillmore and Donelson ticket in 1856, and for Bell and Everett in 1860, and canvassed the county for these officers. He was candidate for the Legislature several times, and once for the Senate, and was defeated in the latter contest. He has left the political arena, prefering to engage in other business more congenial to his nature. Mr. Larkins is a practical surveyor and engineer, and has sawed and sold more plank and lumber than any man in the county.

HENRY LARKINS was born January 27, 1824, in Caldwell (now Lyon) County, Ky. His parents are William and Penelope Larkins. Subject had fair school advantages, and began for himself at the age of twenty-one years. He has been very successful in business, now owning 370 acres of land in Trigg and 254 acres in Caldwell County. He has 280 acres of well-improved land in the two counties. He raises stock and grain, changing from one to the other. He raises all the products grown in this part of the country. His farms are in a good state of cultivation. He was married, in 1850, to Miss Lucy A. Wilcox, of Caldwell County, Ky. Their children are: Charles C., Mary A., Susan F., Sarah E., L. Alice, Henry F., William S., Walter E., Laura E., Albert E. Mary is the wife of John R. Carney; Charles C. is married to Mary G. Hayden; their children are Edna G. and Lucy M. The Misses Sallie and Alice are both teachers of several years' experience. They have had good success in teaching, and like the business very well. Their services have given general satisfaction to employers, parents, pupils and all concerned. Both Mr. and Mrs. Larkins, with six children, are members of Bethesda Methodist Episcopal Church South.

JOHN C. LARKINS, son of William and Penelope Larkins, was born in Trigg County, in 1843. His parents were well and favorably known as among the best people of the county. Though dead many years, their good influence still lives. Our subject began for himself at the age of twenty-one; farming and carpentering have engaged his attention. He, with his sisters, Martha and Eliza live at the home farm. The good influences and generous hospitality that characterized the parents still follow the children. The brother and sisters are members of the Bethesda Methodist Episcopal Church South. John has about seventy-five acres of land under cultivation. He is farming about twenty-two acres of corn, ten of tobacco and eight acres of wheat. His outlook is very encouraging.

BENJAMIN P. MITCHELL was born February 7, 1844, in Trigg County, Ky. He is a son of James and Celia (Pearl) Mitchell. The father was a native of North Carolina. He was a farmer, carpenter and wheel-wright; he came to this country in early childhood. He died in this county in 1873, aged sixty-nine years. These parents had seven children, five of whom are now living. The mother is still living with her son Benjamin. Her general health is very good, and her powers of mind and body well preserved. Benjamin began for himself on the farm at the age of nineteen years. He now owns about 175 acres, 120 of which are well improved. He has been quite successful, and is counted among the good business men of the precinct. The past year he raised 1,800 pounds of tobacco, 100 barrels of corn, 150 bushels of wheat, 210 bushels of oats, besides hay. He has been raising cattle the past year. His outlook is very encouraging. He was married, August, 1863, to Lindsey A. Smith, of this county. Her parents are James and Lucinda (Pitkins) Smith. Six children have blessed this union, viz.: Amos, Celia, Iceloan Mark, Cerona and Willa R. Celia is the wife of Elijah Ladd. Both Mr. and Mrs. Mitchell are members of the Baptist Church.

CALEDONIA PRECINCT.

WALTER C. ANDERSON was born September 27, 1846, in Hanover County, Va. His parents are Dr. Monroe and Nancy E. (Harris) Anderson, elsewhere mentioned. Our subject began for himself at the age of twenty-one years. He has been very successful in farming, and his farm of 182 acres is well improved. He raises generally about 30,000 pounds of tobacco, 250 barrels of corn, and an average of about 500 bushels of wheat. His farm is located on the Christian County line one mile southeast from Caledonia, and about due south from the road leading from Caledonia to Hopkinsville. His farm is among the best of its size of any in Trigg County. He is counted among the extensive farmers of the county. His present prospect for wheat is excellent, better than it has been since 1874. Few persons in the county have so flattering a prospect for wheat as Mr. Anderson. He was married November 16, 1868, to Miss Susan V. Baker, of Christian County. Her parents are Ellison C. and Betsie (Quisenberry) Baker. The father was a native of Kentucky, the mother of Illinois. The father died October 20, 1862, aged fifty years. The mother died January 12, 1867, aged fifty-four years. To Mr. and Mrs. Anderson were born seven children, viz.: Dovie, Daisey (deceased), Monroe, Ellison (deceased), Mattie, Nettie and Alex. Mrs. Anderson is a member of the Christian Church.

E. I. ANDERSON, farmer, was born January 26, 1860, in Christian County, Ky. His parents are Dr. Monroe and Nancy E. (Harris) Anderson, both natives of Virginia. The father was a farmer and trader in cotton. He practiced medicine for many years and was a most successful physician and surgeon. His death took place in St. Louis in 1863, aged forty-five years. The mother died in 1871, at the age of fifty-three years. These parents had eight children, seven of whom are now living. Monroe, the sixth child, came to his death by the accidental discharge of a pistol on Christmas day. Our subject began for himself at the age of twenty years. Farming has been his business. He now owns 200 acres of land, besides horses, mules and sheep. He depends on raising crops rather than stock. He raised 1,300 bushels of potatoes, 25,000 pounds of tobacco, 400 barrels of corn, and ten acres of oats the past year. His outlook is most encouraging. He was married January 7, 1880, to Miss Nannie Coffey, daughter of Acey and Sidney Coffey, natives of Kentucky. They were married here and settled in Washington County, Ill. Later they moved to Christian County, Ky. To Mr. and Mrs. Anderson is born one child—Charles Rascoe. Mrs. Anderson is a member of the Christian Church.

WILLIAM G. BLAIN, farmer, was born July 27, 1829, in Halifax County, Va. His parents are Ephriam and Keziah Blain, both natives of same county and State. The father was second cousin of Hon. James G. Blaine. He was a farmer and came to Montgomery County, Tenn., in 1838, and settled, in 1847, at Roaring Springs, Ky. He left and went to Graves County, Ky., in 1857, and there yet lives at the age of seventy-eight. He is a member of the Methodist Episcopal Church South. The mother died while in Tennessee, in 1844, aged thirty-two; she was a member of the Methodist Episcopal Church. Our subject began for himself at the age of nineteen, not having a dollar. He farmed two years, and procured money enough to attend school for several years. He then taught school for nine years with good success. Farming next engaged his attention, in which he has been attended with good success. He now owns a comfortable home and has reared a family of twelve children. He was married in 1856 to Mary E. Smith, of this county. They have had seventeen children, viz.: George W., William B., Joseph B. (deceased), Jefferson D. (deceased), Julia A. (deceased), John T., Mattie P. and Robert P. (twins), Adam C., Charles W. (twins, deceased), Lizzie O. Martha C. (deceased), (twins, unnamed, deceased), Commie H., Mellie B. and Benjamin B. George W. is married to Fanny E. Averitt. Mina D. is their only child. Mr. and Mrs. Blain are both members of the Methodist Episcopal Church South. The former is also a member of the Masonic order. He has been Justice of the Peace twelve years. Mr. Blain is a practical surveyor, and has followed that calling the past thirty years, in Trigg and surrounding counties. He has the best reputation as a surveyor of any man in this part of the State. He frequently has calls to Montgomery and Stewart Counties in Tennessee.

THOMAS J. HAMMOND, merchant and farmer, was born August 24, 1835. He is a son of Thomas W. and Margaret R. (Daniel) Hammond, natives respecti/ely of Virginia and North Carolina. The father was a soldier in the war of 1812, and took part in the battle of New Orleans. He was a farmer and an early pioneer settler in the county. He studied law in early manhood and practiced successfully for some years. He took quite an interest in the affairs of the county. In politics he was a Clay Whig. He was Sheriff of this county in 1844–1845. He served in the State Senate from 1862 to 1866. He possessed the happy faculty of being able to make a speech and talk to the point on almost any subject. It was generally conceded that his official career was one of brilliancy, usefulness and very satisfactory to his constituency. He and his wife were worthy members of the Methodist Episcopal Church South. His death occurred in March, 1872, at the age of seventy-nine years. His wife died in May, 1871, at the age of seventy-one years. They had eight children, only two of whom are now living. Our subject, on reaching his majority, began for himself on the farm. He has been in the mercantile business the past eighteen years. He now owns a store in Caledonia; also one in Pee Dee. In the latter Mr. Wall is his partner. In Caledonia he keeps a stock of staple and fancy dry goods, notions, queensware, etc. In the Pee Dee store is kept the same with the addition of family groceries, farming implements, etc. In both stores he is doing a good and increasing business. Mr. Hammond also owns a nice farm of 250 acres where he lives, and his business outlook is most encouraging. He is classed among the best men in the county. May 24, 1871, he was joined in wedlock to Miss Josephine Cunningham of this county. Three children have blessed this union, viz.: Willie R., Walter and Hugh. Mrs. Hammond is a member of the Baptist Church. Mr. Hammond is a member of the Methodist Episcopal Church South; also of the I. O. O. F.

R. S. LEWIS was born in 1834, November 26, in Trigg County, Ky. His parents are Leonard Mary (Sims) Lewis, both natives of Virginia. The father was a farmer, also a teacher. His mortality ended in 1879, at the age of eighty-three. He was a member of the Methodist Episcopal Church South. The mother died with the closing hours of 1834, aged thirty-two years. She was a member of the Presbyterian

Church. These parents had nine children, four of whom are now living. Our subject was an orphan at an early age. He made his home with his grandparents—Richard and Margaret Sims. To these aged people he feels that he owes a debt of gratitude that would be difficult to pay. Richard Sims was a soldier in the war of 1812. He was strictly honest and a man of unflinching integrity. He was born July, 1776, being contempory with the Declaration of Independence. He died in June, 1857, his age, eighty-one years. His wife died in 1864, at the age of eighty-six years. Mr. Lewis' business has been teaching and farming. He has taught about ten years and in that profession has an enviable reputation, having in the main given general satisfaction. He owns 100 acres of some of the very best land in Trigg County. This competence he has accumulated largely by his own exertions. His outlook is very encouraging, and he has a host of good friends. His farm is located on the Sinking Fork of Little River. He is a member of the Methodist Episcopal Church South ; also of the Masonic order.

WILLIAM R. PEAL was born August 28, 1839, in Trigg County, Ky. His parents are Dennis and Eugene (Ramey) Peal, both natives of Caldwell, now Trigg County, Ky. The father was a farmer; his death occurred in 1870, aged fifty-eight years. He was a member of the Baptist Church, also of the Masonic order. The mother died in 1858, aged forty-two years; she was a member of the Baptist Church. Our subject began for himself at the age of twenty-one; he farmed for five years, was in the mercantile business two years, then clerked for E. B. Jones at Paducah, Ky., four years, then taught school in Trigg County for several years with good success. Not liking the business, he kept books and was salesman for D. Hillman & Sons five years, at Trigg Furnace. He was Deputy Sheriff under Capt. W. M. Campbell, of Trigg County, in 1875. During the year 1876 he drummed for G. Magee & Co., Evansville, Ind., then returned to Empire Furnace and kept books for one year. In 1878 he was candidate for Sheriff of Trigg County, and was elected by a large majority. He served in that capacity two years, and later kept books at the flouring-mill at Cadiz. Last year he leased the mill on Sinking Fork. He has bought property and will move to Caledonia soon, and open out cabinet business and cooper shop ; he has been quite successful in business. He was married, in 1863, to Miss Lucy A. Childress, a native of Trigg County, Ky. Three children have blessed this union, viz.: James E., George H. and Minnie O. Both parents are members of the Methodist Episcopal Church South. Mr. Peal is a member of the Masonic order, also of the I. O. O. F. Their son, George Hilson, died of cholera in 1873, at Rock Castle, aged five years.

DAVID C. WOOTTON was born July 16, 1824, in Virginia. His parents are David C. and Frances (Brame) Wootton, both natives of Virginia. The father was a farmer, and came to Christian County, Ky., in 1830. His death occurred in 1864, aged seventy-six years. He and wife were both devoted members of the Presbyterian Church. The mother died in 1868, aged about seventy-two years. Twelve children were born to these parents, only five of whom are now living. Our subject, the sixth child, began for himself at the age of eighteen years; he had a small start; he engaged in the mercantile business for a time, subsequently in the farming business. He has made farming a good success, but has lost money by paying security debts; he now owns 500 acres of land, and is counted among the good men of the precinct. In December, 1849, he was married to Miss Mary F. Coleman, of this county. These parents had six children, viz.: James D., deceased; Thomas W.; Joseph I., deceased; Jeff D., deceased; Nannie C. and Fannie. James D., at the time of his death, was a practicing physician of much promise; he had previously married Miss Lydia Malone. Thomas is engaged in the drug business in Christian County. Nannie C. is the wife of Joseph Ledford, of this county; Nellie is their only child. Miss Fannie is living with her parents, at home. Thomas married Miss Ozella Tuggle, of Trigg County; James and Thomas C. are their children.

TRIGG COUNTY, KY.
INDEX

Prepared by
Sammie Williams
Pittsburgh, Texas